In memory of the people who taught me how to drink, eat, and revel with wild abandon in North Beach—the late Rose Pistola, Freddie Kuh, Sean Mooney, and Bruno Iacopi.

—P. K.

This book is dedicated to Rose "Pistola" Evangelista and to Scott and Peggy, who share her legacy with me.

"I am rough, I am tough, I'm from North Beach—that's enough."

We miss you Rose . . .

—R. H.

THE Rose Pistola COOKBOOK

Reed Hearon &
Peggy Knickerbocker

Black-and-White Photographs by Henrik Kam

& Color Photographs by Laurie Smith

Broadway Books New York

THE Rose Pistola COOKBOOK

140 Italian Recipes from San Francisco's

Favorite North Beach Restaurant

BROADWAY

Library of Congress Cataloging-in-Publication Data

Hearon, Reed.
The Rose Pistola cookbook : 140 Italian recipes from San Francisco's favorite North Beach restaurant / Reed Hearon and Peggy Knickerbocker ; black-and-white photographs by Henrik Kam and color photographs by Laurie Smith. — 1st ed.
p. cm.
Includes bibliographical references and index.
ISBN 0-7679-0250-5 (hc)
1. Cookery, American—California style. 2. Cookery, Italian. 3. Pistola, Rose. I. Knickerbocker, Peggy. II. Title.
TX725.A1H357 1999
641.59794—dc21 99-26468
CIP

FIRST EDITION

Book design by Pei Loi Koay
Black-and-white photographs by Henrik Kam and color photographs by Laurie Smith.

99 00 01 02 03 10 9 8 7 6 5 4 3 2 1

Page ii: Horse-drawn carriages looking south from Chestnut Street on Columbus Avenue in the early 1900s. *Courtesy J. B. Monaco Photography.*

Page iii: Lunch on the sidewalk at Rose Pistola.

Contents

THE
Rose Pistola
COOKBOOK

North Beach: A Little History

Enterprising Ligurians and other Italians fled their homeland in the mid-nineteenth century in hopes of striking it rich in the California Gold Rush. The gentle climate and accommodating landscape of San Francisco's northern waterfront offered respite to those whose dreams didn't pan out. North Beach reminded them of home. But the new land was so much greener and richer; it was more abundant on land and at sea. It was not the land of tiny terraced parcels to farm, but a land of wide expanses and deep blue horizons. They could fish, grow vegetables, eat well, and often earn enough money to go back to Italy or to send for their families. Many stayed on to establish what would become one of the most famous Italian quarters in America.

Paesani sunning in Washington Square circa 1900.
Courtesy J.B. Monaco photography.

Because many of these immigrants were (or quickly became) fishermen, it was natural that they'd settle in the cheap housing near the bay at the end of Columbus Avenue in Fisherman's Wharf. By the turn of the century, a line of caffès and simple restaurants extended from the wharf up Columbus Avenue, slicing into the heart of what soon became the thriving community of North Beach. There, and in surrounding neighborhoods, Ligurians (many from the port town of Genoa) grew the familiar produce of their homeland—eggplants, artichokes, chicory, rosemary, basil, garlic, lettuce, and tomatoes. Horse-drawn carts transported the goods to a central market in the heart of San Francisco that was frequented by restaurant chefs and Italian housewives looking for bargains and food that would make their families less homesick. Neighborhood artisans and craftsmen became famous for their Old World skills, and Italians from North Beach helped rebuild much of San Francisco after the devastating earthquake and fire of 1906. In the shade of sycamore trees, old men played bocce ball in the crushed oyster shell courts that had sprung up in the neighborhood parks and around Catholic churches.

If they wanted, Italians could live a lifetime in North Beach without ever speaking a word of English. Even today, Mass is held in Italian in Saints Peter and Paul Church on Washington Square, across the street from the original Rose Pistola's (now Washington Square Bar and Grill). Here, they could do virtually everything they would have done back home: Besides producing familiar food, they could cook, bake, paint, sculpt, write poetry, sing opera, and make wine. Wealthy neighbors talked disparagingly of "dago blood" running in the gutters. Later it was revealed that the "blood" was actually harvesttime spillover from the basement wineries that were then all over North Beach, using grapes shipped down to the Embarcadero from the Napa Valley in open railway cars.

After World War II, as some of the more prosperous Italians started "moving up" and out of the neighborhood, North Beach began attracting non-Italian writers and artists and other bohemian types, drawn by the same pleasant climate and inexpensive living quarters that had appealed to their predecessors. The European style and way of life established by the early Italians has been attracting creative souls ever since. In the 1950s, local bars, caffès, and restaurants (invariably Italian, and cheap) became the meeting ground for the loosely knit group of poets and writers who became known as the Beat Generation—Jack Kerouac, Allen Ginsberg, Gregory Corso, Lawrence Ferlinghetti, Michael McClure—and the Beats added another layer of culture to the area, one still vital today.

North Beach is arguably the incubator of what has become known internationally as California cuisine. When the Ligurians first settled here, they found the fertile ground of what became a source of unparalleled bounty. Sophisticated and worldly, yet notoriously parsimonious, Ligurians had created, in Italy, a cuisine of tremendous elegance and simplicity. When this approach was transplanted to Northern California, with its spectacularly abundant agriculture, fishing, and viticulture, a new cuisine was born—a cuisine rooted in the seasonal, ingredient-inspired cooking of Liguria and other parts of Italy, and in the recipes these early settlers developed from what was available in their new home.

Today, life in North Beach is perfumed by food, is driven by food, is about food. You can't walk down the street without inhaling the savory aromas of roasting coffee, baking bread, sizzling garlic and onions. Almost every second storefront has something to do with food or drink. Shopping for food in North Beach is like shopping in the Old Country—a leisurely pursuit liberally fueled with coffee (and maybe, later in the day, with wine), involving stops at a dozen places, each one specializing in something different. It is a neighborhood whose vendors still wrap focaccia, cheese, and lovely chalky salami in paper and string.

Food is not the only appetite that drives people to North Beach. Never very far below the surface is the sense that something sexy is happening in the neighborhood. Is it any wonder that the topless craze started on bawdy Broadway in the 1960s? Today, old Italian ladies, with the scent of the marriage bed still fresh in their minds, can still be seen shuffling down the hill to buy something nice for their husbands at one of the remaining Italian stores. The bars and restaurants are filled with poets and lovers, musicians and artists, all looking for the same thing that North Beach has offered for over a century and a half, the fragrance of adventure and the lust-driven freedom to consummate it.

Saints Peter and Paul Church, site of Rose Pistola's funeral; Coit Tower is in the background.

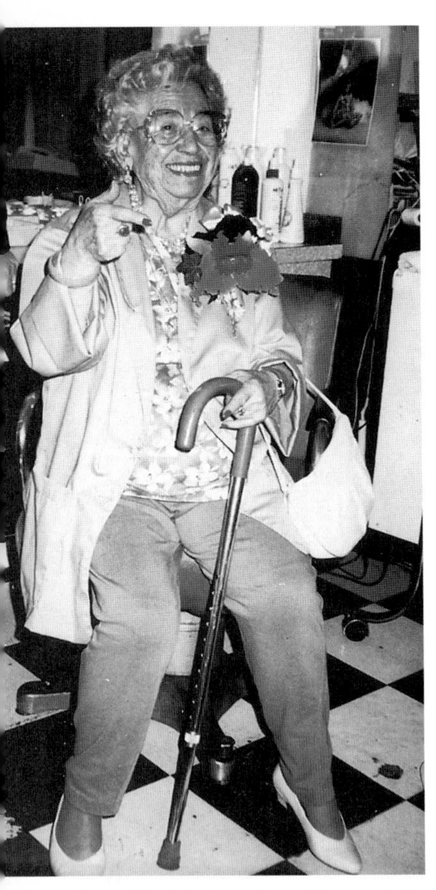

Rose at the beauty parlor, getting ready for the opening of Rose Pistola, March 1996.

If an invitation came in from Rose Pistola, you hopped. You didn't need to get dressed up or bring presents; all you needed was a huge appetite and a willingness to participate in an evening full of raucous tales and drinking. The aromas that swirled down her front steps to greet you at her house on Lombard Street, across from the old North Beach Plunge, smelled so good they made you want to weep. There she'd be stirring her gravy (tomato spaghetti sauce) or stuffing squid with her old hard-worked fingers. She'd often have a basil leaf stuck in her cleavage. "Men like a woman who smells as if she knows how to cook," she'd tease. Not much had changed since the days of Rose-Pistola-the-saloon; things just moved a little more slowly toward the end of Rose's long, gracious, and feisty life.

A legendary bar owner and renowned North Beach cook, Rose Pistola lived in North Beach for ninety years. She was born on Vanderwater Street, which, at the time, was on the water's edge (the area has since been filled in). Her Sicilian father was a fisherman and her mother was a fantastic cook. She made brown-bag lunches for ten children with sandwiches of breaded eggplant or fresh tomatoes, often stolen from horse-drawn vegetable wagons by Rose, the youngest of the ten. "A young girl could not go out alone in those days," Rose explained, "so I was always home helping my mother cook. She taught me all I know. When I got a little older, I quit school and picked asparagus on the Sacramento Delta before going to work for Del Monte at the peach-canning factory on Sansome Street."

Later she worked at a cannery. "I'd get in terrible fights with the other girls there over the best spot to stand." She put up her fist and laughed. "I knocked the hell out of one big blond girl one day, and every day after that, the other workers would bet on who'd win between us. I always did."

Rose was already an independent woman by the age of nineteen, but her parents found it necessary to arrange a marriage for her. She had other fish to fry, so she eloped with her true love, a man who drove a fish truck be-

tween Eureka and San Francisco. After a brief marriage, sadly, his truck ran off the narrow, twisty Highway 1, and he was killed.

Years passed before Rose met Fred Evangelisti, a terse North Beach waiter who was first known as Smiling Fred the Stone Face. He'd earned his name, Pistola, because one day he got so mad at the cook at a long-gone Broadway restaurant that he came downstairs brandishing a pistol to scare him. From then on, he was called Fred Pistola, and she took on the name too.

In the early 1950s, the Pistolas bought a bar on Washington Square and named it Rose Pistola's. There, they became hosts to a legendary array of longshoremen, writers, musicians, poets, actors, and garbagemen. "I danced and sang and drank and sometimes I'd cook," Rose reminisced. But as neighborhood habitués such as Lou the Glue, present-day custodian of the Dolphin Club, remember it, "If Rose invited you to stay at the bar for dinner, you knew you had arrived." She only invited people she liked, and she'd kick people out with a broom, a meat cleaver, or a gallon wine jug if she didn't. She never charged her friends for the huge platters of pasta with tomato sauce, veal chops, or stuffed calamari that she'd set up on the long Formica tables in her no-frills saloon. The austere ambience of the joint was not a reflection of Rose's nature—she was warm, tough, motherly, and funny.

When North Beach restaurateur Ed Moose became interested in buying her saloon, he was invited to negotiate over a bowl of pasta. In the middle of the discussion, a pool ball inadvertently landed in the dish. "She just picked it right out of there and threw it back," said Moose, who eventually bought the spot and resurrected it as the Washington Square Bar and Grill.

Rose remained active in the community, playing bingo at Saints Peter and Paul Church, taking fre-

Rose Pistola at her eponymous bar on Washington Square in the 1950s: "I'm rough and I'm tough, I'm from North Beach and that's enough."

quent bus trips to gamble in Reno, and cooking for her daughter, three grandchildren, and four great-grandchildren.

In 1996, Peggy wrote an article that appeared in the first issue of Saveur *magazine, called "Old Stoves of North Beach." "Old stove" is gentle, complimentary North Beach slang for someone who has put in a lot of time in front of a lot of old stoves in his or her day. Old stoves are sometimes restaurant chefs or retired restaurant chefs—but more often they are simply home cooks, with many years of experience making savory dishes for themselves, their families, and their friends.*

At the same time, Reed was looking for a name for a restaurant that he was planning to open in North Beach. He loved Rose's name, her attitude, and her joyfulness, so Peggy arranged for an introduction. After the initial meeting, Reed said, "I wanted to bring back the spirit of North Beach, and Rose has spirit to spare." His offer to her, in exchange for using her name, was that she, her family, and her friends would always have a table and a meal waiting at her namesake restaurant. Rose celebrated her ninetieth birthday at the restaurant, in a room filled with well-wishers, just months before her death.

During the last years of her life, Rose lived at On Lok Senior Health Center, where she always had a bottle of olive oil and a can of Parmesan on her table. Rose died in the summer of 1998, and the entire neighborhood attended her funeral and wake. At the funeral, a few of her longtime friends sneaked a bottle of booze, a pack of cigarettes, and two heads of garlic into her casket. At the wake, which was held at the restaurant, was a photograph of Rose reveling at her old bar with her garter belt and the tops of her stockings exposed. Reed said, "Rose is a link between North Beach's past and future. She personifies what I love about the neighborhood: its bawdy sense of history and its wry acknowledgment that it's futile to take ourselves too seriously."

Basic Recipes and Techniques

The cooking techniques in this book are based on home-cooking traditions—nothing fancy, nothing complicated. Some of those traditions—saving pasta water and making homemade ricotta—have long been forgotten and we revive them here, giving careful attention to the description of their execution.

Black Point Cove circa 1920s. Today it is called Aquatic Park and is the site of the Dolphin Club. To stretch their budgets, North Beach mothers would send their sons out to gather mussels off the rocks and pilings along the edge of the bay.

Basilade

1 garlic clove
Pinch of kosher or sea salt
15 basil leaves
1/4 teaspoon grated lemon zest
2 tablespoons extra virgin olive oil

Makes 1/4 to 1/3 cup

This basic basil sauce adds a wonderful burst of freshness to the Braised Oxtails with Asparagus (page 172) or other long-cooked or reheated dishes, such as Seafood Lasagnette (page 114).

Place the garlic, salt, basil leaves, and lemon zest in a mortar and, using the pestle, pound it with the olive oil. Alternatively, you can use a blender or a mini food processor, but the mortar and pestle works best here, releasing more of the basil's perfumed essence.

Biga (Sourdough Starter)

1/8 teaspoon active dry yeast
3/4 cup all-purpose flour

Makes 3 1/2 cups

The night before you plan to bake focaccia or any of the pizzas in this book, make the biga, *or sourdough starter. Biga adds a more complex flavor and texture to breads.*

In a bowl, stir 1/2 cup warm water (approximately 100°F), the yeast, and flour together until smooth. Cover and refrigerate overnight. Remove from the refrigerator about 1 hour before using and let come to room temperature. Proceed as directed in recipes using biga.

Bread Crumbs

Fresh bread crumbs are made from fresh bread. Dried bread crumbs are made from bread that is at least a day old. To make either fresh or dried bread crumbs: Remove the crusts from a few slices of bread. Tear them into pieces, put them in the food processor, and process until the bread is ground to the desired size.

When measuring fresh bread crumbs, do not pack them tightly into the measuring cup, or they will lose their airy texture.

Pesto

- 1 garlic clove
- 1/2 teaspoon kosher or coarse sea salt
- 3 cups basil leaves
- 1/3 cup extra virgin olive oil (plus extra if storing)
- 2 tablespoons pine nuts
- 1/3 cup freshly grated pecorino

Makes 1 cup

Pesto has a superior flavor and texture when made with a mortar and pestle rather than in a food processor. Put the garlic and salt in a mortar and pound together until a creamy paste forms. Add one or two of the basil leaves at a time and pound to a rough paste. Add a couple of drops of the olive oil and continue to pound until a smooth emulsion is formed. Continue adding basil and olive oil in this fashion until all of the basil and oil are used. Pound in the pine nuts and, if you are ready to use immediately, stir in the cheese. Otherwise, put the pesto in a small, opaque container, float a small amount of olive oil on the surface, and refrigerate until you are ready to use it. Stir in the cheese before serving.

Hazelnut Pesto

1 teaspoon kosher or coarse sea salt
1 garlic clove
1 cup flat-leaf parsley leaves
4 basil leaves
½ cup extra virgin olive oil
½ cup hazelnuts, toasted and peeled (see page 191)

Makes ¾ to 1 cup

The method for making this stunning sauce is much the same as for making a basil pesto. We recommend making it in a mortar, but a mini food processor works as well. Serve with Lasagnette of Artichokes, Wild Mushrooms, and Hazelnut Pesto (page 112).

Place the salt and garlic in a mortar or a mini food processor and pound or blend together. Add the parsley leaves a few at a time, pounding or pulsing as you go. Add the basil leaves and pound or pulse until they are well incorporated. Add the olive oil and blend with the pestle or process in the food processor. Add the hazelnuts and just bruise them in the mortar or coarsely chop in the processor, breaking them up a bit while you combine them with the other ingredients.

Herbs

Early Italian settlers in North Beach regularly cooked with a profusion of herbs, grown from seeds carried from the old country or found wild in the hills. The herbs were planted in truck gardens along the perimeters of the neighborhood and sold at the old produce market not far from where Rose Pistola stands today.

Many of the recipes in this book call for a generous measure of fresh herbs, including marjoram, thyme, rosemary, sage, and basil. We usually throw the whole herb stem into a dish and leave it in for service. But some recipes call for leaves; if so, just tear them off the stem. We usually tear basil leaves to top pizzas. Sometimes we grind or pound leaves into an emulsion with other ingredients.

Fresh herbs are readily available everywhere. If you use dried herbs, replace them often as they quickly go stale.

Herb Butter

½ pound (2 sticks) unsalted butter, at room temperature
¼ cup chopped shallots
¼ cup minced chives
1 garlic clove, finely chopped
Juice and grated zest of 1 lemon
3 anchovy fillets, finely chopped
1 teaspoon freshly cracked black pepper

Mix all the ingredients together in a mixer, or combine in a medium bowl and beat together with a spoon. Place in a small bowl, cover tightly, and refrigerate until ready to use.

Makes 1 cup

Homemade Ricotta

1 gallon whole milk
¼ cup fresh lemon juice
Kosher or sea salt

Makes about 2 cups (½ pound)

It is so easy to make whole-milk ricotta cheese in just a few hours.

When the cheese is ready, simply unmold it from the cheesecloth, sprinkle with a little salt, and store, covered, in the refrigerator until you are ready to serve it. Try it on pizzas, toast with jam, or in the Roasted Sweet Peppers with Ricotta and Basil (page 36).

Heat the milk with the lemon juice in a stainless steel or other nonreactive pot over medium-low heat only until the curds separate from the whey; do not let the milk scorch.

Line a colander with three layers of cheesecloth. Pour the mixture into the colander. Bring the ends of the cheesecloth together and tie them securely with kitchen twine. Tie the twine to a wooden spoon handle. Rest the spoon with the cheesecloth bag over a deep bowl. Depending upon the consistency you desire, allow the bag to hang for 2 to 3 hours in the refrigerator. The longer you leave it, the stiffer the curds will become.

When it is ready, unmold the cheese. Season with salt and store in an airtight container in the refrigerator for 3 days. You might also season the ricotta with minced chives or green garlic, cracked black pepper, and a little olive oil.

Sue Conley of the Cowgirl Creamery at Tomales Bay Foods in Point Reyes, California.

Marinated Anchovies

Keep these on hand for whenever a recipe calls for anchovies. They bear no resemblance to the anchovies found swimming through oceans of cheese on the tops of many pizzas.

*These are easy to marinate, but you must start with salt-packed anchovies, such as the Sicilian brand called Agostino Recca. You can order them by mail (**see Sources, page 264**), or look for them in Italian grocery stores or specialty food stores.*

1 can salt-packed anchovies (about 1 pound, 5 ounces)
2 cups extra virgin olive oil
1 clove
1 bay leaf
10 black peppercorns

Makes 1 pound

Gently rinse the anchovies several times in water until barely salty. Fillet the anchovies with your fingers: Slip your thumb into the belly of each one and gently ease the fish open to reveal the spine. Carefully lift out and discard the spine. Lay the fillets on a clean kitchen towel or paper towel and place another towel on top. Press down with your hand to squeeze out the water. Pat any excess moisture with another towel.

Arrange the fillets in layers in a clean jar just large enough to hold them. Pour in the olive oil to cover and add the clove, bay leaf, and peppercorns. Keep refrigerated until ready to use. Remove only the number of anchovies that you will need for a specific recipe and bring them to room temperature. The anchovies will keep for 3 weeks in the refrigerator.

Pizza Tomato Sauce

¼ cup extra virgin olive oil
1 garlic clove, bruised
2 cups peeled, seeded, and chopped fresh or canned tomatoes
2 basil leaves
¼ teaspoon crushed red pepper flakes
Kosher or sea salt

Makes 2 cups

The secret to the fresh, clean flavor of this tomato sauce is briefly cooking it over high heat.

Heat the olive oil and garlic in a large heavy-bottomed sauté pan over medium-high heat until the garlic sizzles and is fragrant. Increase the heat to high, add the tomatoes, and cook, stirring frequently, for 3 to 4 minutes, or until the tomatoes begin to break down. Add the basil and red pepper, season to taste with salt, and remove the garlic. Let cool before using.

Polenta

Choose a coarse-grain stone-ground polenta for the best flavor and texture. (See Sources, page 264.) Stone-ground polenta that still has its germ tastes best, but it can also go rancid quickly, so store it in the refrigerator and use it up in a month or two.

There is no getting around it; the best polenta is made by fairly constant stirring on top of the stove for forty-five minutes to an hour. The longer you cook the grain, the more the corn flavor will develop. Quite good results come also from cooking the polenta in a 350°F oven, stirring occasionally, after starting it on top of the stove. If the polenta is done before the rest of the meal is ready, or if you would like to hold it for a while before serving, cover it and keep it warm.

Either way you make it, eat it in its soft form first and then, if you have any left over, pour it onto an oiled sheet pan, spreading it out evenly about ¾ inch thick. It will firm up nicely. Refrigerate it, covered, for up to a few days, and slice it for grilling or fry it in a pan with a little olive oil.

Serve polenta with any fish, fowl, or meat that has a nice, juicy sauce, such as Braised Calamari with Polenta (page 161) or Roast Sage-Stuffed Quail with Walnut Sauce (page 201).

1 cup coarse-grain cornmeal
1 teaspoon kosher or sea salt

Makes 4 servings

Bring a pot with 4 cups salted water to a boil. Whisk in the polenta, stirring to avoid lumps. Allow the water to return to a boil. Lower the heat to a simmer and continue to cook, stirring forcefully on and off with a wooden spoon, for 30 to 50 minutes. Or, put the pot in a 350°F oven, stirring it from time to time. In either case, scrape down the sides of the pan frequently.

When the polenta becomes shiny and starts to stiffen, it is almost done, but the best doneness test is to taste. The cornmeal will be smooth with no hard grains.

Note
This recipe works well when doubled or tripled.

White Beans

- ½ cup extra virgin olive oil, plus extra for drizzling
- 1 garlic clove, crushed
- 2 rosemary sprigs (about 4 inches long)
- 3 cups dried white beans (about 1½ pounds)
- ¼ pound prosciutto with fat, diced, optional
- 2 ounces prosciutto rind, optional
- 2 ounces Parmigiano-Reggiano rind, optional

Makes 7½ cups

Plump emergo beans (or large white runner beans), gigandes, cannellini, and cranberry and borlotti beans are the base of many dishes at Rose Pistola. Beans are used in White Bean Soup with Braised Greens (page 64), Grilled Sea Bass with Lemon and White Beans (page 148), Roasted Pork Loin with White Beans, Artichokes, and Salsa Verde (page 186), Grilled Octopus with Broccoli Rabe and White Beans (page 166), and Seafood Salad with Cranberry Beans (page 85).

We cook dried beans in our wood-burning oven because they develop a deep flavor and do not break up as easily as they might if cooked on top of the stove. Since that technique is out of the question for most people, cook beans at a low temperature in a conventional oven. Keep your eye on them, though, to make sure they don't dry out, and add water as needed.

The beans served at Rose Pistola are not soaked before cooking, because we buy our beans from a purveyor with a brisk turnover, guaranteeing a supply of fresh beans. The fresher the beans, the faster they cook. Carefully pick over all dried beans to remove any pebbles and rinse them well.

Beans from Phipps Ranch, in Pescadero, an hour south of San Francisco on the coast, are my favorite, because they hold together well and make for a dramatic presentation. You can mail-order these beans (see page 265), or use cannellini or Great Northern beans, which are available everywhere.

Ask your butcher to save you prosciutto rinds, and save the rinds from Parmigiano-Reggiano. Throw them into beans as they cook; they provide a hauntingly deep flavor.

If you are planning to serve the beans with fish, then omit the prosciutto and the Parmigiano rind.

Preheat the oven to 275°F.

Heat the olive oil, garlic, and rosemary in a heavy ovenproof pot over medium-high heat. Sauté until the garlic perfumes the oil and starts to turn golden. Add the beans and 4 cups water. Raise the heat to high and add the diced prosciutto, prosciutto rind, and Parmigiano rind, if using. Stir well and bring to a simmer.

Cover the pot and transfer to the oven. Bake until the beans are tender when pierced with a fork, 1½ to 2 hours. Check periodically and add water as needed to keep the beans barely covered.

Use as directed in individual recipes or serve as is, adding a splash of olive oil at the table. If draining the beans before use or serving, save the water to use in a soup or for braising greens.

Sweating the Aromatics and Perfuming the Oil

Almost every warm savory dish in this book begins by infusing warm high-quality olive oil with aromatics, such as onions, garlic, fresh and dried herbs, salty components such as olives or anchovies, citrus zest, hot pepper, mushrooms or other vegetables, and/or cured meats.

This technique differs from the French method of sautéing because all the ingredients, including the oil, are started in a cold or cool pan over medium-high heat, allowing the ingredients to warm up in the oil and thereby release their fundamental qualities into the oil. This way, garlic and onions won't burn and other ingredients retain their flavor. Just how long to cook the ingredients is determined by sight, smell, and touch. Garlic, for instance, should be cooked until it begins to color very slightly and releases an assertive aroma. Parsley and other fresh herbs quickly release their fragrance and should be heated just until they sizzle and the oil begins to take on their color. If vegetables such as carrots, mushrooms, or onions are cooked until they caramelize and turn brown, they impart a nutty richness to the dish quite different from the more delicate sweetness they would if not browned.

Once we have made this aromatic oil base, we add the principal ingredient of the dish and often gently sweat it with the aromatics so that the base takes on its character. The principal ingredient, in turn, will take on the flavor and characteristics of the aromatics.

Adding an Acidic Backbone

A great many of the sauces, braisings, pastas, and other dishes in this book call for a dry Italian white wine. The ideal wines are Vermentinos, such as those from Liguria, or any clean, tart, nonoaky California white, such as a Pinot Blanc or a not overly grassy Sauvignon Blanc. The wine is added to the aromatics and infused oil, the heat is increased to high, and, usually, the wine is reduced, or boiled down, by half. The purpose of this somewhat inexact technique is to boil off the alcohol and to concentrate the acidity and flavor of the wine.

Creating Body

Once the oil is perfumed and an acidic foundation has been built, it's time to create the body of the sauce or other dishes. As the dishes in this book are home-style cooking, we don't rely on complex restaurant-style, single-purpose stocks. Instead, we provide body to the sauces in one of three ways. First, we extract it from ingredients added to the infused oil, often by adding meat trimmings—prosciutto or pancetta—or anchovy in order to provide a savory foundation. Second, for many of the sauces, we use a tomato puree. This is a simple, pure puree of fresh or canned tomatoes that provides a light tomato note. Three, we sometimes add a broth, a "home kitchen"-style broth—that is, a broth made by using trimmings from roasts, leftover meats, prosciutto ends and trimmings, Parmesan rinds, dried wild mushrooms or mushroom trimmings, etc. This creates a rich meaty broth full of character and flavor. (Unlike neutral restaurant stocks, this broth is never reduced until it thickens.)

Reducing and Marrying Ingredients

In our home-style cooking, meats and seafood are typically cooked in the sauces that accompany them—taking on the characteristics of the sauce and giving up their flavor to the sauce. During this cooking time, the three components of the sauce—the aromatics, the acid backbone, and the base, or body—typically reduce in volume. There are three goals in this reduction: to concentrate flavor, to build texture by thickening through the process of reduction, and to blend, or marry, flavors. The violent boiling of liquids lets the aromatic olive oil become incorporated into the sauces in the form of tiny droplets, which both slightly thicken the sauces and give an unctuous body to them. This sort of reduction is very different from more typical restaurant sauce techniques in that it relies on the body of vegetables, or perhaps the slight starchiness of pasta water, for thickening, rather than the gelatin in stock or the fat in cream and butter.

Optional Accents

Often when we finish a sauce, at the last minute, we will add in a finely chopped or pounded mixture of ingredients. For example, in a long-cooking dish like the Braised Oxtails with Asparagus (page 172), we add a mixture of basil, lemon zest, and garlic pounded together with a little olive oil and salt as a fresh, bright counterpoint to the rich flavors of the slow-cooked beef. Or, for the Roast Sage-Stuffed Quail (page 201), we pound together walnuts, bread crumbs, garlic, salt, and sage and simmer it in the sauce until the bread and nuts thicken the sauce. In the pesto recipes, a little bit of pasta water transforms the pesto into a miracle of creamy summer flavor.

Antipasti

In the early days of North Beach, antipasti, served in uncomplicated working-class restaurants, meant a platter with peperoncini, olives, pickled carrots and cauliflower, and green onions. If the place had class, the platter might include a few slices of homemade salami, mortadella, coppa, and dry Monterey Jack or teleme. It was a matter of economics to keep things simple. Courses that followed were huge, with enormous communal bowls of pasta and large platters of whole fish, food to feed men who worked ten-hour days, six days a week.

Today antipasti are more than just a nibble before the meal. They are also an option for a light supper or a late-afternoon snack with a glass of wine.

We love antipasti at Rose Pistola. The first thing customers see upon entering the restaurant is a colorful array of seafood and marinated vegetable antipasti on long, oval platters at the end of the open kitchen's counter. Many diners make a meal of a combination of hot and cold antipasti. We have loads of recipes in this book for antipasti—marinated olives, fried, sautéed, and poached fish, and a lovely selection of shaved raw, braised, and marinated vegetables. There's a splashy assortment of crostini; something for everyone. Have an antipasti party or incorporate a wonderful small dish or two before the pasta or the main course.

Asparagus ready to be cooked.

Marinated Olives

Serve these with drinks before lunch or dinner. Offer a little dish alongside for the pits. It is nice to include an assortment of olives, with some green Bella di Cerignola mixed in with a variety of black olives, because they look and taste so good.

- 1 pound assorted olives, such as Niçoise, Gaeta, San Remo, and green olives such as Bella di Cerignola or Picholine
- 1/4 pound sun-dried tomatoes, thinly sliced
- 1/4 cup extra virgin olive oil
- Grated zest of 1 lemon
- 1 garlic clove, bruised
- 1/4 cup basil leaves

Drain the olives and toss in a bowl with the sun-dried tomatoes, olive oil, lemon zest, garlic, and basil. These can be served after marinating overnight in the refrigerator, or stored for up to 2 weeks. Bring to room temperature before serving.

Serves 8 to 12

A platter of marinated olives at Rose Pistola.

Fried Olives

- 4 cups olive oil, for deep-frying
- 2 cups (1 pound) assorted olives, such as Niçoise, Gaeta, San Remo, Picholine
- 1 large egg
- 1 cup whole milk
- 1 teaspoon thyme leaves
- 1/4 teaspoon cayenne pepper
- 1 cup pastry flour

Serves 4 to 6

Olives are the perfect food to nibble alongside an apéritif. This recipe uses an assortment of olives. If you use pitted olives, many varieties of stuffed ones are available that will make these fried olives unique. Unpitted olives tend to have a more pronounced olive flavor. Whichever ones you decide to use, easy-to-make fried olives will delight your guests.

Enjoy with a Pinot Grigio wine.

In a Dutch oven, preheat the oil (at least 1 inch deep) to 350°F on a thermometer. Drain the olives. Whisk together the egg, milk, thyme, and cayenne in a medium bowl. Toss the olives in the flour to coat. Shake off the excess flour, dip the olives in the milk, and then coat in flour again. Fry until golden brown and hot throughout, about 4 minutes. Serve.

Tuna Tapenade

This flavorful, versatile spread can be served on the Tomato, Goat Cheese, and Tapenade Crostini (page 29) or on flatbread, or as a dip for raw vegetables. Or use it in Crisp Salmon with Fennel and Tapenade (page 144). However you plan on using it, the flavorful spread will keep well under a float of a few tablespoons of olive oil, well covered, in the refrigerator for up to two weeks. Bring it back to room temperature before using.

3/4 cup Niçoise olives, pitted
1/4 cup green olives, pitted
1 garlic clove
3 tablespoons capers, drained
1 teaspoon thyme leaves
1/4 teaspoon rosemary leaves, chopped
One 6 1/2-ounce can Italian olive-oil-packed tuna, drained
Grated zest and juice of 1 lemon
1 tablespoon Cognac
About 1/2 cup extra virgin olive oil

Pulse the olives, garlic, capers, and herbs together in a food processor. Then pulse in the tuna until it is combined. Place the ingredients in a bowl and add the lemon zest, lemon juice, and Cognac. Slowly mix in the olive oil, a little at a time, until the tapenade has a coarse texture. It should not be smooth. Cover and refrigerate until needed; serve at room temperature.

Makes about 1 1/2 cups

Pitting Olives

Lay a clean kitchen towel on a flat surface and place about five olives on top. With the flat side of a heavy knife, whack each of the olives so that they split open. Ease the pit out with your fingers, set the pitted olives aside, and proceed until all the olives are pitted.

Crostini of Asparagus, Prosciutto, and Teleme

- 12 thick asparagus spears, trimmed to about 5 inches long, or 20 pencil asparagus spears
- 1 tablespoon extra virgin olive oil
- Kosher or sea salt and freshly cracked black pepper
- 4 long slices country-style bread, the same length as the asparagus
- ¼ pound ripe teleme or crescenza cheese
- 4 thin slices prosciutto

Serves 4

In both this antipasto and in Asparagus Carpaccio (page 33), we combine asparagus, cheese, and prosciutto, yet the results are markedly different. Here the asparagus is grilled, taking on a slightly bitter, smoky flavor.

If you don't have a grill lighted and ready, you can use a stovetop grill pan or a very hot oven. Make this to nibble on while you fix the rest of the meal. It only takes about ten minutes from start to finish.

A glass of Arneis Bruno Giacosa would be good with these crostini.

Prepare a medium-hot fire in a grill, preheat a stovetop grill pan, or preheat the oven to 550°F (or to the highest setting).

Toss the asparagus with the oil, then season to taste with salt and pepper. Place the asparagus on the grill rack, in the grill pan, or on a sheet pan in the oven and cook, turning frequently, until nicely browned, about 5 minutes.

Meanwhile, toast the bread on the grill rack or in the grill pan or oven, turning once, until golden on both sides.

To serve, spread each piece of toast with a thick layer of cheese. Lay the prosciutto on top and arrange the grilled asparagus over it.

Asparagus fresh from Ferry Plaza Farmers' Market.

Fava Bean Puree Crostini

The texture of this fava bean puree is as delightful as its color is. The way to get it right is simple—mix peeled and unpeeled fava beans.

In Italy, fava beans are small and rarely need peeling once they are released from their pods. But many Americans let favas grow Texas-style.

This is the same recipe we use to stuff ravioli. It is great in omelets and as a sauce for pork or rabbit.

- ¼ cup fava beans (see page 195)
- ¼ cup baby or immature fava beans (see page 195)
- 1 teaspoon lemon thyme leaves or 1 teaspoon thyme leaves mixed with ¼ teaspoon grated lemon zest
- ¼ cup plus 1 tablespoon extra virgin olive oil
- ¼ teaspoon kosher or sea salt
- ½ teaspoon chopped green garlic or 1 small garlic clove, chopped
- 4 slices country bread

Serves 4

Combine the fava beans, thyme, ¼ cup of the olive oil, the salt, and garlic in a food processor and puree just until blended. The puree should be smooth but not silky; it should still have a little crunchy texture.

Toast or grill the bread. Brush with the remaining 1 tablespoon olive oil, spread the fava bean puree on top, and serve.

Crostini of Figs, Crescenza, and Prosciutto

4 ripe figs, cut in half
4 slices country bread
¼ pound crescenza cheese or teleme
4 thin slices prosciutto
A handful of arugula leaves

Serves 4

To start a late summer meal, serve these crostini when figs are ripe and plentiful. Grilling the figs caramelizes them and enhances their sweetness. The slightly tangy flavor of the crescenza cheese, the saltiness of the prosciutto, and the sweet figs are a memorable combination. If crescenza is hard to get in your area, use teleme or a soft, mild cheese like fresh ricotta.

These are delicious with a Dolcetto wine.

Prepare a medium-hot fire in a grill or preheat a skillet over medium-high heat.

Place the fig halves cut side down on the grill or in the skillet and grill for a few minutes, until the cut sides start to caramelize.

Meanwhile, grill or toast the bread.

Spread each slice of bread with the crescenza. Place 2 fig halves on each slice of bread. Lay a slice of prosciutto over the figs, scatter a few arugula leaves on top, and serve.

Reed Hearon (left) discusses the making of crescenza cheese with cheesemaker Liam Callahan (right) at Bellwether Farms.

Tomato, Goat Cheese, and Tapenade Crostini

If you have some tapenade in the refrigerator, you're almost there. If not, tapenade is quick and easy to make, or you could use a good commercial variety. This is just the thing to munch on while cooking dinner or to put together when friends drop by.

Enjoy with a glass of rosé.

4 slices country bread
2 tablespoons extra virgin olive oil
6 ounces goat cheese, at room temperature
1 tablespoon plus 1 teaspoon Tuna Tapenade (page 25)
1 large ripe tomato, thickly sliced

Serves 4

Preheat the broiler. Brush the bread with the olive oil. Broil the bread, turning once, until golden brown and crusty on both sides. Drizzle with the oil. Spread each slice with the goat cheese and then the tapenade, top with a tomato slice, and serve.

Sea Salt

Although I prefer cooking with sea salt, you can certainly substitute kosher salt. Sea salt is much more than sodium chloride (the salt in table salt). Sea salt contains the full spectrum of minerals present in ocean water and hence has a much broader, more complex range of flavors. It's also a great source of trace minerals such as calcium, magnesium, and zinc. It simply has the greatest flavor of any salt.

Shaved Artichokes with Fava Beans and Parmesan

1 lemon, halved, plus a few drops of lemon juice
16 baby artichokes
¼ cup extra virgin olive oil
½ cup fava beans (see page 195)
Kosher or sea salt and freshly cracked black pepper
A ¼-pound wedge Parmigiano-Reggiano

Serves 4

Here is one of the most irresistible antipasti served at Rose Pistola; it couldn't be simpler. Artichokes are very versatile (see, for example, Griddled Artichokes and Potatoes, page 207, and Fried Artichokes with Parmesan, page 32), and when thinly shaved, and served raw, they are delicious. Their crunchy, slightly bitter flavor stimulates the appetite and palate.

Enjoy this antipasto with a Vermentino or Pigato from Liguria.

Fill a large bowl with water and squeeze in the juice from the lemon, then toss in the squeezed halves. Peel off and discard the outer leaves from each artichoke until you reach the part that is yellowish-green. Trim off the top, peel off the tough outer layer at the bottom, and cut the artichoke in half. Remove the small thistle if it has started to form in the middle. As each artichoke is trimmed, put it into the lemon water.

When all the artichokes are prepared, pour the olive oil into a serving bowl. Drain the artichokes and cut each in half lengthwise. Then lay the halves cut-side down on a cutting board, and, using a sharp stainless steel knife, slice into lengthwise slices as thin as possible. Alternatively shave them with a mandoline, being very careful of your fingertips. Put the slices in the bowl with the olive oil as you finish them, tossing to coat to prevent discoloration.

Add the fava beans, toss well, and season with salt and pepper and a few drops of lemon juice. Shave shards of the cheese over the top with a vegetable peeler and serve.

"Vicious," or spiky, artichokes from Knoll Farms in Brentwood, California.

Preparing Artichokes

Artichokes discolor if they come into contact with air, iron, or aluminum. To avoid discoloration always use stainless steel knives and cookware or glass pots. If preparing just one or two artichokes, rub the exposed area with lemon juice to preserve the green color. Or, when preparing a large batch, drop the trimmed artichokes into a bowl of water to which has been added the juice of two lemons along with the squeezed lemon halves, or with one-third lemon juice or white vinegar. Cover the artichokes with a clean kitchen towel to submerge them under the water.

To trim a medium or large artichoke, cut the black tip off the base of the stem. Then, using a small knife, peel off the stringy outer layer of the stem. If you wish to discard the stem, cut it off flush with the bottom. We usually leave the trimmed stem connected to the heart. Pull off any small leaves surrounding the base. Break off at least three or four layers of leaves until you reach the pale green or pale lavender interior leaves.

Place the artichoke on its side and slice about one inch off the tops of the leaves to remove the sharp, pointed tips. Cut the artichoke in half lengthwise (or into quarters if large) and use a grapefruit spoon or melon baller to scoop out the prickly choke and tiny, sharp inner leaves. Immediately slip the halves into lemon water.

Just before using them, drain thoroughly and pat dry. If sautéing or frying, cut them as directed in individual recipes. (If adding the artichokes in a soup or braise, drying isn't necessary.)

Fried Artichokes with Parmesan

1 lemon, halved
16 baby artichokes
4 cups olive oil, for deep-frying
2 tablespoons finely chopped flat-leaf parsley
1 teaspoon minced spring garlic or 1 garlic clove, bruised
Kosher or sea salt and freshly cracked black pepper
A 3-ounce wedge Parmigiano-Reggiano

Serves 4

Artichokes are surprising, because they behave differently at different times, sometimes acting as a starchy vegetable, as is the case here, sometimes as a green vegetable. Frying artichokes to potato-chip-crispness and a mahogany color brings out the nuttiness of the vegetable. Serving them raw accentuates their slightly bittersweet flavor, reminiscent of raw peas or fava beans.

Pour a Prosecco wine.

Squeeze the juice of the lemon into a large bowl of water and then toss in the squeezed halves. Trim the artichokes as directed on page 31 and cut each artichoke lengthwise into quarters; as you cut each artichoke, drop the wedges into the lemon water.

Heat the oil to 350°F in a large heavy pot. Drain the artichokes and pat dry with paper towels. Fry half of the artichoke wedges in the hot oil until golden, about 7 minutes. Lift out with a wire skimmer or slotted spoon and drain on paper towels. Pat off most of the surface oil with additional paper towels. Repeat with the remaining artichoke wedges. (This can be done a few hours ahead of serving; set the pan of hot oil aside in a safe place.)

Just before serving, heat the oil to 365°F. Briefly refry the artichokes, all at one time, until brown and crisp, about 2 minutes. Lift out and drain again on paper towels.

Toss together the parsley and garlic in a large bowl. Add the hot artichoke wedges, season to taste with salt and pepper, and toss again. Arrange the artichokes on a platter, shave the cheese over the top, and serve hot.

Asparagus Carpaccio

When raw asparagus is thinly shaved, the texture becomes interesting, as in this crisp salad. The lemony oil and the rich nutty cheese wonderfully neutralize the strong grassy flavor of the raw vegetable. The trick to the dish is to slice the asparagus as thin as possible; if you have a mandoline, use it.

"O" olive oil is a California oil made by crushing olives with Meyer lemons. The result is a fragrant blend of lemon and olive flavor. Unlike infused oils, this product actually is made with the oil of lemons. It was inspired by similar Italian citrus olive oils, such as Agrimato brand.

Pour an Italian or California Sauvignon Blanc with this dish.

1 pound large asparagus spears
1 to 3 tablespoons Meyer lemon-flavored "O" olive oil, another lemon-flavored olive oil, or very good extra virgin olive oil
Kosher or sea salt and freshly cracked black pepper
A 3-ounce wedge Parmigiano-Reggiano
4 very thin slices prosciutto, optional

Serves 4

Trim the asparagus spears by breaking the ends off where they give way naturally. Trim the jagged ends so that they are even. Peel the stalks to within 3 inches of the tips with a vegetable peeler. Cut the tips off the stalks and set aside. Slice the stalks as thin as possible on a mandoline or with a sharp knife. Slice the tips lengthwise in half and then into small bits. Place the asparagus in a bowl with the olive oil, season to taste with salt and pepper, and toss well.

To serve, divide the asparagus among individual plates and, using a vegetable peeler, shave the cheese over each serving. If desired, lay a prosciutto slice on top of each, and season with pepper. Or, if you would like to serve the salad on a platter, place the asparagus on the platter, shave most of the cheese over the top, and toss gently to mix, then shave the remainder over the top. Arrange the prosciutto slices, if using, around the edge of the platter.

Baby Fava Beans and Pecorino

1 cup baby fava beans (see page 195)
½ pound Pecorino Sardo or Pecorino Toscano, preferably with peppercorns

Serves 4

Fava beans are large fleshy beans with an outer pod that holds several beans and an inner skin that wraps each bean. When the bean is mature, the inner pod is disagreeably tough and bitter, but when immature, this little bean, skin and all, tastes like spring smells. Its slightly bitter flavor contrasts perfectly with a young sheep's milk pecorino, such as Pecorino Sardo from Sardinia. It is particularly good with one that has whole peppercorns imbedded in the cheese.

Try this dish with a medium-bodied California Dolcetto.

Arrange the beans and cheese on a plate in whatever form pleases you. Enjoy the taste of spring.

Shaved Raw Mushrooms, Endive, and Parmesan

The perfume of raw mushrooms can be extraordinary. They have a particular affinity for cheese, taken advantage of here. If porcini are available, use them. If not, portobellos, with their black gills trimmed off, will also work.

Belgian endive works well here, as would thinly shaved fennel. Either one adds a nice crispness that counterpoints the softer mushrooms and cheese.

A Prosecco di Valdobbiadene, Ruggeri, Veneto, is recommended.

2 heads Belgian endive

1/2 pound mushrooms, preferably portobellos, stemmed, cleaned, gills removed with a spoon, and thinly sliced

2 tablespoons extra virgin olive oil

Kosher or sea salt and freshly cracked black pepper

A 3-ounce wedge Parmigiano-Reggiano

A few drops of fresh lemon juice

Serves 4

Cut the endive leaves into long julienne. Divide among four plates. Top with the mushroom slices. Drizzle with the olive oil. Season with salt and pepper. Shave the Parmesan over the top and drizzle with a few drops of lemon juice.

Roasted Sweet Peppers with Ricotta and Basil

- 1½ pounds assorted red and yellow bell peppers (about 6 medium or 4 large peppers)
- 1 cup Homemade Ricotta (page 12) or fresh ricotta
- ½ cup extra virgin olive oil
- 20 basil leaves
- 1 garlic clove, bruised
- Kosher or sea salt
- 8 Cured Fresh Sardines (page 50) or ¼ cup capers or olives (Niçoise or other black imported olives)

Serves 4

When you see stall after stall at the farmers' market with still-life displays of peppers in every color conceivable, buy them and put them to use for an antipasto or a light lunch as generations of North Beach residents have. Roasted and stuffed with fresh ricotta and basil, they taste as good as they look.

You can make your own ricotta or buy a good local brand. Similarly, for the topping you can make Cured Fresh Sardines or buy a good brand of sardines or anchovies. They provide a nice salty counterpart to the cheese, but you can leave them out and serve with capers or olives instead, so the dish has some contrast.

Serve with a Prosecco di Valdobbiadene, Ruggeri, Veneto.

Grill the peppers over a gas flame or under the broiler, turning them with tongs, until all sides are blistered. Place in a bowl, cover with a kitchen towel, and let stand for about 15 minutes.

Slip off the pepper skin, pull out the cores, and brush off the seeds. Do not wash, or the flavor of the peppers will be diluted.

Stuff the peppers with the ricotta—if the peppers are large, split them in two and stuff, re-forming them as if each half were a single pepper. Place the peppers on a serving platter and cover the peppers with the olive oil, scatter the basil leaves and garlic over them, and sprinkle with salt. Arrange the sardines or scatter the capers on top. Let sit for a short while to let the basil and garlic flavor the peppers. Discard the garlic and serve.

Crispy Fried Zucchini

Fried zucchini is one of the old standards of traditional Italian restaurants. When we opened Rose Pistola, we offered a lighter version of that classic dish, which was achieved by slicing the zucchini paper-thin. This is easy to do using the thin slicing blade of a food processor or a mandoline. To make these as light as possible, do use pastry flour, for a crisp delicate coating. For a nice zesty note, we add thin lemon slices and a few basil leaves, fried and tossed in at the very end. These will disappear faster than you can possibly imagine.

They are delicious with a Corsican Vermentino wine.

- 4 cups olive oil, for deep-frying
- 1 cup pastry flour
- Kosher or sea salt and freshly cracked black pepper
- 1 pound large firm zucchini, sliced into paper-thin rounds
- 1 lemon, cut into paper-thin slices
- 1/4 cup chopped flat-leaf parsley
- 1 teaspoon finely minced green garlic or 1 garlic clove, finely minced
- 15 basil leaves

Serves 4 to 6

Heat the oil in a heavy saucepan or a deep-fat fryer to 350°F. Season the flour with salt and pepper. Toss the zucchini and the lemon slices in the flour and shake off any excess flour. Working in batches, deep-fry the zucchini and lemon until golden brown. Keep the slices moving in the oil with a slotted spoon or tongs so they don't clump together; watch carefully, as they burn easily. When golden brown, remove with the spoon or tongs to a wire rack placed over paper towels to drain briefly. Transfer to a bowl, toss with the parsley and garlic, and season to taste with salt and pepper.

Fry the basil leaves until crisp and lightly browned, a few seconds. Toss with the zucchini and lemons and serve at once.

Ricotta with Arugula Puree and Grilled Bread

- 1 garlic clove
- ¼ teaspoon kosher or sea salt, plus more to taste
- 2 tablespoons extra virgin olive oil
- 2 bunches arugula, tough stems removed (about 4 cups)
- 1 cup Homemade Ricotta (page 12) or fresh ricotta
- 1 sprig rosemary
- 1 large egg, beaten
- Freshly cracked black pepper
- 8 slices country bread

Serves 6 to 8

This dish combines three classic Northern Italian and Northern Californian flavors in a very simple and straightforward way. The creamy, bland ricotta bakes until it's brown on the outside and is served with a slightly bitter puree of arugula and lots of grilled country bread.

Enjoy with a young Chianti or a California Sangiovese.

Preheat the oven to 500°F.

In a mortar or a food processor, pound or process the garlic, salt, olive oil, and arugula until a coarse puree is formed.

Pack the cheese into a small bowl to shape it into a dome. Unmold onto a small nonstick baking sheet. Using the rosemary sprig as a brush, brush the cheese all over with the egg. Season the outside generously with salt and pepper and bake until brown and crusty all over, about 20 minutes. Let the cheese cool slightly while you toast the bread.

Serve the cheese with the arugula puree in a ring around it and the toasted country bread on the side.

Since the mid-1800s, the bocce courts, bars, and caffès of North Beach have been the domain of Italian men. For more than eighty years, the San Francisco Italian Athletic Club (SFIAC), just down the block from Rose Pistola, has been a gathering place for social and cultural events, as well as for sports. It started in 1917, when a group of young Italian North Beach residents wanted to have a spot to relax together after a hard day's work. Most of them had fled devastating poverty in the Old Country to create better lives for themselves. Many had come alone, hoping eventually to make enough money to bring over their wives and families.

To combat homesickness and loneliness, the men started a club called Circolo Recreativo Italiano, holding their meetings in a series of different houses. Life was isolating in North Beach, and many residents spoke only Italian. Regional barriers that had divided men in the Old Country broke down in their new home. Tuscans, Sicilians, and Ligurians mingled, playing sports, working, drinking, and eating together. Eventually, these men formed the Unione Sportivo Italiano, which met in a club room on Mason Street between Green and Vallejo. All sorts of sporting events were supported by the club, including fencing, boxing, soccer, and the oldest running race in San Francisco, the Statuto Race.

The only thing missing at the clubhouse was a kitchen (and women, of course). So members began to meet at a neighborhood restaurant located where Columbus Avenue meets Stockton Street, not far from where Rose Pistola stands today. They called it the U.S. Caffè for Unione Sportivo. The barbershop that popped up next door quickly became known as the U.S. Barber Shop.

Hungry sportsmen and other neighborhood Italians flocked to the caffè to eat fluffy artichoke frittatas, salt cod in tomato sauce, and perfectly fried calamari. The restaurant has changed hands a few times over the years, but it has been operated by Maria Borzoni and her family for about the last thirty years. Borzoni, who has survived happily in North Beach without ever speaking English, cooked in front of the old stove well into her eighties. Her daughter, Anna Cipollina, and son-in-law, Al, worked by her side. The women are some of the true "old stoves" of North Beach. "Old stoves" are cooks with years of experience cooking Italian food in the North Beach tradition. They are old souls, well aged, and well loved because they have provided thousands of meals for family and friends. "Old stoves" can be restaurant chefs, active or retired, but usually they are just good simple home cooks.

Today the Italian Athletic Club, whose old-time members still remember the original U.S. Caffè, boasts some twelve hundred members, who regularly attend weddings, dances, and banquets in a building that continues to preserve many of the neighborhood traditions. Men still also go to the club to play cards, take steam baths, speak Italian, and worry about the fate of the younger generation.

Pickled Crab

1 Dungeness crab (1½ to 2 pounds)
½ cup plus 2 tablespoons red wine vinegar
½ cup extra virgin olive oil
2 small inner celery stalks with leaves, finely diced
1 medium carrot, finely diced
1 small red onion, finely diced
3 garlic cloves, chopped
1 tablespoon chopped flat-leaf parsley
Kosher or sea salt
Dash of cayenne pepper

Serves 4

When I first met Rose Pistola, with a conspiratorial wink, she told me about this recipe. "Sell it in your restaurant," she said, "and you'll make lots of money off it." Much as I loved Rose, her grasp of restaurant economics had eroded over the years. Crab is expensive and hence not a moneymaker, but she's right about one thing: This is a dynamite dish.

You can make it with cold precooked crab, but this dish is at its absolute peak when the vinaigrette goes straight onto still-warm, freshly cooked and cracked Dungeness crab.

Pour a Chardonnay or Arneis, Bruno Giacosa, Piedmont, 1997, and serve with country bread and a tossed green salad.

Bring a large pot of salted water to a boil. Add the crab, submerging it completely, return to a boil, and cook until cooked through, 8 to 10 minutes. Remove the crab to a work surface and, when cool enough to handle, clean, section, and crack as directed on page 157.

Whisk together the vinegar, olive oil, celery, carrot, onion, garlic, parsley, salt to taste, and cayenne in a large bowl. Add the crab pieces and toss to coat well. Let marinate in the refrigerator for at least 1 hour and up to 2 days, tossing occasionally.

Serve the crab with nutcrackers, picks, and finger bowls.

Freshly caught crabs.

Grilled Oyster Brochettes Wrapped in Pancetta

San Francisco Bay used to be teeming with oysters, especially the tiny native Olympias. During the Gold Rush, these briny little treats were so popular that they were essentially eaten into extinction. It is hard to imagine that at one point raw oysters were so plentiful and so much in favor that people used to eat twelve dozen or more at a seating.

An exciting discovery in early 1999 of a small colony of what experts believe to be Olympias made front-page news. Up and down the California coast, oyster farms still raise uniquely flavored Pacific oysters, which are shipped across the United States. If you can't get these, use what is available in your region. Typically of larger Japanese seed stock, these oysters are noted for their clean, cucumbery flavor. This wonderfully simple brochette is a nice alternative to the raw oyster tradition.

- 4 sprigs rosemary (about 8 inches long)
- 12 large Pacific or Blue Point oysters, freshly shucked
- ¼ pound pancetta, sliced as thin as possible
- 1 lemon, sliced paper-thin

Serves 4

Strip the leaves from all but the top 1 inch of each rosemary sprig. Reserve the leaves for another use. Cut an angled piece off the bottom of each sprig to create a sharp point. Skewer 3 oysters (through the length of the oyster) onto each sprig. Wrap the oysters tightly with the strips of pancetta, making a spiral. (The oysters can be prepared a few hours ahead to this point and refrigerated.)

Prepare a fire in a grill or preheat a grill pan over medium-high heat. Grill the oysters until browned on all sides, about 4 minutes. Shingle the lemon slices on a plate, arrange the skewers across the top, and serve.

True Bay Shrimp in Olive Oil

Kosher or sea salt
1 piece nori (Japanese dried seaweed)
3/4 pound fresh bay shrimp
1/4 cup highest-quality extra virgin olive oil, preferably Ligurian
1 lemon, cut into quarters

Serves 4

San Francisco Bay used to be filled with tiny, brownish shrimp called grass shrimp. They were caught at a series of thirty-some Chinese camps set up around the periphery of the Bay. The Chinese had come to California during the Gold Rush and later, in the mid-1860s, settled in fishing camps around the Bay. Huge numbers of grass shrimp were salted, dried, and shipped to China, and local cooks used them as well. Eventually, a method for mechanically peeling these tasty shrimp was invented. Unfortunately, it involves freezing the shrimp and abrading the shells off the meat. In the process, they are so roughly treated that nearly all their tender flavor is lost. These are the disappointing shrimp-cocktail shrimp you see on airplanes.

While fresh, unpeeled bay shrimp are much harder to find than they used to be, they do still exist. They are usually quite inexpensive. If you cannot find fresh bay shrimp, substitute the smallest fresh shrimp you can find. A splash of the best Ligurian extra virgin olive oil and a squeeze of lemon juice is all these shrimp need. You'll want some good crusty bread to sop up the juices. The nori provides an extra burst of flavor.

A delicate Pinot Bianco, such as Alois Lageder, Alto Adige, 1997, wine would be great.

Heat a pot of seawater or well-salted tapwater, along with the nori, to a rolling boil. Cook the shrimp for 2 minutes or until pink. Drain, let cool, and peel them.

Divide the shrimp among four chilled plates. Drizzle on the olive oil and serve with a lemon quarter on each plate.

Rick Knoll in the fields at Knoll Farms in Brentwood, California. Knoll Farms is known for its artichokes and green garlic.

Grilled Spiced Shrimp

Inspired by our popular Whole Roasted Crab Crusted with Garlic and Red Pepper (page 154), chef Erik Cosselmon applied a similar approach to the wonderful live shrimp we get from neighboring Chinatown. On and off during the year when shrimp come in, a deliveryman walks a hand truck up from Chinatown to Rose Pistola. On the truck is a bucket of seawater with shrimp literally jumping into the air. The sweet shrimp can be peeled or eaten head, shell, and all, after you work your magic on them as Erik does at the restaurant. Frozen shrimp are fine; defrost them slowly in cool salted water.

1 teaspoon crushed red pepper flakes
2 tablespoons marjoram leaves
1 teaspoon fennel seeds, crushed
2 garlic cloves, chopped
½ teaspoon kosher or sea salt
¼ cup extra virgin olive oil
1 pound fresh shrimp with heads

Serves 4

Prepare a hot fire in a grill or heat a grill pan over high heat. Combine all the ingredients except the shrimp and puree to make the marinade. Rub the marinade onto the shrimp. Grill on one side until the shells blister and turn pink, then turn and grill on the other side until done. Serve hot.

The only reason anyone would leave Italy, the most beautiful country in the world," explains art history professor Ray Mondini, "was to escape dire poverty." Born and raised in North Beach, Mondini is one of a disappearing breed of third-generation Italians who still live and work in the neighborhood. His house is a short walk from the Art Institute, where he teaches—and from the flat off Columbus Avenue where he was born. He tells of the food of a neighborhood that was born out of frugality.

As he lifts weights in the Dolphin Club exercise room, a room that has remained almost unchanged since he was a boy, Mondini remembers what it used to be like in the neighborhood. "During World War II, Roosevelt encouraged Americans to plant victory gardens, and being good new Americans, many Italians were happy to comply." On the roofs of the apartment buildings of the neighborhood were little wooden-box gardens. The boxes sprouted familiar Old Country produce: lettuces, greens, herbs, tomatoes, and peppers. Dandelion greens grew wild around Coit Tower and kids were sent out to pick them for ravioli stuffing and for braising.

"My relatives didn't eat out much and they didn't go to bars." The wives cooked with crab and squid, which were cheap and plentiful. They made polenta with Monterey Jack cheese, and coteghino and breaded veal cutlets. They cooked tripe on Thursdays, boiled beef with fedelini or pastina in a beef broth on weekends, cioppino for New Year's, and ravioli for Christmas. Baccalà, salt cod, was a staple in most houses, because most were without refrigerators, and it didn't have to be kept cool. "I remember the ice man in his leather vest, with his big ice pick, making a weekly delivery of a huge piece of ice."

Risotto was a cheap and commonplace meal, made simply with stock, a little cheese, and some wild mushrooms if the family was lucky enough to have a father who went foraging in Marin or Sonoma county. There he could find all the deer, duck, and mushrooms he and his family could possibly eat. Backyards were little barnyards, where rab-

bits and chickens were kept in pens. Many families aged cheese in their cool basements. They'd buy a wheel of Monterey Jack, rub it with pepper and olive oil, and wait for it to get hard enough to grate. Parmigiano-Reggiano was unheard of in the neighborhood at the time. Meals were big and hearty to fuel the men, many of whom worked two or more hard manual jobs, fishing, cooking, farming, collecting garbage, or tending grocery stores and bakeries. The tradition of the big family-style meals started then in the neighborhood, a tradition that is carried on at Rose Pistola today. The focaccia at the Liguria Bakery is the same today as it was in 1948, and the window display hasn't changed much in fifty years either.

Mondini remembers the ultimate patriarchal pastime—wine making. During the fall harvest, when the trains brought grapes down from Napa, flatbed trucks would pick up loads from the railroad tracks on the Embarcadero and deliver the grapes to cellars around the neighborhood. "There were not a lot of garages at that time, so the street-level basements were reserved for wine making. The gutters looked as if blood was running in them, but it was just 'Dago red.' My father would take me with him sometimes," Mondini reminisces. "We'd go to our neighbors and there the men would discuss the merits of one wine and its vinegar over another. They'd always worry that if I got too close, I'd breathe in the fumes and get drunk."

When Mondini was a boy, he was sent on errands to the Italian groceries in North Beach. In those days there were Celli Brothers, Molinari, and Panelli Brothers, all with huge barrels of olives. Panama and Florence Ravioli rolled out the best pasta in the neighborhood, and two of the bakeries still provide pastries for family celebrations today. Victoria Pastry remains the place to go for St.-Honoré birthday cakes, and if all its rum cream, cream puff pastry, and mille-feuilles *are too much, there is always Stella Pastry for airy, intoxicating sacripantina, a sponge cake with zabaglione filling.*

Skillet-Roasted Mussels

1 pound mussels, scrubbed and debearded
Kosher or sea salt and freshly cracked black pepper
4 tablespoons unsalted butter, melted

Serves 2

Mussels have long been part of the culinary traditions of North Beach. Up until a few decades ago, when Italian housewives needed to stretch the food budget, they'd send their children out to pick mussels off the pilings on the piers along the edge of the Bay. Aquatic Park was a favorite spot for finding mussels, because children, and adults for that matter, could wade into the calm, cold water at low tide and pick off the mussels that grew on the stones flung into the Bay during the building of the railway and tracks. They had to be careful, though—there was an official quarantine on wild mussels from May 1 until the first of November.

Mussels appear in cameo roles in cioppinos, pastas, and sandwiches, but at Rose Pistola, they star, pure and simple, on a searing-hot plancha, *or iron skillet. This signature dish is one of our simplest, most satisfying dishes, and it's very easy to prepare at home. The mussels' own juices provide the lovely smoky flavor.*

Today much of the mussel crop is aquacultivated in Washington State or along the East Coast. These cleaned and debearded mussels generally can be purchased in little net bags. There are some great planchas available in restaurant supply stores and gourmet stores. They come with small wooden boards upon which to rest the hot skillet at the table and make for a great, straightforward presentation. You can always use a cast-iron skillet.

A chilled bottle of Barbera from California or Italy is just the thing to go with mussels.

Heat the plancha or cast-iron skillet over high heat (or over a hot wood fire) until it is extremely hot; when a bead of water dances across the surface and the pan is almost white, it's ready. Spread the mussels in one layer in the pan: The heat will cause the mussels to open. Their juices will first pool and then burn on the surface of the pan, at which point they are ready to serve, 4 to 5 minutes cooking time. Season the mussels generously with salt and pepper and serve from the pan at the table, with the melted butter on the side.

Octopus with Potatoes and Baby Green Beans

Octopus is perhaps the most tender and succulent of all shellfish. Its sweet, rich flavor is much like that of lobster and is best enjoyed either by itself or in simple combinations. Here we combine it with earthy potatoes and tender fresh green beans.

Serve with a nice light Pigato.

- 3/4 pound Yellow Finn or fingerling potatoes
- 1/4 pound tender young green beans
- 1½ cups cooked octopus, about 1½ pounds (see cooking instructions in Grilled Octopus with Broccoli Rabe and White Beans, page 166)
- 1/4 cup extra virgin olive oil
- Juice of 1 lemon
- 20 flat-leaf parsley leaves
- Kosher or sea salt and freshly cracked black pepper

Serves 4

Cook the potatoes in boiling salted water to cover until tender when pierced with a knife. Remove from the water and cook the green beans in the same water until tender; drain.

While they are still warm, scrape the peels off the potatoes and cut them into ⅓-inch-thick rounds.

Cut the octopus into 1-inch lengths. Warm it in the olive oil in a medium saucepan over medium heat. Add the potatoes and green beans, toss with the lemon juice and parsley, and season to taste with salt and pepper before serving.

Seafood Fritto Misto

- 4 cups olive oil, for deep-frying
- 12 mussels, scrubbed and debearded
- 2 cups flour, preferably 00 *farina di grano tenero* from Pastiticio (see Sources, page 264) or a flour such as Wondra
- Kosher or sea salt and freshly cracked black pepper
- ½ pound calamari, cleaned and cut into rings and tentacles (see page 163)
- ½ pound large shrimp
- ¾ pound small fish, such as fresh anchovies, whitebait, fresh sardines, small sole, and/or sand dab
- 1 recipe Salt Cod Fritters (without the salad; page 52), optional
- 1 lemon, thinly sliced
- ½ cup seaweed, optional

Serves 6 as an antipasto, 3 as a main course

Once you get the hang of it, deep-frying is no big deal. Fritto misto, or "mixed fry," can be lots of fun. Don't restrict yourself to seafood: All sorts of vegetable combinations also work. Here we combine calamari and shrimp, small whole fish, and salt cod fritters (optional). A garnish of fried lemon slices and seaweed adds unexpected crunch and color to the dish. Look for seaweed at Japanese fish markets, or ask your favorite fish restaurant or fish store to save you the seaweed lobster is packed in for shipping. The type we use is called limu *in Hawaiian,* wakame *in Japanese.*

This dish works equally well as an antipasto or as a main course. Enjoy it with a Brut Reserve Champagne, Billecart-Salmon, or a Blanc de Blanc from California.

Preheat the oven to 250°F. Heat the oil in a large heavy pot to 350°F.

Meanwhile, steam the mussels in ¼ cup water in a large sauté pan, covered, over high heat until they just open. Remove from the pan and let cool.

Whisk together the flour with salt and pepper to taste in a shallow dish. Working in small batches, toss the mussels, calamari, shrimp, and fish in the seasoned flour, shake off any excess, and fry until golden brown, about 3 minutes. Remove with a skimmer to a wire rack placed over paper towels to drain, then keep warm in the oven until all the fish is cooked.

Toss the lemon slices in the flour. Fry the seaweed with the lemon slices until brown and crisp, about 3 minutes. Serve alongside the fried seafood. Enjoy while hot.

Swordfish Brochettes with Salsa Verde

When days are mild, grill these brochettes over a charcoal fire. In the winter, you can cook them on a stovetop grill pan, although you'll miss the flavor from the grill.

Firm fish, such as sea bass, mackerel, salmon, mahi mahi, and halibut, can be substituted. If you do not have rosemary stems for skewering the fish, you will need to soak wooden skewers in water for about thirty minutes before skewering so they won't burn on the grill.

Serve with Asparagus Carpaccio (page 33) and a crisp Cortese di Gavi, "La Rocca," Luigi Coppa, Piedmont, 1997, wine.

For the Salsa Verde

- 1 cup loosely packed flat-leaf parsley leaves
- 1 tablespoon capers, rinsed and drained
- 1 tablespoon red wine vinegar
- 1 garlic clove
- 2 anchovy fillets
- 1 tablespoon dried Bread Crumbs (page 9)
- 1/4 cup extra virgin olive oil

- 1/4 pound swordfish steak
- 1 tablespoon extra virgin olive oil
- Kosher or sea salt and freshly cracked black pepper
- 8 sprigs rosemary (6 inches long) or 8 wooden skewers, soaked in water for 30 minutes

Serves 4

For the Salsa Verde

Combine all the ingredients in a blender or food processor and process until smooth. Set aside.

For the Brochettes

Prepare a fire in a charcoal grill, or heat an oiled stovetop grill over medium-high heat. Cut the fish into bite-sized pieces, about 1 inch × 1 inch. Place the fish in a bowl, add the olive oil and salt and pepper to taste, and toss to coat. Thread 1 or 2 pieces of fish onto the rosemary or wooden skewers.

Place the brochettes on the oiled grill rack 6 to 8 inches above the hot coals and cook, turning to brown on all sides, until nearly opaque throughout, about 1 minute per side. Or, cook the brochettes on the stovetop grill for about 1 minute on each side. Serve at once on individual plates, with the Salsa Verde spooned over the top.

Cured Fresh Sardines

¼ cup fresh lemon juice
¼ cup dry Italian white wine
¾ teaspoon kosher or sea salt
½ pound fresh sardines (or anchovies)
Extra virgin olive oil, preferably Ligurian, to cover
A few Niçoise olives
Thyme leaves

Serves 6 to 8

The first thing our guests see upon entering Rose Pistola is a lovely array of olive oil-cured fish. Thin slices of raw salmon, halibut, and swordfish, along with whole anchovies and sardines, rest in graceful long white serving dishes, ready to be eaten as a light antipasto.

This ancient method of preservation yields a delicate, bright, pure seafood flavor. First lemon juice, white wine, and salt "cook" the fish in the same way that citrus juice cooks a ceviche. The seafood is then covered in olive oil to preserve it. There are several variations here, to cure different kinds of fish.

Lately there has been a lot of discussion about the way swordfish is caught. In respect to the limits of wild populations of swordfish, we only use swordfish caught on long lines in California waters.

Serve with other antipasti, such as Marinated Olives (page 23) and Shaved Artichokes with Fava Beans and Parmesan (page 30). A Pinot Blanc or Pigato, Colle dei Bardellini, Liguere, 1997, would go nicely with this dish.

For the Sardines

Combine the lemon juice, white wine, and salt in a glass bowl. Fillet a sardine or an anchovy by cutting off the head and making a slit down the belly of the fish with a small, sharp knife. With your thumb, ease open the sides and pull out the spine and any innards. Cut the fish in half, leaving the tail on, add to the bowl with the lemon juice mixture, and proceed with the curing process. Refrigerate and let the fish "cook" until opaque throughout, about 2 hours.

Cover a wire rack with a clean kitchen towel. Remove the fish from the marinade, place it on the towel-covered rack, and top with a second towel. Press down on the towel to remove excess moisture. Transfer the fish to a glass or ceramic dish, cover with olive oil, and add the olives and thyme leaves. You can serve immediately or refrigerate, covered, for up to 4 days.

Cured Tuna

- 1/4 cup fresh lemon juice
- 1/4 cup dry Italian white wine
- 3/4 teaspoon kosher or sea salt
- 1/2 pound tuna, thinly sliced about 1/4-inch thick (sashimi-sized pieces)
- Extra virgin olive oil, preferably Ligurian, to cover
- 1 fennel bulb, thinly sliced

For the Tuna

Combine the lemon juice, white wine, and salt in a glass bowl. Add the tuna. Refrigerate and let the fish "cook" until opaque throughout, about 2 hours.

Cover a wire rack with a clean kitchen towel. Remove the fish from the marinade, place it on the towel-covered rack, and top with a second towel. Press down on the towel to remove any moisture. Transfer the fish to a nonreactive dish and cover with olive oil. You can serve immediately or refrigerate, covered, for up to 4 days. Arrange the fennel slices on top just before serving.

Cured Swordfish

- 1/4 cup fresh lemon juice
- 1/4 cup dry Italian white wine
- 1/4 teaspoon kosher or sea salt
- 1/2 pound swordfish, thinly sliced
- Extra virgin olive oil, preferably Ligurian, to cover
- 1 tablespoon drained green peppercorns

For the Swordfish

Combine the lemon juice, white wine, and salt in a glass bowl. Add the swordfish. Refrigerate and let the fish "cook" until opaque throughout, about 2 hours, turning once.

Cover a wire rack with a clean kitchen towel. Remove the fish from the marinade, place it on the towel-covered rack, and top with a second towel. Press down on the towel to remove any moisture. Transfer the fish to a ceramic dish and cover with olive oil. You can serve immediately or refrigerate, covered, for up to 4 days. Shower the green peppercorns on top just before serving.

Salt Cod Fritters with Tomato Salad

½ pound skinless, boneless salt cod
1 cup milk
½ white onion, chopped
3 sprigs thyme (3 inches long)
½ pound Yellow Finn potatoes, peeled and cut into quarters
¼ cup extra virgin olive oil
¼ cup heavy cream
4 cups olive oil, for deep-frying
2 medium eggs
½ cup Bread Crumbs (page 9), made from day-old bread

Serves 4

One of the ingredients that immigrants brought to North Beach was salt cod. Salt cod is not at all like fresh cod. It is incredibly versatile and has always been an essential ingredient in good Italian cooking. Salt cod is a bit like prosciutto, a salt-cured product. In both cases, the salting was originally intended as a preservative, but the flavor caught on and the preparations have endured, now out of demand rather than necessity.

Salt cod originated in Scandinavia, where cod was salted and dried in the northern latitudes. Salt cod will be rock hard when you buy it. It must be soaked in cold water to reconstitute it, usually for about thirty-six hours. Place it in a container slightly larger than the fish and change the water four times. Cooking with salt cod is an old North Beach tradition. In every North Beach delicatessen, wooden boxes spill over with hard dried sides of salt cod.

These simple fritters can be served as part of an elaborate Seafood Fritto Misto (page 48) or served simply with the salad of lettuces, olives, and tomatoes.

Put the salt cod in a large bowl with cold water to cover. Cover and refrigerate for 36 hours, changing the water at least four times.

Drain the cod, place in a large saucepan, and pour in the milk plus enough water to just cover. Add the onion and thyme and bring to a simmer over medium heat. Adjust the heat to maintain a gentle simmer and poach until tender, about 10 minutes. Lift out the cod with a slotted spoon and set aside. The fish may break into pieces, which is okay. Leave the cooking liquid in the pan.

Add the potatoes to the cooking liquid and simmer until tender when pierced with a fork, about 15 minutes. Drain, discarding the liquid, thyme sprigs, and onion.

Bring the ¼ cup olive oil and cream to a simmer in a small saucepan over high heat. Remove from the heat, add the cod and potatoes, and whisk together to form a thick mash. Let the mixture cool, then roll into balls a little smaller than a golf ball and place on a large dish.

Heat the oil for deep-frying in a large heavy pot to 350°F. Lightly beat together the eggs and a splash of water in a shallow dish. Place the bread crumbs in a second shallow dish. A few at a time, dip the cod balls in the egg mixture and then in bread crumbs to coat and fry until crusty and brown. Drain the cod balls on paper towels. Keep warm as you make the salad.

For the Salad

- 3 tablespoons extra virgin olive oil
- 1 tablespoon red wine vinegar
- 1 garlic clove, bruised
- Scant ¼ teaspoon kosher or sea salt
- 1 large ripe tomato, peeled, seeded, and roughly chopped
- 20 Niçoise olives, pitted
- 2 cups dandelion greens or mesclun

For the Salad

Whisk together the oil, vinegar, garlic, and salt in a salad bowl. Add the tomatoes, olives, and dandelion greens, toss to coat, and serve alongside the hot cod fritters.

Stuffed Roasted Sardines

8 fresh sardines
½ cup extra virgin olive oil
1 small white onion, finely chopped
1 garlic clove, crushed
1 sprig rosemary (3 inches long)
4 anchovy fillets, chopped
1 cup mixed greens (see headnote)
Kosher or sea salt and freshly cracked black pepper
½ cup coarse fresh Bread Crumbs (page 9)
1 tablespoon chopped flat-leaf parsley

Serves 4

Monterey Bay used to abound with sardines that were used in North Beach cooking—remember Steinbeck's Cannery Row? *Today a revival in sardine fishery is occurring. Here is a great recipe with which to celebrate its rebirth. If you have only had canned sardines, please don't think the fresh ones are at all the same. The difference is like the difference between canned and fresh tuna. Fresh sardines look (and taste) a lot like small fresh tuna.*

You will need to fillet and butterfly the sardines. You could have your fish dealer do this, but be sure he leaves the tails intact. To accompany them, compose a medley of wild greens such as dandelion, nettles, and milk thistle or domestic greens such as cavolo nero, chard, kale, or even spinach.

A Vermentino di Sardegna, "La Cala" Sela & Mosca, 1997, is recommended.

To prepare the sardines, cut off the heads. Make a 3-inch slit down the belly of each fish and open the fish out flat. With your fingers, carefully lift the backbone away from the flesh and discard it, along with the innards. Leave the tail on. Rinse and drain on paper towels.

Preheat the oven to 500°F. Oil a baking sheet with 1 tablespoon of the olive oil.

Combine 2 tablespoons of the olive oil and the onion in a medium saucepan over medium heat and sauté until the onion becomes translucent, about 5 minutes. Add the garlic and rosemary. Continue to cook until the rosemary sizzles and the garlic is fragrant, about 3 minutes more. Add the anchovies and sauté, pressing on the anchovies with a fork until they melt into the oil, about 2 minutes. Remove the rosemary and garlic and discard.

Blanch the greens in salted boiling water for 3 to 4 minutes. Drain and, when cool enough to handle, squeeze out as much moisture as possible.

Add the greens and 2 tablespoons of the olive oil and cook in the same pan as the anchovies, stirring often until the greens are tender, about 4 minutes longer. Season with salt and pepper. Remove to a plate and let cool slightly.

Combine the bread crumbs, parsley, 1 tablespoon olive oil, and salt to taste in a small bowl. Mix well.

Arrange the sardines skin side down on the prepared baking sheet. Season each with salt and pepper to taste and drizzle with about 2 tablespoons olive oil. Divide the stuffing among the sardines, sprinkling each fish with a light coating of the mixture and patting it down as you go. (At this point the fish can be refrigerated, covered, for up to 1 hour before baking.)

Bake until the bread crumbs are golden brown and the fish are cooked through, 5 to 8 minutes. Transfer to a platter and serve.

Tuna Carpaccio with Slivered Artichokes

1 lemon

½ pound very fresh albacore or yellowfin tuna

About 2 tablespoons extra virgin olive oil

4 baby artichokes, trimmed (see page 31), halved, and sliced

½ teaspoon kosher or coarse sea salt

Serves 4

This recipe takes full advantage of one of the cornerstones of our simple cooking at Rose Pistola: the use of lemon juice and olive oil to heighten and enrich flavors in food.

Here we poach a lemon in order to render all of its flesh tender and edible. Paper-thin slices of it provide a high note for the rich, slightly oily tuna and the cleansing freshness of raw artichokes. A little coarse salt on top at the end adds its crunch.

Pour a Pigato or Sémillon from Rosenblum Cellars, Livermore, California, 1997.

Poach the lemon in barely simmering water for 10 minutes over medium-low heat. Drain and let cool.

Slice the tuna into 4 slices, cutting across the grain. Spread out a 12-inch sheet of plastic wrap on a work surface. Brush olive oil over the plastic wrap and place a tuna slice on top. Drizzle a little more olive oil over the top and cover with a second sheet of plastic wrap. With a rolling pin, roll the tuna into a thin sheet about 6 inches in diameter. Transfer to a chilled plate. Repeat with the remaining slices, adding a little more olive oil as you go if necessary.

Cut one half of the lemon, including the rind, into paper-thin slices. Scatter the lemon and artichoke slices over the tuna. Squeeze the juice from the remaining lemon half over both the fish and the artichoke slivers. Season with a few grains of coarse salt and serve.

Soups

In North Beach, soup often replaces pasta in the meal. The best home-style soups are often long simmered and full of vegetables, with rich, deep flavors. Many of the soups in this chapter are bean- or bread-based—the starch playing the role of a meat substitute in this healthy, frugal fare.

The Spring Vegetable Minestrone, the Ribollita, the White Bean Soup with Braised Greens, the Calamari and Borlotti Bean Soup, and the Fava Bean and Porcini Soup are seasonal variations on the same principle. They are all basically bean soups with changing ingredients depending on what is fresh, local, and seasonal. The simple soup of mussels and bread in a tomato sauce base is perfect at almost any season—fragrant of the sea and rich with the flavors of the home kitchen. The Summer Tomato Soup makes use of an abundance of juicy ripe tomatoes, when they all seem to become ripe at the same time. Green Garlic Soup can be made with fresh spring garlic or garlic cloves; it's a light, simple broth powerful enough to help sufferers get over an early spring cold. The Homemade Kitchen Broth can be enjoyed as is or is used as the base for other recipes in the book.

Ladles in the kitchen at Rose Pistola.

Spring Vegetable Minestrone

- ½ pound fresh morels, chanterelles, porcini, or other wild mushrooms, cleaned and cut into bite-sized pieces, or 1 ounce dried porcini mushrooms plus ½ pound fresh white mushrooms, cleaned and cut into bite-sized pieces
- 4 large asparagus spears
- 1 pound fava beans in the pod
- 3½ cups Homemade Kitchen Broth (page 70), pasta water (see page 69), or water
- ⅓ pound tiny potatoes
- 4 small carrots, peeled and cut into bite-sized pieces
- 2 spring onions, greens trimmed off, or ½ white onion, chopped
- 2 small zucchini, cut into 1-inch chunks
- 1 cup English peas (about 1 pound in the pod)
- Kosher or sea salt and freshly cracked black pepper
- ¼ cup Basilade (page 8)

Serves 4 to 6

There is a moment in the spring, usually in late March, when I know winter is behind us. Spring shouts its arrival in shades of green. The long-cooked, layered flavors of winter give way to bright, brilliant tastes. Each week at the farmers' markets, I see more and more evidence of this delicate season. It can be almost overwhelming after winter's limited palate.

This soup is a celebration of spring. Its components may vary, as different ingredients come into season. You can make this sort of soup throughout spring and well into summer, changing the ingredients as asparagus goes out and tomatoes come in. Add pasta, preferably a small tubular shape, and it is a main course. Add slivers of roasted chicken or spring lamb and you have a very hearty meal.

Serve with a crisp Italian Dolcetto.

If using dried porcini, soak in warm water to cover for 30 minutes to soften, then drain. Strain the soaking liquid through a cheesecloth-lined sieve and reserve.

Trim the asparagus spears by breaking the ends off where they give way naturally, then trim the spears so the ends are even. Peel the spears almost up to the tip, then thinly slice them on the diagonal, into ½- to 1-inch pieces.

To shell the fava beans, remove the beans as you would peas from a pod. Bring a saucepan filled with water to a boil. Add the fava beans and blanch for 1 minute. Drain and immerse the fava beans in ice water so they retain their bright green color. Drain again and peel the skin off each fava bean. (If the beans are very small and tender, you need not peel them.)

Bring the broth to a boil in a large saucepan. If you are using dried porcini, add the reserved soaking liquid. Add the potatoes, reduce the heat to low, and simmer uncovered until they are tender when pierced with a fork, 5 to 7 minutes. Add the carrots, onions, zucchini, mushrooms, and asparagus and simmer until all the vegetables are tender, about 5 minutes. Add the fava beans and peas and simmer for 2 minutes longer. Season with salt and pepper. Ladle into warmed soup bowls and top each with basilade. Or serve in a tureen and pass the basilade at the table.

Ribollita

Ribollita is a Tuscan soup, a creation of frugal housewives who never abandon stale bread or cooked vegetables. The name translates as "reboiled," acknowledging the custom of reheating leftover vegetable soup, with the addition of day-old bread. Here is our version, not made with leftovers.

At Rose Pistola, this soup cooks in a cauldron on a hook suspended over a wood fire for days on end, until meltingly tender, soft, and rich. We add fresh ingredients daily to make up for what we have served. As the seasons change, so does the soup. In summer, vine-ripe heirloom tomatoes, still warm from the sun, join fresh shell beans, zucchini, mature lettuces, and other produce from the garden.

Serve with Stuffed Roasted Sardines (page 54), a Bowl of Iced Summer Fruit (page 233), and a good Barbera for a perfect late-summer or early fall dinner.

¼ cup extra virgin olive oil, plus extra for drizzling
3 pale inner celery stalks with leaves, chopped
1 fennel bulb, chopped
1 red onion, chopped
1 garlic clove, bruised
2 cups fresh shell beans, such as cranberry beans or black-eyed peas, or 2 cups dried cannellini beans (see page 16)
1 cup dry white wine
6 large tomatoes, peeled, seeded, and chopped
1 Parmesan rind (about ¼ pound; see page 70)
Kosher or sea salt and freshly cracked black pepper
⅓ pound day-old coarse country bread, cut into 1-inch cubes (about 2 cups)
3 zucchini, coarsely chopped
12 basil leaves

Serves 4 to 8

Heat the olive oil in a heavy saucepan over medium heat. Add the celery, fennel, onion, and garlic and cook, stirring occasionally, until tender, 10 to 15 minutes.

Add the beans, white wine, tomatoes, and Parmesan rind. Pour in water just to cover the vegetables and bring to a simmer. Season to taste. Cook, uncovered, over low heat (or in a preheated 275°F oven) until the beans are meltingly tender, 2½ hours, depending upon the freshness of the beans.

Add the bread, 2 more cups water, and the zucchini and cook for about 25 minutes longer, until the ingredients are very tender.

Add the basil leaves, season to taste with salt, and serve. Drizzle with olive oil. (The soup is even better reheated.)

Summer Tomato Soup

6 pounds very ripe tomatoes
⅓ cup extra virgin olive oil, plus extra for drizzling
2 garlic cloves, crushed
3 slices day-old country bread, preferably ciabatta, crusts removed
Kosher or sea salt and freshly cracked black pepper

Serves 4 to 6

We make this sensational soup when tomatoes are at their peak, plump and ripe and full of sweetness. Use only ripe, juicy tomatoes. This is a great soup when you have a lot of tomatoes on hand and are afraid you won't be able to eat them all before they are over the hill. Of course, you can always prepare the soup just for the love of ripe tomatoes.

Dunk the tomatoes in a large pot of boiling water for 30 seconds to loosen their skins. Slip the skins off the tomatoes and cut the tomatoes crosswise in half. Place a strainer over a bowl. With your fingers, scoop out the tomato seeds and pulp into the strainer so that the juices fall through into the bowl. Set the seeded tomato halves aside and reserve the strained juice.

Heat the olive oil in a large saucepan over medium heat for 1 minute. Add the garlic and cook just until the cloves turn barely golden. Remove and discard. With your hands, crush the tomato halves into the garlic oil. Bring to a simmer. Tear the bread into pieces the size of small tomatoes and toss into the soup. Add the strained tomato juice and bring to a simmer. Season to taste with salt and pepper.

Ladle the soup into bowls and just before serving, drizzle with a thread of olive oil over the top.

Reed Hearon in the field with assorted heirloom tomatoes at J. K. Smith's Farms, home of the Heirloom Tomato Company, in Brentwood, California.

Calamari and Borlotti Bean Soup

During a recent trip I took to Provence, one of the many culinary highlights was a simple salad that one of our hosts made with calamari and fresh shell beans. When I returned to San Francisco, I took the same ingredients and flavors and made this delightful soup. If you choose to soak the beans, the cooking time will be less.

Pour a light-style Chianti and serve with Giant Ravioli of Soft Egg and Wild Greens (page 108).

2 tablespoons extra virgin olive oil, plus extra for drizzling
1 sprig rosemary
¼ cup chopped flat-leaf parsley
3 garlic cloves, chopped
1 pound calamari, cleaned and cut into tentacles and rings (see page 163)
Pinch of crushed red pepper flakes
1 cup dry Italian white wine
2 cups fresh shell beans, such as borlotti (cranberry beans) or black-eyed peas, or 2 cups dried beans cooked for 1 hour
1½ cups tomato puree (made from processing drained canned peeled whole tomatoes or peeled fresh whole tomatoes)
Kosher or sea salt

Heat the olive oil, rosemary, parsley, and garlic in a skillet over high heat until the parsley sizzles. Add the calamari and red pepper flakes and cook until the calamari is opaque, 3 to 5 minutes. Add the white wine and beans and cook until the wine has reduced by half.

Add the tomato puree and enough water to cover, lower the heat, and simmer until the beans are tender, about 1 hour for fresh beans. Season to taste with salt.

Just before serving, drizzle with a little extra virgin olive oil.

Serves 4 to 6

Fava Bean and Porcini Soup

1¼ ounces (1 cup) dried porcini
¼ cup extra virgin olive oil, plus extra for drizzling
1 medium white onion, finely diced
2 garlic cloves, bruised
2 sprigs rosemary
1 sprig sage
1 sprig thyme
1 sprig marjoram
¾ cup dry Italian white wine
2 cups dried fava beans
Kosher or sea salt

Serves 6 to 8

Erik Cosselmon, our executive chef, was preparing fava bean puree one day when in walked Lorenzo, the mushroom forager, with a bag of fresh porcini. Eric immediately decided to use the fava bean puree as a soup base and add the mushrooms for flavor and texture. I usually don't like pureed soups because they often seem to become monotonous as you eat them, each bite just like the previous one, but I was won over by this combination, which now appears regularly on our menu.

Without a forager like Lorenzo, fresh porcini are hard to come by, but you can use dried ones to the same effect. Try to find small dried fava beans that are peeled—they are called favettes *in Middle Eastern markets and* habas *in Mexican markets. If you can only get the unpeeled variety, soak them overnight in a bowl of water and slip off the skins before proceeding.*

Pour a full-bodied Pigato to complement this soup. Serve with Roast Sage-Stuffed Quail with Walnut Sauce (page 201) and Persimmon Pudding (page 244).

Soak the dried porcini in warm water for 30 minutes. Drain the mushrooms, but retain the soaking water. Pour the water through a very fine strainer lined with cheesecloth to remove the grit. Save.

Heat 2 tablespoons of the olive oil in a large heavy pot over medium heat. Add the onion and 1 garlic clove. Tie the herbs together with a piece of kitchen twine, add them to the onions, and cook until the onions and garlic are completely soft. Add ½ cup of the white wine, the fava beans, ¼ cup of the soaked and drained porcini, and enough water to cover generously. (Depending upon the size of your pot, you will probably need 5 to 6 cups of water.) Cook until the beans are completely tender, stirring occasionally, 45 minutes to 1 hour. Add the strained porcini water to the soup. You may need to add an extra cup or two of water as the beans cook.

Remove and discard the herb bundle. Puree the bean mixture in a food processor, a third at a time. Pass through a fine sieve or a food mill into a bowl. Set aside and keep warm.

Heat the remaining 2 tablespoons olive oil in a skillet over medium heat. Add the remaining garlic clove and mushrooms and cook until the mushrooms are tender and fragrant, about 10 minutes; shake the pan and stir often. Remove the mushrooms to a dish and set aside.

Splash in the remaining ¼ cup white wine to deglaze the pan, scraping up the crispy bits. Return the fava bean puree to the pan in which the beans cooked, add the mushrooms and the contents of the deglazed skillet, and season to taste with salt. If the soup appears to be too thick, add a little warm water. Heat the soup until it is hot, and serve at once. Drizzle a little olive oil over the top of each serving.

White Bean Soup with Braised Greens

For the Beans

1 ounce (1 cup) dried porcini

2 large sprigs rosemary (each about 5 inches long)

3 garlic cloves, bruised

½ cup olive oil

2 cups dried cannellini beans

1 cup dry Italian white wine

Kosher or sea salt

Serves 4 to 6

This simple, thick white bean soup, fragrant with rosemary and olive oil, becomes more complex with the addition of braised greens flavored with pancetta and onion. As the textures of the two come together, they make each bite of soup slightly different—and totally delightful. While I don't soak the beans at Rose Pistola, do so if you like.

Serve with a big red wine such as a Dolcetto, a great loaf of bread, and a wedge of Parmesan and some dates.

For the Beans

Preheat the oven to 275°F.

Soak the dried porcini in warm water for 30 minutes. Drain the mushrooms, but retain the soaking water. Pour the water through a very fine strainer lined with cheesecloth to remove the grit. Save.

Sauté the rosemary and garlic in the oil in a heavy ovenproof pot over medium heat until fragrant. Add the beans, porcini, and wine and bring to a boil. Add water to cover, cover, place in the oven, and cook until meltingly tender, about 2½ hours.

Remove the rosemary and puree the soup until smooth in a blender. Season to taste with salt.

For the Greens

Blanch the greens in salted boiling water for 3 to 4 minutes. Drain and, when cool enough to handle, squeeze out as much moisture as possible and coarsely chop the greens.

Meanwhile, in a second large heavy pot, sauté the onions, garlic, and pancetta in the oil until the onions are tender and the pancetta has rendered its fat. Pour off most of the fat and add the sage, greens, and enough water to generously cover. Braise over low heat until the flavors have melded and the pancetta is tender, about ½ hour. Season to taste with salt.

To serve, ladle the beans into a soup tureen or individual bowls and swirl in the braised greens. Serve with olive oil for drizzling and a peppermill on the side.

For the Greens

- 2 cups mixed greens
- 1 large white onion, cut lengthwise in half and then into half-moons
- 1 garlic clove, bruised
- ½ pound pancetta, cut into batons ¼ inch × ½ inch
- 2 tablespoons olive oil, plus extra for drizzling
- 8 sage leaves
- Kosher or sea salt
- Freshly cracked black pepper

Green Garlic Soup

- ½ cup extra virgin olive oil
- ½ pound green garlic, cut into ¼-inch-thick rings (about 2 cups)
- ¼ pound crusty country bread, crusts removed and cut into 1-inch cubes
- 1 cup dry Italian white wine
- 5 cups Homemade Kitchen Broth (page 70) or canned low-sodium chicken broth
- 4 large eggs
- ¼ pound Parmigiano-Reggiano, shaved with a vegetable peeler
- Kosher or sea salt and freshly cracked black pepper

Serves 4

This flavorful soup is light yet satisfying. Finished with poached eggs and Parmigiano-Reggiano shavings, it would make a good late-night supper or light lunch with Focaccia (page 134) and a good dry Italian white wine.

Use a wide shallow pan for cooking the soup so that the eggs do not sink to the bottom when they are added. They should almost float on top of the bread. Serve with Capponada (page 76).

Heat ¼ cup of the olive oil in a wide heavy shallow saucepan over medium-high heat until it begins to thin, about 1 minute. Add the green garlic and sauté until light golden brown, stirring constantly. Remove with a slotted spoon to a dish.

Add the remaining ¼ cup olive oil to the pan, reduce the heat to medium, and add the bread cubes. Sauté just until they become crisp and begin to turn color. Reduce the heat to medium-low and add the white wine. Cook until it reduces slightly, about 1 minute.

Add the broth and garlic and simmer for 2 minutes longer. One at a time, crack the eggs and carefully drop them evenly in the center of the soup. Scatter some of the cheese over the top. Simmer until the egg whites are set and the yolks are glazed, about 4 minutes. You may need to ladle a little broth over the eggs to help them along. Season to taste with salt and pepper.

Ladle the soup into warmed soup bowls, giving each person an egg, and add the rest of the Parmigiano-Reggiano on top of each one.

Green Garlic

Green garlic resembles green onions but it has a slightly rounder bulb, each containing tiny "pearls" of garlic. The stems sometimes reach a foot in length and deliver a flavor that is unmistakably garlicky but less intense and hot than ordinary garlic. Green garlic marks the middle stage in the life of a garlic plant, falling between the days of the very tender early spring garlic and the familiar papery mature cloves. Look for it at farmers' markets.

Knoll Farms in Brentwood, in the northern part of the San Joaquin Valley, is renowned in Bay Area culinary circles for its green garlic. The Knolls have bred their garlic expressly for this stage. In early spring, their fields are filled with the scruffy, floppy pale green and white stalks. During the spring, they sell between six and eight hundred pounds of green garlic weekly to restaurants, retailers, and wholesalers. At Rose Pistola, we use it for studding spring lamb, in ravioli, and in spring vegetable ragouts. (Regular garlic tends to be dry and hot in the early spring, so the tender, moist green garlic is a flavorful alternative.) The whole plant can be used. The little pearls and chopped stems are great thrown into vegetable sautés or scattered on top of pizzas, and they add crunch to pastas.

Store green garlic stalks in the refrigerator covered with a plastic bag. Or wrap the stalks in paper towels and put them in a plastic bag in the vegetable bin.

Mussel and Bread Soup

1 small white onion, finely chopped
¼ cup extra virgin olive oil
1 garlic clove, bruised
4 anchovy fillets
3 sprigs marjoram
4 sprigs parsley
¼ teaspoon crushed red pepper flakes
1 cup dry Italian white wine
4 cups tomato puree (made from processing drained canned peeled whole tomatoes or peeled fresh whole tomatoes)
1 pound mussels, scrubbed and debearded
Kosher or sea salt
4 thick slices country bread, toasted

Serves 4

This simple, delicious soup is typical of the flavorful home-style soups we serve at Rose Pistola. Rather than relying on a prepared broth or stock, you make an aromatic broth with the mussels, wine, and tomato. Stale country bread soaks up the soup in the bowl, turning the broth into a richly satisfying light meal or a great first course.

Sauté the onion in the olive oil in a large pot over medium heat until soft, about 5 minutes. Add the garlic, anchovies, marjoram, parsley, and crushed red pepper and cook until fragrant and sizzling, about 3 minutes. Add the white wine, increase the heat to high, and reduce the wine by half.

Add the tomato puree, bring to a simmer, and reduce the heat. Taste for seasoning and add the mussels. Cover the pot and cook until the mussels open. Discard any that do not open. Season with salt.

Ladle the soup over the bread in four bowls and let sit for about 3 minutes before serving.

Save the Waters

We save the waters at Rose Pistola—pasta waters, that is; this cuisine is not very reliant on stocks. We, and generations of Italian cooks, rely on the starchy, slightly salty waters in which we cook pasta to flavor many dishes. When a little of the pasta water is combined with the sauce that goes over the noodles, it integrates all of the ingredients.

The same approach can be used with the water in which white beans have been cooked, because that water has the essence of the starchy legumes and any herbs or vegetables that were cooked along with them. So, if you are making Grilled Sea Bass with Lemon and White Beans (page 148), use the water from the beans to bring the dish together.

Not all waters have to be used immediately. For example, if you are rehydrating mushrooms by soaking them in hot water, save the mushroom water and add it to polenta or a pasta sauce with mushrooms.

So save your waters. Drain off pasta, bean, potato, dried mushroom, and vegetable water and, if you can't use it right away, refrigerate it or freeze it for the future. (Hint: Mark what's in the container so you don't come across it later and wonder what in the world you so carefully saved!)

Homemade Kitchen Broth

- 1/4 pound Parmesan rind (see below)
- 1/4 pound prosciutto rind
- 1 white onion, chopped
- 2 celery stalks with leaves
- 2 garlic cloves or 2 stalks green garlic
- 2 carrots, peeled
- 2 pounds cooked or roasted meats or poultry and/or meat or poultry bones
- 4 sprigs flat-leaf parsley
- 1 ounce dried porcini, rinsed, or 1 cup mushroom trimmings and scraps
- 1 bunch thyme, tied together with kitchen string

Makes 2 quarts

This is the sort of rich broth that good cooks have always made at home using whatever was available. Vary the ingredients with the season or depending on what you have on hand. Any leftover meat, meat or chicken bones, perhaps a chicken breast, roast drippings, mushroom trimmings, or parsley stems could go into it. Cook it at just below a simmer (at about 180°F) until the meat and vegetables begin to fall apart. Skim off any fat or scum as soon as it rises to the surface. The result will be a crystal-clear, richly flavored, light broth.

Save your Parmesan rinds, and ask your butcher for prosciutto rinds or trimmings to throw into this and other soups and beans.

Put all of the ingredients in a large pot. Cover with cold water and slowly bring to a simmer. Lower the heat and skim all of the scum and fat off the top. Cook at just under a simmer until the vegetables and meat begin to fall apart.

Strain the broth through a fine sieve, discarding the meat and vegetables. Let cool and remove the fat from the top. This freezes well for a couple of months or it can be kept in the refrigerator for about a week.

Parmesan Rinds

Always save the rinds from Parmigiano-Reggiano cheese. Wrap them in plastic and store in the refrigerator. There are several recipes in this book that are greatly enhanced by their rich flavor. Or throw them into the pot with any bean soup that does not have fish in it.

Using Parmesan rinds is another of those frugal housewife's tricks, such as saving the water from cooking potatoes, beans, greens, and pasta. Using these by-products makes economic and gastronomic sense—economic sense because you throw less away, gastronomic sense because they have quite a bit of texture and/or flavor that can enhance other dishes.

Skillet-Roasted

Mussels

(page 46)

Cured Fresh

Sardines

(page 50)

Roasted Beets with

Ricotta Salata

and Arugula

(page 72)

Shaved Artichokes

with Fava Beans

and Parmesan

(page 30)

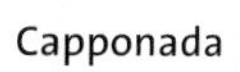
Capponada

(page 76)

Spaghetti with

Clams and

Broccoli Rabe

(page 94)

Ravioli of

Mixed Greens

with Mushrooms

(page 104)

Goat Cheese and

Roasted Pepper Pizza

(page 131)

Salads

No meal in North Beach was or is complete without a salad. In the first caffès and restaurants, salads were slices of tomatoes and torn lettuce leaves thrown together and dressed with a splash of vinegar from homemade wine and olive oil from the Old Country. Ingredients such as radicchio, arugula, and endive, sold at the Ferry Plaza Farmers' Market and considered to be fancy or unusual today, were actually commonplace at the Colombo Market (see page 212). There were also simple seafood combinations like those we serve today at Rose Pistola, such as our Salad of Bay Shrimp and Belgian Endive. We also keep alive the tradition of chopped, or steak house, salads.

The salads at Rose Pistola reflect not only the tradition of early North Beach but also the bounty of the organic movement in the Bay Area today. Our salads change with the seasons, as they did on those old North Beach tables. Many of the salads in this book have short ingredients lists, because we go to great lengths to get the best-quality raw materials, and it is important that each ingredient can be tasted. And don't forget to use the best-quality vinegars and olive oils; they can make or break a salad.

Columbus Day Parade in front of Rose Pistola, on Columbus Avenue—site of the original United States Columbus Day Parade.

Roasted Beets with Ricotta Salata and Arugula

1 pound beets
10 sprigs thyme, plus 1 teaspoon minced thyme
2 garlic cloves, crushed
¼ cup dry Italian white wine
¼ cup fresh orange juice
Kosher or sea salt
3 tablespoons extra virgin olive oil
1 tablespoon red wine vinegar, preferably made from a California Zinfandel or a strong French red wine
¼ teaspoon finely grated orange zest
Freshly cracked black pepper
1 large bunch arugula, tough stems removed and torn into bite-sized pieces
⅓ pound ricotta salata, cubed

Serves 4

This colorful salad is one of the most popular at Rose Pistola. It combines three very simple ingredients—iron-rich beets, lightly bitter, nutty arugula, and ricotta salata—in an appealing balanced composition. You can use either red or golden beets, or a mixture.

Ricotta salata is ricotta that has been salted and molded to preserve it. There are both Sicilian and Sardinian versions, but if you can't find it, substitute a well-drained Greek or French feta.

The beets can be baked and marinated a day ahead, but let them return to room temperature before tossing with the arugula and adding the cheese.

Serve as an antipasto along with Stuffed Roasted Sardines (page 54) and Fried Artichokes with Parmesan (page 32). This would be wonderful before any of the whole roast fish dishes in the book. Pour a fruity, dry Malvasia Bianco from California or Moscato Giallo, Nilo Bolagriani.

Preheat the oven to 400°F.

In a large baking dish, combine the beets with the thyme sprigs, garlic, white wine, orange juice, and ¼ teaspoon salt. Cover with a lid or foil and bake until the beets are tender, about 1¼ hours. Remove from the oven and let cool slightly.

Peel the beets and cut them roughly into 1-inch cubes. (Discard the liquid remaining in the dish.)

Combine the olive oil, vinegar, orange zest, and the minced thyme in a large bowl. Add the beets, season to taste with salt and pepper, and toss well. Add the arugula and toss again. Transfer to a serving platter and scatter the cheese over the top. Serve at once.

Salad of Mushrooms, Endive, and Parmesan

This salad is a wonderful example of the power of using high-quality ingredients simply. Any mushroom combination such as portobello, crimini, or chanterelle will work in this salad—use whatever is available, although I am partial to porcini when available.

This salad is excellent with Corzetti of Fish and Greens (page 110) and Tangerine Tart (page 250). A full-bodied creamy-style Friuli Pinot Bianco wine is recommended.

- ½ pound mushrooms, cleaned
- A ¼-pound wedge Parmigiano-Reggiano
- 2 heads Belgian endive
- 2 tablespoons extra virgin olive oil
- A few drops of fresh lemon juice
- Kosher or sea salt and freshly cracked black pepper

Serves 4

Slice the mushrooms paper-thin and place in a salad bowl. Using a vegetable peeler, shave the cheese on top. Slice the endive on a diagonal from the top down, discarding the core. Add to the salad bowl and toss all of the ingredients with the olive oil, lemon juice, and salt and pepper to taste. Serve at once.

Combining Flavors: Keep It Simple

Great dishes often involve combinations of only two or perhaps three ingredients, such as bread and cheese, prosciutto and melon, tomatoes and basil, hot fudge and vanilla ice cream, and so on. The flavors create a dialogue as your palate goes back and forth between them, one flavor creating tension of a sort, the other flavor resolving that tension.

The dialogue between flavors brings out aspects of each one that might not be apparent when tasted alone. For example, in this Salad of Mushrooms, Endive, and Parmesan, the mushrooms and endive bring out the rich mustiness in each other. At the same time, the underlying creaminess of the Parmesan cheese plays against and highlights the crisp sharpness of the endive and vice versa.

The more ingredients you combine, the more difficult it is to differentiate among and enjoy the power of the pure flavors and textures, and the greater the likelihood that you will get a relationship between ingredients that does not make sense. Keep it simple and elegant.

Olive Oil

Extra virgin olive oil plays a starring role in almost every dish at Rose Pistola. Its excellence is essential to the harmony of our food. Poured or drizzled over fish, vegetables, soups, pastas, and salads, it's the substance that keeps the dialogue between Italy and North Beach vibrant.

Since almost all of our food is Ligurian-inspired, for these recipes, it makes sense to use, as often as possible, a Ligurian oil—one that is fruity, ripe, and both delicate and full of flavor. Just as Tuscan oil flatters the cuisine of that region, boasting of hearty meat and bean dishes, Ligurian oil flatters the bright, light cuisine of coastal Liguria and, in turn, that of coastal North Beach. We are constantly on the lookout for the perfect oil in any given season. Since olive oil is an agricultural product just as wine is, its quality varies from year to year.

Liguria, close to the South of France, is a continuation of the Riviera. The two regions share a similar landscape and climate—one that provides optimum conditions for growing olives to make excellent extra virgin olive oil. Because of their proximity, the regions produce a similar style of olive oil. So really, French extra virgins are much like Ligurian oils. At times, we use a French extra virgin olive oil such as Puget. We like some California oils, too, but Ligurian oils, such as Roi Mosto, Raineri, and Isnardi, are our favorites.

Seek out the finest olive oils (see Sources, page 264) for the recipes in this book. Use the light-colored, somewhat buttery, feathery Ligurian or French oils for finishing pastas, for drizzling on top of fish just before it comes to the table, and for salads, soups, bean dishes, and vegetables. Since the quality of an expensive oil does not withstand high heat, keep an inexpensive workhorse olive oil on hand for sautéing and frying. Should you be concerned with the cost of great olive oil, compare it with the price of a good bottle of wine. A bottle of wine is usually consumed in one sitting, while a bottle of olive oil can last you for a couple of months if stored in a cool, dark spot in your kitchen (never near the stove, and not in the refrigerator).

Chopped Salad

This salad goes so well with the grills and roasts of Rose Pistola. It's very much an Italian-American salad: Italian, because of the absence of the meat, avocado, and bacon used in most American chopped salads. There's a nod to the Italian tricolore salad, with the three colors of the Italian flag (the white endive, red radicchio, and green romaine). It's American, because of the Maytag Blue cheese and chopped texture.

There are endless variations on this sort of salad, although here we use ingredients easy to come by in winter, drawing inspiration from the blue cheese dressing salads of steak houses of my youth. (For that old steak house touch, freeze the salad plates and forks—and wow your guests.) You could use tomatoes, sweet onion, cucumber, mint, and romaine to make a nice summer version of this salad.

Serve with Terrorized Steak (page169) and Sacripantina (page 256). Try the salad with a red wine such as a Barolo or a lager beer.

- 2 tablespoons fresh lemon juice
- 1/3 cup extra virgin olive oil
- Kosher or sea salt and freshly cracked black pepper
- 6 ounces blue cheese, such as Maytag
- 1 romaine lettuce heart, chopped into 1/2-inch pieces
- 1 head radicchio, chopped into 1/2-inch pieces
- 2 heads Belgian endive, chopped into 1/2-inch pieces
- 1 cup chopped watercress sprigs

Serves 4

Whisk together the lemon juice and olive oil in a salad bowl. Season to taste with salt and pepper and whisk again. Crumble in the blue cheese and add the salad greens. Toss well and serve.

Capponada

⅓ pound day-old country bread, crusts removed
¼ cup red wine vinegar
¼ cup extra virgin olive oil
3 tablespoons fresh lemon juice
4 thick asparagus spears, trimmed and thinly sliced
¼ cup Niçoise olives (pitted if you wish)
2 inner celery stalks with leaves, thinly sliced on the diagonal
¼ cup fresh English peas (about ¼ pound in the pod)
¼ cup fava beans (see page 195)
4 baby artichokes, trimmed (see page 31) and thinly sliced, or 1 medium artichoke heart, trimmed (see page 31) and very thinly sliced
6 to 8 radishes, trimmed and thinly sliced
¼ cup halved cherry tomatoes or 1 large tomato, chopped
One 4-ounce can oil-packed tuna or Preserved Tuna (see next page)
¼ cup loosely packed flat-leaf parsley leaves
Kosher or sea salt and freshly cracked black pepper
4 large eggs, boiled for exactly 5 minutes, drained, peeled, and quartered lengthwise
8 bottled, canned, or salt-cured anchovies, rinsed, or 1 ounce bottarga

Serves 4

Capponada is one more example of the ongoing influence of the Ligurian aesthetic on California cooking. It reflects the central importance of fresh vegetables and seafood in Ligurian and North Beach cooking.

This salad is more closely related to salade Niçoise, in that both are most properly made from raw ingredients combined with canned or preserved fish, herbs, and olives, than to the Sicilian caponata, a cooked vegetable dish similar to a sweet and sour ratatouille.

Use this recipe as an outline only. First make the salad in the spring, as peas, baby beans, favas, and asparagus come into season. Vary it as ingredients go out of season and new ones come in (heirloom tomatoes, sweet peppers, cucumbers).

This recipe calls for canned tuna, but seek out a good-quality Italian or French olive oil-packed tuna. At the restaurant, we preserve our own tuna, which is actually easy to do. If you want to try this, instructions are included for doing so. It will need to be made two hours in advance.

A light to full-bodied Pigato would be good with this dish. Serve with Salt-Roasted Prawns with Lemon Aïoli (page 151) and Bowl of Iced Summer Fruit (page 233).

Soak the bread in 1 cup of warm water in a bowl until soft, then squeeze out as much moisture as possible with your hands. Discard the water and return the bread to the bowl. Douse with the vinegar and toss. Tear the bread into pieces the size of a quarter and place in a large shallow serving bowl. Toss with the olive oil and lemon juice. Add the asparagus, olives, celery, peas, favas, artichokes, radishes, and tomatoes.

Drain the tuna and crumble or flake the tuna into the bowl. Add the parsley. Toss and season to taste with salt and pepper. Arrange the eggs on the side of the bowl and top with the anchovies or bottarga. Serve.

For the Preserved Tuna, If Using

Sprinkle the tuna with the salt and pepper and rub in well on all sides. Sprinkle the rosemary and marjoram evenly over the tuna. Put the tuna into the smallest nonstick saucepan that will hold it. Add the wine and let marinate for 1 hour.

Drain the tuna, discard the wine, and add just enough oil so the tuna floats. Poach over medium-low heat until the tuna is opaque and barely pink in the center. Remove from heat and let cool in the oil. (You can follow the same procedure with the tuna in an uncovered glass canning jar in a water bath.) The tuna will keep, refrigerated and covered in the oil, for up to 1 week.

Preserved Tuna

- 1/3 pound tuna, such as tombo or albacore
- 1/4 teaspoon kosher or sea salt
- 1/4 teaspoon freshly cracked black pepper
- Leaves from 1 sprig rosemary, roughly chopped
- Leaves from 2 sprigs marjoram, roughly chopped
- 1/4 cup dry Italian white wine
- About 1/2 cup extra virgin olive oil

Bottarga

Bottarga, a Mediterranean delicacy, is the dried and pressed roe sack of tuna or gray mullet. Once the roe is extracted from the fish, it is salted and weighted in its sac. Once all the moisture is removed and it is compressed, it is hung in a cool, dark spot to dry. Bottarga can be shaved over pasta, in salads, or on omelets to add a haunting, salty flavor. It is sometimes available in powder form, but it is most often in the shape of a small sausage. See Sources (page 264) for availability or buy it on your next trip to the Mediterranean.

Artichoke, Fennel, and Mushroom Salad

Salad

¼ cup plus 2 tablespoons extra virgin olive oil

1 large or 2 small fennel bulbs, cut lengthwise into ¼-inch slices

Kosher or sea salt

½ pound mushrooms, such as chanterelle, cleaned and thinly sliced

1 sprig rosemary (3 inches long)

1 garlic clove, crushed

1 large artichoke, trimmed (see page 31) and thinly sliced, or 8 baby artichokes, trimmed (see page 31) and thinly sliced lengthwise, soaking in lemon water

Serves 4

Like the Salad of Mushrooms, Endive, and Parmesan (page 73), this dish has only three principal elements. We change the fundamental characteristics of these three ingredients using the technique of caramelization. All vegetables contain sugars that, when cooked with high heat, will caramelize, giving the vegetables a complex, nutty flavor. Adding toasted hazelnuts to the dish enhances its nutty undertone. Caramelization also intensifies the vegetables' own natural flavors, because they cook in their own juices.

When creating salads like this, think about the greens in much the same way you might think about the pasta in a pasta dish, the pizza dough in a pizza dish—that is, as providing a unifying backdrop for the main ingredients.

Serve with Grilled Sea Bass with Lemon and White Beans (page 148) and, for dessert, Caramelized Pear and Almond Tart (page 246). Pour a crisp, fragrant Pigato or California Chenin Blanc wine.

Heat 2 tablespoons of the olive oil in a large nonstick sauté pan over medium-high heat. Add the fennel and sauté, stirring, until golden brown, about 10 minutes. (If smaller pieces become brown more quickly, remove them as they are ready.) Season to taste with salt, remove from the pan with a slotted spoon, and drain on paper towels.

Add the mushrooms, rosemary, garlic, and 2 more tablespoons oil to the pan and sauté until the mushrooms are browned, about 6 minutes. Season to taste with salt. Remove with the slotted spoon and drain on paper towels.

Pat the artichoke slices dry and add to the pan, along with the remaining 2 tablespoons oil. Sauté until lightly browned and tender, about 5 minutes. Season to taste with salt, remove from the pan with the slotted spoon, and drain on paper towels.

Red Wine Vinaigrette

Whisk together the vinegar and olive oil in a large salad bowl. Whisk in salt and pepper to taste.

Add the greens and vegetables to the salad bowl and toss well. Sprinkle the hazelnuts over the top and serve at once.

Red Wine Vinaigrette

- $1\frac{1}{2}$ tablespoons red wine vinegar, preferably made from a California Zinfandel or a strong French red wine
- $\frac{1}{4}$ cup extra virgin olive oil
- Kosher or sea salt and freshly cracked black pepper

- 1 head frisée, torn into bite-sized pieces (about 2 cups)
- 1 bunch small dandelion greens, torn into bite-sized pieces (about 2 cups)
- 1 small bunch arugula, torn into bite-sized pieces (about $1\frac{1}{2}$ cups)
- $\frac{1}{4}$ cup hazelnuts, toasted, peeled (see page 191), and roughly chopped

Columbus Day Parade—garbagemen parading with garbage cans.

Vinegar

Look for the same thing in vinegar as you do in wine—flavors that heighten the natural taste of a dish. We use a small-production red Zinfandel wine vinegar from California almost exclusively. There are several widely available alternatives in specialty food stores. L'Estornell packages extraordinarily good Spanish Grenache wine vinegar. There are numerous brands of good-quality French red wine vinegar—look for a strong one that says 7 percent on the label. This indicates that the vinegar is liable not to be diluted with water or otherwise chemically altered. I occasionally use balsamic vinegar, but rarely for dressing lettuce-based salads (except those with game)—it is too sweet.

Roasted Mushroom and White Asparagus or Endive Salad

- 10 white asparagus spears or 2 heads Belgian endive
- 1 pound assorted mushrooms, such as chanterelle, oyster, lobster, shiitake, button, and/or portobello, cleaned and cut into bite-sized pieces
- 1 large red onion, cut into 8 wedges
- 1 garlic clove, bruised
- 2 sprigs thyme or 1 teaspoon dried thyme
- ¼ cup extra virgin olive oil
- Kosher or sea salt and freshly cracked black pepper
- 2 tablespoons red wine vinegar
- 1 bunch frisée, cut into bite-sized pieces
- 1 bunch arugula, torn into bite-sized pieces (about 2 cups)
- 2 ounces shaved Parmigiano-Reggiano

Serves 4 to 6

Roasting vegetables at very high heat causes rapid evaporation of their inherent moisture, concentrating their flavors and caramelizing them to a golden brown. You need very little fat or oil, just enough to coat what you are roasting.

This salad takes advantage of a briefly available seasonal vegetable, white asparagus. It is white because it is grown under completely banked soil; because no sun reaches it, it develops no chlorophyll, which would give it the familiar green color, and it has a different flavor from regular asparagus. If you cannot get white asparagus, substitute quartered whole Belgian endive.

In the spring, serve with Lamb Shanks with Peas and Potatoes (page 182) and Zabaglione with Strawberries in Red Wine (page 232). Pour a Sauvignon Blanc to accompany this salad.

Preheat the oven to 550°F (or the highest setting).

Break the tough ends off the asparagus or trim the Belgian endive and slice it lengthwise into 8 wedges.

Place the mushrooms in a gratin or other baking dish with the asparagus or endive, the onion, garlic, and thyme. Toss with the olive oil and sprinkle with salt and pepper. Roast the vegetables, turning a few times to ensure even browning, for about 20 minutes, or until tender when pierced with a fork.

Transfer the vegetables and their cooking juices to a salad bowl and add the vinegar and a little more salt and pepper if needed. Toss well, taste for seasoning, and add the greens. Toss well. Scatter the Parmigiano on top and serve at once.

Asparagus, Artichoke, and Poached Lemon Salad

Each ingredient in this salad, even the lemon, is poached until meltingly tender, then tossed with high-quality olive oil and radicchio. The ingredients themselves, particularly when they are all simultaneously at their seasonal peak, make this a sure bet. Look for new zucchini: bigger than baby-sized, but barely mature—small enough that the seeds aren't developed, yet big enough to lose the bitterness that baby squash often has. Poach whole until tender. They will become silky and melting, a real treat if you have only experienced them al dente.

Serve this salad warm, giving all the ingredients a couple of minutes to marinate before tossing with the parsley and radicchio and serving. Try it as a generous first course for a vegetarian menu, followed by Trofie with Pesto (page 116).

- 1 garlic clove, crushed
- ¼ cup extra virgin olive oil
- 3 small fingerling or Yellow Finn potatoes
- 1 lemon, halved
- 2 small zucchini (see headnote)
- 2 artichokes, trimmed to hearts (see page 31)
- 12 large asparagus spears, trimmed and peeled
- Kosher or sea salt and freshly cracked black pepper
- 1 head radicchio
- 15 flat-leaf parsley leaves

Serves 4

Bring 6 cups of salted water to a boil in a saucepan. Rub a wooden salad bowl with the garlic clove and discard it. Add the olive oil.

Add the potatoes and lemon halves to the boiling water and cook for 5 minutes. Add the zucchini and artichoke hearts and cook for 5 minutes longer. Add the asparagus and simmer gently. Cook until each vegetable is tender when pierced with the tip of a knife, removing them as they become done and rinsing all the ingredients briefly under cold water to preserve the color.

When the vegetables are cool enough to handle, peel the potatoes and cut into ¼-inch-thick slices. Thinly slice one half of the lemon, and reserve the other half. Cut the zucchini lengthwise in half and then into 1-inch-thick chunks. Slice the artichoke hearts and asparagus into thin pieces. Add the cooked vegetables, while still warm, to the salad bowl. Toss the potatoes, lemon slices, artichoke, asparagus, and zucchini well, then squeeze the juice from the lemon half over the vegetables. Season to taste with salt and pepper.

Right before serving, toss the radicchio and parsley with the vegetables. Divide the salad among four plates and serve.

Tomato Salad with Bottarga or Anchovies

1½ pounds ripe tomatoes in assorted colors (preferably including some striped varieties and some cherry tomatoes)
1 teaspoon thyme leaves
Kosher or sea salt and freshly cracked black pepper
¼ cup extra virgin olive oil
1 sweet onion, thickly sliced, soaked in 1 cup ice water with ½ teaspoon salt for 15 minutes, and drained
2 ounces bottarga or 8 anchovies, packed in oil, rinsed

Serves 4

Tomato seeds from the New World were taken to Italy and then brought back again as Italians immigrated and settled in places like San Francisco. Tomatoes have been a basic in North Beach for over a century and a half, and in the late summer and early fall, everyone gets pretty excited about them. Many natives still grow fog-resistant varieties in yards or in containers on back porches, but the juicy, sweet heirloom varieties really are best when they come from nearby farms, where it gets good and hot.

Tomatoes are always best kept at room temperature; don't refrigerate them. Slice a wild array of tomatoes, including some cherry tomatoes, for this salad, and it will come out of the kitchen looking like a splashy Matisse collage—and taste as good as it looks.

Bottarga—pressed and dried tuna roe—is a wonderful delicacy in many Mediteranean countries. We shave it into Capponada (page 76) and I love it over juicy ripe tomatoes. You could use a few anchovies instead. See Sources (page 264) for bottarga availability.

Serve with Chicken Under a Brick (page 198), and Panna Cotta with Berries (page 251) for dessert.

Core the large tomatoes and slice into ⅓-inch-thick rounds; stem the cherry tomatoes and cut in half. Put in a glass baking dish. Sprinkle with the thyme, salt and pepper to taste, and the oil. Let marinate for about 30 minutes.

Arrange the tomatoes on a platter or on individual plates. Top with the onion slices. Shave the bottarga with a very sharp knife and scatter over the top or lay the anchovies on top and serve.

Heirloom tomatoes from the Heirloom Tomato Company, where conditions are perfect for great tomatoes.

Mussel, Broccoli, and Potato Salad

This unusual combination of flavors and textures is one of the most deeply satisfying, warming combinations I know. We serve this dish as an antipasto or as a main course at Rose Pistola.

Most Americans are in the habit of barely blanching broccoli in boiling water to cook it, but by slowly braising the broccoli, its flavors mellow and soften and gently combine with the potatoes and mussels.

A Stuffed Focaccia (page 136) might set this dish off nicely. Pour a chilled Charbono.

- 3/4 pound Yellow Finn potatoes, peeled and cut into 1/2-inch slices
- 1 large head broccoli, preferably romanesco or purple Venetian, cut into florets (reserve the stalks for another use)
- 1/4 cup plus 2 tablespoons extra virgin olive oil
- 3 anchovy fillets, chopped, or 1 tablespoon anchovy paste
- 2 tablespoons red wine vinegar
- 1 garlic clove, crushed
- Pinch of crushed red pepper flakes
- 3/4 pound mussels, scrubbed and debearded
- 1/4 cup dry Italian white wine
- Small handful of flat-leaf parsley leaves

Serves 4 as a first course, 2 as a main course

In a heavy flameproof casserole with a tight-fitting lid, combine the potatoes, broccoli, 2 tablespoons olive oil, and 3 tablespoons water. Cover and cook over medium-low heat, without stirring, until the potatoes are tender, about 25 minutes. Drain and toss in a salad bowl with the remaining olive oil, anchovies, vinegar, garlic, and crushed red pepper.

Meanwhile, put the mussels and white wine in a large sauté pan with a tight-fitting lid, cover, and steam the mussels open over high heat, 2 to 3 minutes. Discard any that do not open.

Add the mussels and 1/4 cup of the steaming liquid to the potato and broccoli mixture. Toss, season to taste, and toss again. Serve warm or at room temperature, garnished with the parsley leaves.

You may remove the mussels from their shells, but we serve them in their shells at Rose Pistola.

Salad of Bay Shrimp and Belgian Endive

½ pound cooked bay shrimp or other small shrimp
2 heads Belgian endive, leaves julienned and separated
¼ cup best-quality extra virgin olive oil
Juice of ½ lemon
Kosher or sea salt and freshly cracked black pepper
A few drops of white truffle oil, optional

Serves 2 to 4

During the 1870s, competition for fishing rights on the Bay grew fierce between Chinese and Italian factions in San Francisco. The Italian fishermen were among the first to organize in the West. What was organized in 1850 as the Fishermen's Mutual Aid Society had become by 1877 the Fishermen's Protective and Benevolent Association. By 1888, the Italian Fishermen's Association was a true trade union. The Italians battled the Chinese immigrants for fishing rights both in and out of the Bay. In the end, the Chinese sold the Italians shrimp (but dried most of the catch to sell to China) and bought fresh fish from the Italians at Fisherman's Wharf. The real losers were the bay or grass shrimp, tiny shrimp most familiar now as the rubbery, flavorless frozen shrimp in bad shrimp cocktails (see page 42).

We buy our shrimp from an Oregon source who laboriously peels them by hand, and the flavor is unlike anything else. But you can enjoy a similar treat just by buying tiny shrimp already cooked and peeled.

This salad makes a great antipasto before Giant Ravioli of Soft Egg and Wild Greens (page 108). A light and crisp Pigato or Colli di Luni Vermentino would be nice with this.

Place the shrimp and Belgian endive in a bowl. Drizzle with the olive oil and then add the lemon juice. Toss well. Season with salt and pepper and toss again.

Divide the salad among chilled salad plates and serve at once.

Seafood Salad with Cranberry Beans

If you have never cooked with fresh shell beans, you are missing a real treat. Shell beans are fresh beans in a pod. They are the same kinds of beans that you can purchase shelled and dried, but they are harvested before they dry out so they have a much less starchy, more creamy texture and a sweeter flavor. Don't worry if you can't find the fresh beans, though—use dried or, better yet, use fresh peas, black-eyed peas, cubed potatoes, or even cut green beans in this recipe.

Try this for dinner with Gnocchi with Calamari Bolognese (page 120) and Fig Soufflé with Honey and Raspberries for dessert (page 242). A nice Vermentino would be wonderful with the salad.

1 cup shelled fresh cranberry beans (about 1 pound in the pod) or dried beans

½ pound calamari, cleaned and cut into tentacles and rings (see page 163)

¼ cup extra virgin olive oil

½ pound prawns or large shrimp, peeled and deveined

Kosher or sea salt

12 mussels, scrubbed and debearded

12 littleneck or Manila clams, scrubbed

2 tablespoons dry Italian white wine

2 garlic cloves, bruised

¼ cup finely chopped flat-leaf parsley

½ cup (½ pound) cooked octopus (see cooking instructions in Grilled Octopus with Broccoli Rabe and White Beans, page 166), optional

Juice of 1 lemon

Freshly ground white pepper

Serves 4

Cook the cranberry beans, covered, in a pot of simmering salted water until tender, about 45 minutes for fresh, 2 hours for dried. Drain thoroughly and put the beans in a bowl.

Put the calamari in a nonstick pan over medium heat and cook until it releases its liquid, about 2 minutes. Drain and set aside.

Heat 2 tablespoons of the olive oil in a medium sauté pan over medium-high heat. Quickly sauté the prawns until pink and cooked through, about 3 minutes. Season with salt and set aside.

Combine the mussels and clams with the white wine in a medium sauté pan, cover, and steam open over medium-high heat; remove them as they open and set aside. Once all the shells have opened, and the mussels and clams have been removed, strain the cooking liquid through a cheesecloth-lined sieve. Add the cooking liquid to the beans.

Heat the remaining 2 tablespoons oil in a medium sauté pan over medium-high heat and briefly sauté the garlic and parsley until sizzling and fragrant, about 2 minutes. Add the calamari and the optional octopus and sauté until warm and coated with the parsley, about 2 minutes. Add the seafood to the beans, add the lemon juice, and season to taste with salt and white pepper. Serve warm or at room temperature.

Venture no more than forty-five minutes north of the Golden Gate Bridge and you find yourself in the midst of sloping hills that turn from a parched golden brown landscape in summer into a lush green backdrop dotted with acacia during the winter rains. Urban sprawl has produced uniformly disastrous results for the landscape around most of the cities of the world, but on the coast north of San Francisco, a series of farming projects has managed to sustain an unusual group of producers.

Warren Weber of Star Route Farms in Bolinas, California. Warren grows arugula, dandelion, black kale, and all sorts of fresh herbs.

Here, a small group of farmers has made the choice to leave the comfort afforded by mainstream corporate jobs to farm, fish, and forage on the urban fringe, and cooks and consumers in the Bay Area benefit from their dedication. Many of these providers—including Sue Conley at Cowgirl Creamery in Point Reyes, Cindy Callahan at Bellwether Farms in Petaluma, and the owners of Hog Island Oyster Company on Tomales Bay—supply Rose Pistola with extraordinary products. Take Warren Weber, for instance, who lives and works in the old hippie enclave of Bolinas, a hard-to-find farming and fishing village an hour north of San Francisco (inhabitants constantly tear down road signs in a xenophobic attempt to protect their anonymity). Weber had always wanted to be a farmer. He attended Cornell College of Agriculture in Ithaca, New York, but eventually found his way to the University of California, where he got his Ph.D. in English. "I was into growing things," he says, "and when a spot in Bolinas became available, I grabbed it."

In the early days, his neighbors did not understand why he tilled the fields of his hundred-acre farm with plough horses. Nor did they understand later why he harvested his lettuces when they were so young (at the request of Chez Panisse's Alice Waters). Today, Weber is one of the country's most respected and successful organic farmers. We place orders with his Star Route Farms on a daily basis.

"Because we are organic," explains Weber, "we can farm next to civilization." He gestures across neat rows of arugula, dandelion, black Tuscan kale, Yellow Finn potatoes, and herbs—marjoram, sage, thyme—that stretch right up to the walls of a wooden schoolhouse. "This type of farming is safe for people, and no fertile land is wasted.

"To me," he says, "the essence of the organic movement is really the revival of the successful small farm." Since demand for specialty produce from restaurants and farmers' markets is increasing, it is ever more possible for the small farmer to make a living on a farm of less than five acres. "Civilization was built by having farms close to the cities they fed," says Weber. "That was the model in the Middle Ages. It's good for the urban consciousness for people to see where their food comes from."

Warren Weber's truck.

North Beach Salt Cod Salad with Red Onion, Potatoes, and Parsley

- 1 pound boneless, skinless salt cod
- ½ cup extra virgin olive oil
- 1 garlic clove, crushed
- 1 pound Yellow Finn or Yukon Gold potatoes
- 2 cups flat-leaf parsley
- 1 red onion, sliced into thin rings and rinsed
- Kosher or sea salt and freshly cracked black pepper

Serves 4 to 6

This salad could be the true salad of North Beach. Many North Beach cooks—Joe Delgado, Ray Mondini, Flicka McGurrin, and Peggy—learned a version of this dish from Rose Pistola when she had her bar. This warm salad is not for the timid. That's why Rose loved it so much; she felt this dish separated the men from the boys.

Salt cod, or baccalà, is available in most Italian, Spanish, and Scandinavian specialty markets. Allow a day or a day and a half to soak the cod and transform it from its stiff dried, salted state to the tender, succulent fish that is the basis for this dish.

Serve with a good crusty country bread and a full-bodied Arneis or light-bodied Pinot Grigio wine. The salad is also great served with Roasted Sweet Peppers with Ricotta and Basil (page 36).

Place the salt cod in a large bowl of cold water to cover. Refrigerate for 24 to 36 hours, changing the water 4 times.

Bring a pot of water to a boil. Add the salt cod and cook at a simmer until tender, 10 to 15 minutes. Do not overcook, or the fish will toughen. Using a slotted spoon, remove the salt cod from the water, leaving the cooking water in the pot. Set the salt cod aside to cool.

Break up the cooled salt cod into flakes. Remove any stray bones or pieces of skin, and toss with the olive oil and garlic.

Bring the cod water back to a boil and cook the potatoes until they are tender when pierced with a fork, about 20 minutes. Drain.

When the potatoes are cool enough to handle, slip off their skins and cut into thin slices. Toss with the fish, parsley, and onion. Season to taste with salt and pepper and serve.

Steak House Salad

This salad uses ingredients found in traditional Italian cooking, chopped and tossed together very casually. It is reminiscent of the early days of North Beach, when vegetables came from Italian farmers who trucked their produce right into North Beach, or from natives' backyards. Nothing fancy was expected in the steak houses and early Italian restaurants, just good honest food for hard-working people.

Full of bold flavors, this is almost a meal in itself. Feel free to vary the ingredients with the season, although this salad is at its best in the summer, when tomatoes are at their peak. We use lemon-cured green olives at the restaurant, but other tangy green olives will do well too.

You can assemble the salad ahead of time and add the watercress, romaine, and avocado at the last minute. The other ingredients can marinate in the vinaigrette for a few hours.

I like to serve this old-fashioned salad with Terrorized Steak (page 169) and Griddled Artichokes and Potatoes (page 207).

1 red or yellow bell pepper, cored, and chopped into ½-inch pieces
½ red onion, peeled and chopped into ½-inch pieces
1 garlic clove, finely chopped
½ cup pitted and chopped lemon-cured Greek green olives or other green olives, with ¼ cup of their brine
1 large tomato, cored and chopped into ½-inch pieces
2 small pale inner celery stalks with leaves, chopped into ½-inch pieces
8 anchovy fillets, chopped
1 teaspoon fresh oregano leaves, or ½ teaspoon dried
Juice of ½ lemon
2 tablespoons red wine vinegar
½ cup extra virgin olive oil
Kosher or sea salt and freshly cracked black pepper
1 bunch watercress, chopped into ½-inch pieces
1 heart romaine, chopped into ½-inch pieces
1 avocado, peeled, pitted, and chopped into ½-inch pieces

Serves 6

Combine the pepper, onion, garlic, olives and their brine, the tomato, celery, anchovies, oregano, lemon juice, vinegar, and olive oil in a salad bowl. Season to taste with salt and pepper. Toss with the watercress, romaine, and avocado and serve.

Heirloom tomatoes from the Heirloom Tomato Company.

Pasta

Cries of "*Buon appetito*" and "*Buon gusto*" have been heard through the open windows and doors of North Beach since the Italians first settled here. Emblematic of the spirit of the neighborhood, they are the words of the song that has attracted outsiders for over a century and a half. Food, and in particular pasta, has been North Beach's secret to success. When people in the city get hungry, they head to North Beach for a big bowl of pasta.

The early immigrants pinched pennies to save on everything but food staples. Even the poorest families splurged on pasta, olive oil, sausages, cheese, and bread. By 1912, while earning less than an average of $900 a year, the city's Italians spent more for food, per capita, than any other nationality. While living and working conditions might have been wearisome, time spent at the table was full of laughter and good cheer.

Huge steaming bowls of pasta have long been associated with the good life in North Beach. Its first pasta factory was established as early as 1855 and by the 1890s the Pacific Consolidated Paste [*sic*] Company was shipping superior-quality products throughout the west. By 1917, nineteen pasta factories were producing literally tons of dried pasta annually.

Since many of the early immigrants in North Beach were from Liguria, they brought with them the practice of making stuffed and other varieties of pasta, the most popular being ravioli. The little filled dumplings are to the Genoese—and their North

Henry Fautz's North Beach Café, a saloon at the corner of Taylor and Chestnut Streets and Columbus Avenue, circa 1908. *Courtesy J. B. Monaco Photography.*

Beach descendants—a party dish, often served at Christmas, New Year's, or whenever a celebration is in order. Today, ravioli is still one of North Beach's favorite dishes, stuffed with wild greens, meat (sometimes including sweetbreads, calf's brains, and marrow), fish, artichokes, or mushrooms.

Many of the sauces in this chapter can be served with quality dried pasta. We make a lot of fresh pasta at Rose Pistola and offer a recipe so that you can cook the same pastas we enjoy serving at the restaurant. Our style of pasta preparation, common in the neighborhood, reflects the community's preference for light, fresh tastes and the ability to make use of readily available and affordable ingredients.

Pasta Dough

- $2\frac{1}{2}$ cups 00 *farina di grano tenero* from Pastiticio (see Sources, page 264) or all-purpose flour
- 3 large eggs
- 1 large egg yolk
- $\frac{1}{4}$ teaspoon kosher or sea salt

Makes 1 pound

Although pasta can be made with all-purpose flour, we suggest trying an imported Italian flour, such as 00 farina di grano tenero *from Pastiticio. Use a hand-cranked pasta machine for best results when rolling out the dough; then you'll be ready with sheets of pasta to assemble into ravioli or to cut into long or wide shapes such as the noodles for the lasagnette.*

Making fresh pasta really is easy. Give yourself plenty of time, be patient, and have fun.

Fresh pasta makes such a difference in the dishes at Rose Pistola. We use this recipe for tagliarini, spaghetti, lasagnette, and ravioli; we have a ravioli assembly line that turns out hundreds of plump, fresh ravioli every day. Use the dough for Ravioli of Mixed Greens with Mushrooms (page 104), Ravioli of Fava Beans and Lemon Thyme (page 106), Giant Ravioli of Soft Egg and Wild Greens (page 108), Lasagnette of Artichokes, Wild Mushrooms, and Hazelnut Pesto (page 112), and Seafood Lasagnette (page 114).

Mound 2 cups of the flour on a clean work surface. With two fingers, create a well in the center. Add the eggs, egg yolk, and salt.

With a fork, mix the eggs and salt together, incorporating the flour from the inside of the well and bringing up the flour from the bottom. Using a pastry scraper, scrape any unmixed flour into the moist dough. Knead the dough, adding a little more flour as necessary to obtain a stiff, pliable dough. After 2 to 3 minutes, the dough should feel fairly smooth and no longer sticky. Pat the dough into a disc and place it in a plastic bag. Refrigerate for 30 minutes or up to 24 hours before rolling it out. (If the dough is refrigerated for longer than 30 minutes, bring it to room temperature before rolling.)

To Roll Out the Dough

Divide the dough into 4 equal pieces; shape into balls. Work with one at a time, keeping the others refrigerated.

Flatten the ball with your hands so it will fit between the rollers on the pasta machine. Set the rollers at the widest opening and pass the dough through once. Then set at the next setting and pass the dough through again. Finally set the rollers at the third-widest setting and pass the dough through another time. Fold the dough over itself and repeat the procedure with the same three settings. Dust the dough with flour as necessary to keep it from getting sticky. Finally, roll it out through progressively narrower settings until it becomes almost transparent, up through the last, or second-to-last, setting on most machines. If you are not using the dough immediately, lay a clean kitchen towel out on a flat surface and place the pasta on the towel. Cover it with a slightly damp cloth. Or let the pasta sheet air-dry on a floured work surface.

Proceed as directed in each recipe. Roll out the remaining dough balls after you have filled (in the case of ravioli) or cut (in the case of flat noodles) the first sheet portion.

Spaghetti with Clams and Broccoli Rabe

- 1 bunch broccoli rabe, trimmed of tough stems
- 3 tablespoons extra virgin olive oil
- 2 garlic cloves, crushed
- ¼ teaspoon crushed red pepper flakes
- 2 tablespoons anchovy paste or 6 anchovy fillets, chopped
- ½ pound spaghetti
- 1 pound small Pacific littlenecks, rock clams, or Manila clams, scrubbed
- ½ cup dry Italian white wine
- ⅓ cup tomato puree (made from processing drained canned peeled whole tomatoes or peeled whole fresh tomatoes)
- Kosher or sea salt

Serves 2 to 4

Before it was called Fisherman's Wharf, the wooden moorings at the cove in North Beach (near the present-day Francisco Street) were named after the nefarious Henry Meiggs, a scheming businessman. His enterprise, Meiggs Wharf, had been constructed to accommodate the lumber trade; later, it was used by fishermen, swimmers, and sunbathers. The most popular dining spot of the day was Abe Warner's Cobweb Palace, a bizarre saloon known as much for its menagerie of wild animals as for its booze, crab, and clam chowder. This is just the sort of dish that would have been served there in the late fall, when broccoli rabe is in season. Pasta, seasoned clams, and broccoli rabe are all tossed together in the same pan, with the brininess of the clams and the sharpness of the red pepper and garlic exciting the bitter, intense flavor of the broccoli rabe.

Pacific littlenecks, or rock clams, have been harvested along the West Coast for thousands of years. Long before the Spaniards and Italians, clams were a staple in the Native American diet. Substitute mussels for the clams if desired.

Start with Shaved Artichokes with Fava Beans and Parmesan (page 30) and serve Persimmon Pudding (page 244) for dessert. Pour a Grechetto, Falesco, Umbria, 1997.

This recipe can easily be doubled.

Bring a large pot of salted water to a boil. Add the broccoli rabe and simmer until tender, about 5 minutes. Remove the broccoli rabe, leaving the water boiling, and set aside.

Heat the olive oil in a sauté pan over medium heat. Add the garlic and red pepper flakes and sauté until the garlic begins to turn golden, 3 to 5 minutes. Remove and discard the garlic. Add the anchovy paste and press on it with the tines of a fork until it melts into the olive oil, about 2 minutes. Toss in the broccoli rabe and remove from the heat.

Add the spaghetti to the boiling water and cook 10 to 12 minutes or until al dente. Drain the spaghetti and set aside, saving a ladle of the pasta water.

Return the sauté pan to high heat, add the clams and white wine, and shake the pan. Cook over high heat until the clams begin to open and the wine is reduced by half, about 3 minutes. Add the tomato puree, a splash of the saved pasta water, and the spaghetti. Cook until the sauce thickens and the pasta is just coated with the sauce, 2 to 3 minutes. Discard any unopened clam shells. Serve immediately.

Capellini with Crab

- 2 cups dry Italian white wine
- 1 Dungeness crab (2 to 2½ pounds)
- ¼ cup extra virgin olive oil
- ½ small white onion, chopped
- 1 garlic clove, crushed
- 1 sprig marjoram
- ¼ cup chopped flat-leaf parsley
- ¼ teaspoon harissa
- 1 tablespoon anchovy paste or 3 anchovy fillets, chopped
- 1 cup tomato puree (made from processing drained canned peeled whole tomatoes or peeled fresh whole tomatoes)
- ½ pound capellini
- 2 large egg yolks, lightly beaten

Serves 2

This sauce uses not just the meat of the crab, but the whole crab—including the shell and fat—to capture every nuance of its flavor. It is not necessary to present this pasta in the shell, but it makes for a dramatic dish when it is. Begin with impeccably fresh crab. Harissa is a North African red pepper paste available in a tube (see Sources, page 264).

Serve with Grilled Sea Bass with Lemon and White Beans (page 148) and Chocolate Budino (page 252). Pour a Quinterelli white wine.

Bring the wine to a boil in a large nonreactive saucepan with a tight-fitting lid. Add the crab, cover the pan, and steam over medium heat until the shell turns bright orange, 8 to 10 minutes. Remove the crab to a work surface and let cool. Set aside the pan with the cooking liquid in it.

When the crab is cool, remove the back in one piece, scooping out any fat from the corners of the shell. Reserve the crab fat and the back shell for presentation. Clean and section the crab and remove the meat (see page 157); you should have 1 to 1½ cups of crabmeat. Place the shells in the pan used for cooking the crab, place the pan over medium-high heat, and reduce the wine by half. Strain the wine though a fine sieve, pressing down on the shells to remove as much liquid as possible, and set the wine aside.

Bring a large pot of salted water to a boil. Preheat the broiler.

Place the olive oil and onion in a medium saucepan over medium heat and sauté until the onion becomes translucent, about 5 minutes. Add the garlic, marjoram, parsley, and harissa and cook until the parsley sizzles and the garlic is fragrant, about 3 minutes. Add the anchovy paste and sauté, pressing on it with the tines of a fork until it melts into the sauce, about 2 minutes longer. Remove and discard the garlic and marjoram. Add the reduced wine and the tomato puree, stir well, and simmer until the mixture thickens slightly, about 5 minutes.

While the sauce is simmering, add the capellini to the boiling water and cook 5 to 6 minutes or until al dente. Drain.

Transfer the sauce to a sauté pan, add the pasta, stir well, and cook over high heat until the sauce thickens and the pasta is just coated with the sauce, 2 to 3 minutes. Add the crabmeat and crab fat and warm it through. Remove the sauté pan from the heat and add the egg yolks. Toss until all the ingredients are well mixed.

To serve, place the reserved crab shell on its back on a heat-proof platter and fill it with the pasta, letting any extra overflow onto the platter. Broil until the top is bubbly and browned, about 1 minute. Serve from the platter.

Biordi Italian Ceramics on 412 Columbus Avenue, down the block from Rose Pistola, is famous for its pasta bowls and other hand-painted Italian dishes.

Bruised Garlic

One of the clichés about Italian cooking is that it uses too much garlic. We get a wonderful whisper of sweet garlic flavor by bruising or crushing whole (unpeeled) cloves of garlic and then sautéing them in oil. The oil picks up its perfume without letting the garlic overpower the dish. For a rustic presentation, add the cooked garlic to the serving platter.

Spaghetti with Spicy Seafood Sauce

¼ cup extra virgin olive oil
1 small white onion, finely chopped
1 garlic clove, bruised
¼ cup chopped flat-leaf parsley
1 tablespoon anchovy paste or 3 anchovy fillets, chopped
½ teaspoon harissa (see Sources, page 264)
12 mussels, scrubbed and debearded
12 clams, scrubbed
¼ pound white fish fillet, such as sea bass, snapper, or lingcod, cut into 1-inch cubes
¾ pound calamari, cleaned and cut into rings and tentacles (see page 163)
¼ pound peeled large shrimp, such as Santa Barbara prawns
¼ pound cooked octopus, chopped (see cooking instructions in Grilled Octopus with Broccoli Rabe and White Beans, page 166)
¾ pound spaghetti
½ cup dry Italian white wine
1½ cups tomato puree (made from processing drained canned peeled whole tomatoes or peeled fresh whole tomatoes)
Kosher or sea salt

Serves 4

This classic dish of spaghetti with seafood and tomato sauce is the essence of North Beach cooking. When the Italian settlers first arrived, they didn't have much money, so they used shellfish and fish in place of costly meat in many sauces. (Today, the tables have turned, and seafood can be as expensive as meat.) A fisherman would bring home a handful or two from the day's catch, his wife would have a pot of water for pasta on the stove ready to go, and soon, the entire family would feast.

Substitute whatever local seafood you have available in your area. The choices in this recipe are just a suggestion to get you going. Try for a balance of shellfish and fresh fish. If the octopus is too much to deal with, omit it, but it adds a great flavor. It is available, already cooked, in some Asian, Latino, and Italian markets, and in San Francisco in Japanese stores.

Start off with Shaved Artichokes with Fava Beans and Parmesan (page 30) and Crostini of Asparagus, Prosciutto, and Teleme (page 26). Pour a Cinsaut "Alegria Vineyard," Acorn Winery Russian River, 1997.

Bring a large pot of salted water to a boil. Meanwhile, place the olive oil and onion in a medium saucepan over medium heat and sauté until the onion becomes translucent, about 5 minutes. Add the garlic and parsley and cook until the parsley sizzles and the garlic is fragrant, about 3 minutes. Add the anchovy paste and harissa and press with the tines of a fork until melted into the olive oil, about 2 minutes. Increase the heat to high, add all of the shellfish and seafood, and cook until the seafood turns opaque and begins to release a little juice, 2 to 3 minutes.

Add the pasta to the boiling water and cook 10 to 12 minutes or until al dente. Cook the pasta while the seafood cooks.

Meanwhile, add the white wine to the seafood and reduce by half, about 2 minutes. Add ½ cup of the pasta water to the seafood and continue to reduce until about ⅓ cup of liquid remains, about 4 minutes more. Add the tomato puree and continue to reduce by one-third.

When the pasta is cooked, drain it and add it to the sauce. Stir well (or toss, if you're daring) to coat the noodles and continue to cook until the noodles absorb most of the liquid and the oil begins to separate, about 3 minutes more.

The staff eats lunch in the pasta-making room at Rose Pistola.

Spaghetti with Calamari Meatballs

¼ cup plus 1 tablespoon extra virgin olive oil, or more if needed
1½ white onions, chopped
2 garlic cloves, bruised
2 sprigs marjoram
½ cup chopped flat-leaf parsley
1 tablespoon plus 1 teaspoon harissa
14 anchovy fillets
1 pound calamari, cleaned and cut into rings and tentacles (see page 163)
¼ pound pancetta, cut into small cubes
1 large egg white, fresh
½ cup Bread Crumbs (page 9)
¾ teaspoon kosher or sea salt, or more to taste
1 cup dry Italian white wine
1 cup tomato puree (made from processing drained canned peeled whole tomatoes or peeled fresh whole tomatoes)
2 tablespoons calamari ink (see Sources, page 264)
1 pound spaghetti

Serves 6

Spaghetti and meatballs is the most classic of Italian-American dishes. Here, the meatballs are made with that classic meat substitute—calamari. If you can't find calamari ink, leave it out, but it does add color and a richer flavor.

Serve with Steak House Salad (page 89) and Sacripantina (page 256).

Heat 1 tablespoon of the olive oil in a heavy skillet over medium-high heat. Add two-thirds of the onions, 1 garlic clove, 1 marjoram sprig, ¼ cup of the parsley, 1 tablespoon of the harissa, and 10 of the anchovy fillets and sauté until the onion becomes translucent. Let cool. Remove the marjoram sprig.

Pulse all the calamari and pancetta, in small batches, in a food processor, keeping the mixture coarse, not smooth. Add the egg white and pulse to mix. Place the mixture in a bowl and stir in the bread crumbs, salt, and the cooled onion mixture. Form into golf ball-sized balls (using two soupspoons works well).

Heat 2 tablespoons of the olive oil in a large heavy skillet over medium-high heat and brown the calamari balls on all sides, adding more olive oil if needed. (You do not need to cook them all the way through, as they will finish cooking in the sauce.) Drain on paper towels.

Heat the remaining 2 tablespoons olive oil in a large, heavy sauté pan over medium-high heat. Add the remaining onions, garlic clove, marjoram sprig, ¼ cup parsley, 1 teaspoon harissa, and 4 anchovy fillets and sauté until the onion becomes translucent. Add the wine and cook until reduced by half. Add the tomato puree and stir well. Dilute the calamari ink with 1 cup pasta water or tap water and stir it into the sauce. Add the calamari balls and simmer for about 30 minutes. Taste for seasoning. This can be done ahead of time to this point.

Meanwhile, bring a large pot of salted water to a boil. Cook the spaghetti 10 to 12 minutes or until al dente. Drain.

Bring the sauce back to a simmer. Add the spaghetti, stir well, and simmer over medium-high heat in the sauce until the sauce has reduced enough to coat it, about 2 more minutes.

Pappardelle with Broccoli Rabe and Mushrooms

Luciano Repetto, the unofficial mayor of North Beach and owner of Graffeo's, a third-generation coffee roastery on Columbus Avenue, came to California from Liguria when he was ten. He loves to talk about food when customers come to buy his coffee. Luciano says the food, especially this dish, at Rose Pistola reminds him of his mother's cooking.

The long flat wide pappardelle noodles make a nice bed for the broccoli rabe and mushrooms. Make the noodles yourself according to the directions on pages 92–93 and cut them 1 inch wide, or have your pasta shop cut the noodles fresh for you. You can, of course, use dried pasta, such as fettuccine, instead.

Serve with the Roast Guinea Fowl with Pancetta (page 202) and Caramelized Fall Vegetables (page 218), and Caramelized Pear and Almond Tart (page 246) for dessert. Pour a Pinot Noir such as Edmeades, Anderson Valley, 1997.

3 tablespoons extra virgin olive oil
1 garlic clove, crushed
1 sprig rosemary (about 4 inches long)
3/4 pound mushrooms, such as porcini, chanterelle, hedgehog, crimini, portobello, and/or button, cleaned (black gills removed from portobellos) and sliced
1 bunch broccoli rabe, trimmed of tough stems
1 pound fresh pappardelle (see headnote) or 3/4 pound dried egg fettuccine
1/4 cup freshly grated Parmigiano-Reggiano
Kosher or sea salt and freshly cracked black pepper

Serves 4

Heat the olive oil in a heavy nonstick skillet over medium-high heat. Add the garlic and rosemary and cook until the garlic is fragrant and the rosemary starts to sizzle, about 1½ minutes. Add the mushrooms and cook until they start to brown, about 10 minutes; shake the pan and stir often. Remove from the heat and keep warm.

Meanwhile, bring a large pot of salted water to a boil. Add the broccoli rabe and simmer until tender, about 5 minutes. Remove the broccoli rabe and set aside. Add the pasta to the same boiling water and cook until al dente, about 2 minutes for fresh pasta, or as directed on the package for dried. Drain the pasta, leaving a little water clinging to it.

Add the pasta, broccoli rabe, and cheese to the skillet with the mushrooms and toss together. Season to taste with salt and pepper. Serve.

Anna-Maria and Luciano Repetto in front of their third-generation family-owned Ligurian North Beach business, which is the oldest coffee-roasting company in the neighborhood. Luciano Repetto is the unofficial mayor of North Beach.

Sautéed Penne with Mussels

2 cups dry Italian white wine
1½ pounds mussels, scrubbed and debearded
3 garlic cloves, bruised
¼ teaspoon kosher or coarse sea salt
½ cup basil leaves
½ cup extra virgin olive oil
1 small white onion, chopped
¼ cup chopped flat-leaf parsley
1 tablespoon anchovy paste or 3 anchovy fillets, chopped
½ teaspoon crushed red pepper flakes
3 cups tomato puree (made from processing drained canned peeled whole tomatoes or peeled fresh whole tomatoes)
½ pound penne
Kosher or sea salt and freshly cracked black pepper

Serves 2

San Francisco, depicted in a well-known television commercial with cable cars ringing their bells, is linked with a sautéed rice and pasta dish, "the San Francisco treat." In this caricature of our city, as in most caricatures, there lies a kernel of truth. The San Francisco treat has its roots in the technique of cooking dried pasta much like risotto. The pasta is first sautéed and then simmered in a sauce so it cooks through and takes on the sauce's flavor. You could substitute any number of other ingredients, such as mushrooms or asparagus, for the mussels in their light broth.

Serve with Roasted Mushroom and White Asparagus or Endive Salad (page 80) and Mixed Citrus Compote with Vanilla Ice Cream (page 234). Pour a Soave, Anselmi, 1997.

Combine the white wine and 1 cup water in a medium saucepan and bring to a boil. Add the mussels, cover, and cook until they open, 2 to 3 minutes. Remove the mussels from the pan, strain the mussel liquid, and set aside. When they are cool, shell the mussels and set aside.

Put the 2 garlic cloves and salt in a mortar and pound together or puree in a food processor to a creamy paste. Add one or two of the basil leaves and pound or pulse to a rough paste. Add a couple of drops of the olive oil and continue to pound or process until a smooth emulsion, or liquid, is formed. Continue adding basil and olive oil in this fashion until all of the basil and 2 tablespoons of the oil are used.

Place the 2 remaining tablespoons of the olive oil and the onion in a medium saucepan over medium heat and sauté until the onion becomes translucent, about 5 minutes. Add the remaining garlic and parsley and cook until the parsley sizzles and the garlic is fragrant, about 3 minutes. Add the anchovy paste or the anchovies and red pepper and sauté, pressing on the anchovies with the tines of a fork, until the paste or anchovies melt into the oil, about 2 minutes. Add the mussel liquid and bring to a rolling boil. Add the tomato puree and simmer about 3 minutes longer. Keep the sauce over low heat.

Meanwhile, heat the remaining ¼ cup olive oil in a large pot until a drop of water added to it sizzles. Add the uncooked penne and cook over medium heat, stirring constantly, until it changes color all over, about 5 minutes. Just as if you were making risotto, add a ladleful of the tomato-mussel broth and stir to incorporate. Keeping the liquid at a bare simmer, continue to add the broth a ladleful at a time, stirring frequently and cooking until the noodles absorb the liquid, then add another ladle. Keep the broth just below the level of the top of the noodles. As with risotto, you should stir the noodles in one direction only: Stirring only in one direction lines up all of the noodles in one direction, so they will be less likely to break and become gummy. When most of the liquid has been absorbed, begin to taste the pasta, and continue to cook until the pasta is al dente. If you think you will run out of tomato-mussel liquid, thin it with a little water. Stir in the mussels and the basil puree, season to taste with salt and pepper, warm through briefly, and serve.

Ravioli of Mixed Greens with Mushrooms

2 tablespoons extra virgin olive oil
1 small white onion, finely chopped
1½ cups mixed greens (see headnote), blanched and squeezed dry
¼ teaspoon kosher or sea salt, or more to taste
⅛ teaspoon freshly ground white pepper, or more to taste
1 cup Homemade Ricotta (page 12) or fresh ricotta
1 large egg
½ cup freshly grated Pecorino Sardo or Parmigiano-Reggiano
1 egg yolk
4 sheets (1 recipe) Pasta Dough (page 92)
4 tablespoons (½ stick) unsalted butter
2 tablespoons pine nuts
4 sprigs marjoram
1½ cups wild mushrooms, optional

Serves 8 as a first course, 4 as a main course (makes approximately 4 dozen ravioli)

In northwestern Italy and among the Italian immigrants to Northern California, a favorite ingredient in many dishes is a mixture of wild greens called preboggion, *which makes an intensely good ravioli filling. At Rose Pistola, we make this with mature, strong-flavored greens such as dandelion and arugula, in addition to wild nettles, borage, milk thistle, and more typical braising greens such as kale and chard. All of these are brought to us by local Bay Area growers, who grow them much the same way as they have been for decades.*

There's no need to head for the hills. You can easily forage for kale, dandelion, chard, and arugula in your supermarket. This basic composition of greens is also used at Rose Pistola for soups and vegetable braises—it is subject to endless variation.

Serve with Roast Sage-Stuffed Quail with Walnut Sauce (page 201) and Lemon and Pomegranate Snow Cones (page 239). Pour a Pigato such as La Torratta, Colle dei Bardellini, 1996.

Place the olive oil and onion in a medium saucepan over medium heat and sauté until the onion becomes translucent, about 5 minutes. Add the greens, salt, and white pepper and sauté briefly. Transfer the greens to the bowl of a food processor and let cool slightly. Add the ricotta, egg, and ¼ cup of the pecorino to the greens. Process to a smooth puree, taste for seasoning, and set aside.

Prepare an egg wash by whisking the egg yolk with 1 tablespoon water. Make sure all the flour is brushed off the pasta sheets, then lightly brush one side of each sheet with a thin coating of the egg wash. On 2 of the sheets, place tablespoon-sized balls of the filling 3 inches apart so that you have an 8-ball by 3-ball grid on each sheet. Lay 1 of the remaining 2 sheets of pasta, egg-washed side down, over each sheet, starting at one end and draping the sheet successively over the piles of greens. (This draping method prevents excess air bubbles from being trapped in the ravioli.) Press down between the mounds of filling and along the edges to seal the ravioli. Cut into squares with a sharp knife or a ravioli crimper. Squeeze out any air pockets and pinch together any open edges. Lay the ravioli on a wire rack to air-dry for 30 minutes before cooking. (Once they have dried a little, you can toss the ravioli with rice flour and store overnight in the refrigerator, or freeze the ravioli first individually on a baking sheet and then store in a plastic container in the freezer for up to 2 weeks.)

Bring a large pot of salted water to a boil. Tap off any excess flour from the ravioli if they have been stored, drop them into the water, and cook for about 3 minutes, until they float to the top and the pasta is cooked through.

Meanwhile, in a medium sauté pan over medium-high heat, melt the butter with the pine nuts and marjoram until the butter is sizzling and the marjoram, wild mushrooms (optional), and pine nuts are fragrant, 2 to 3 minutes. Remove the pan from the heat.

Drain the ravioli and transfer them to the sauté pan, along with the few drops of water that cling to them. Shake well. Toss together with the remaining ¼ cup cheese and serve immediately.

Ravioli of Fava Beans and Lemon Thyme

1 cup fava beans, peeled (approximately 1 pound fava beans in the pod)
1 cup baby or immature fava beans (see page 195)
1 teaspoon lemon thyme leaves, plus 2 sprigs lemon thyme (see headnote)
¼ cup extra virgin olive oil
½ teaspoon chopped green garlic or 1 small garlic clove, chopped
1 cup freshly grated Pecorino Sardo or Parmigiano-Reggiano
¼ teaspoon kosher or sea salt
1 egg yolk
4 sheets (1 recipe) Pasta Dough (page 92)
¼ pound pancetta, cut into matchstick-sized pieces

Serves 8 as a first course, 4 as a main course (makes approximately 4 dozen ravioli)

One of the great things about mastering a few basic techniques such as this way of making ravioli is that, once you learn how to do it, it's open to almost endless variation. The rich, slight bitterness of fava beans, particularly those that are very young and don't need to be peeled, is one of the classic flavors of spring. If lemon thyme isn't available, substitute regular fresh thyme mixed with a pinch of grated lemon zest, or chopped basil.

Serve with Tuna Carpaccio with Slivered Artichokes (page 56) and Zabaglione with Strawberries in Red Wine (page 232). Pour a full-bodied Pigato.

Combine the fava beans, 1 teaspoon lemon thyme leaves, olive oil, garlic, cheese, and salt in a food processor and puree until smooth.

Prepare an egg wash by whisking the egg yolk with 1 tablespoon water. Make sure all the flour is brushed off the pasta sheets, then lightly brush one side of each sheet with a thin coating of the egg wash. On 2 of the sheets, place tablespoon-sized balls of the fava filling 3 inches apart so that you have an 8-ball by 3-ball grid on each sheet. Lay 1 of the remaining 2 sheets of pasta, egg-washed side down, over each sheet, starting at one end and draping it successively over the piles of fava filling. (This draping method prevents excess air bubbles from being trapped in the ravioli.) Press down between the mounds of filling and along the edges to seal the ravioli. Cut into squares with a sharp knife or a ravioli crimper. Squeeze out any air pockets and pinch together any open edges. Lay the ravioli on a wire rack to air-dry for 30 minutes before cooking. (Once they have dried a little, you can toss the ravioli with rice flour and store overnight in the refrigerator, or freeze the ravioli first individually on a baking sheet and then store in a plastic container in the freezer for up to 2 weeks.)

Bring a large pot of salted water to a boil. Tap off any excess flour from the ravioli if they have been stored, drop them into the water, and cook for about 3 minutes, until they float to the top and the pasta is cooked through.

Meanwhile, in a medium sauté pan over medium heat, cook the pancetta until it has rendered its fat and is brown and crisp. Immediately add the 2 lemon thyme sprigs and cook just until they sizzle, which should happen almost immediately.

Drain the ravioli and transfer them to the sauté pan, along with the few drops of water that cling to them. Toss together and serve immediately.

Giant Ravioli of Soft Egg and Wild Greens

¾ cup mixed greens
1 tablespoon extra virgin olive oil
½ small white onion, finely chopped
¼ teaspoon kosher or sea salt, or more to taste
⅛ teaspoon freshly ground white pepper, or more to taste
2 large egg yolks
½ cup Homemade Ricotta (page 12) or fresh ricotta
¼ cup freshly grated Pecorino Sardo or Parmigiano-Reggiano
4 sheets (1 recipe) Pasta Dough (page 92)
8 large eggs
3 tablespoons unsalted butter
¼ cup shaved Parmigiano-Reggiano
White truffle, optional

Serves 4 as a first course, 2 as a main course

When you cut into your first bite of this huge round ravioli, the egg yolk will spill out onto the plate, bringing along with it a taste of wild greens, soft pasta, and melted Parmesan cheese. It is an amazingly luxurious combination of texture and flavor.

If ever there were a dish that cried out for a few slices of shaved white truffle, this is it. Use it if you can get it, but it is optional.

If you wish, you can use store-bought pasta sheets or, in a pinch, wonton wrappers. If you buy the pasta, ask that the pasta be cut into four strips, each fifteen inches long by three inches wide, if possible.

This is a perfect first course to follow with a rich main course, such as Hazelnut Coteghino with Lentils (page 190), and Lemon and Pomegranate Snow Cones (page 239) for dessert. Pour a Prosecco wine.

Blanch the greens in salted boiling water for 3 to 4 minutes. Drain and, when cool enough to handle, squeeze out as much moisture as possible.

Place the olive oil and onion in a medium saucepan over medium heat and sauté until the onion becomes translucent, about 5 minutes. Add the greens, salt, and white pepper and sauté briefly. Transfer the greens to the bowl of a food processor and let cool slightly. Add 1 of the egg yolks, the ricotta, and pecorino. Process to a smooth puree, taste for seasoning, and set aside.

Prepare an egg wash by whisking the remaining egg yolk with 1 tablespoon water. Make sure all the flour is brushed off the pasta sheets, then lightly brush one side of each sheet with a thin coating of the egg wash. Place 4 mounds of filling down the center of each of 2 of the pasta sheets, spacing them 6 inches apart. Spread each mound of mixed greens out to create a ring with a hole in the center about 1½ inches in diameter (large enough to hold an egg yolk), shaping the ring so that the outside diameter is about 3 inches. Separate the eggs one at a time, carefully placing an unbroken egg yolk in the center of each ring of greens.

Lay 1 of the remaining 2 sheets of pasta, egg-washed side down, over each sheet of greens, starting at one end and draping it successively over each pile. (This draping method prevents excess air bubbles from being trapped in the ravioli.) Press down between mounds of filling and along the edges to seal the ravioli. Cut out each ravioli with a wide-mouth wineglass or a cookie cutter about 4 inches in diameter. Press together the edges of each ravioli with your fingertips, squeezing out any trapped air and being careful to leave the egg yolk unbroken. Lay the ravioli on a wire rack to air-dry for 30 minutes before cooking.

Bring a large pot of salted water to a boil. Carefully place the ravioli in the water and cook for 1½ to 3 minutes.

Meanwhile, melt the butter in a large sauté pan over medium heat. Carefully remove the ravioli from the water with a slotted spoon and add to the sauté pan. Then slide the ravioli out of the sauté pan onto serving plates and pour any remaining butter over the top. Add some Parmigiano-Reggiano shavings to each ravioli. If the gods have smiled on you and you have a white truffle, shave it on top as well. If you are not so fortunate, grind a little white pepper over the top instead.

Corzetti of Fish and Greens

1 pound mixed greens, such as spinach, chopped chard, arugula, and dandelion greens
2 tablespoons extra virgin olive oil
1 small onion, finely diced
1 garlic clove, bruised
1 sprig marjoram (about 6 inches long)
3/4 pound firm white fish fillets, such as halibut or sea bass, cut into 1-inch chunks
1/4 teaspoon kosher or sea salt
Pinch of freshly ground white pepper
Pinch of freshly grated nutmeg
1 large egg
2 1/2 cups all-purpose flour

For the Sauce

2 tablespoons unsalted butter
1/2 small white onion, finely diced
1/2 cup dry Italian white wine
1 1/2 cups tomato puree (made from processing drained canned peeled whole tomatoes or peeled fresh whole tomatoes)
Kosher or sea salt and freshly cracked black pepper

1 tablespoon unsalted butter, melted

Makes 40 pieces; serves 4 to 6

Unlike ordinary pasta dough, this dough has greens and fish mixed right into it to flavor it, so the sauce is only a light accent. The dough is then rolled and stamped into small flat rounds; with a texture almost like that of a biscuit, it gives the sauce something to cling to. The dish is clearly a bridge between stuffed pastas and plain cut pasta. We serve it with a delicate tomato sauce that sets off the green of the pasta.

Corzetti have their origins in medieval Italy, when the rounds of pasta were stamped with the heraldic seals of important households. Corzetti stamps are made of wood and have two parts. The round bottom has a sharp ring that is used to cut the rounds of dough; the tip of the bottom piece has a design cut into it. The round top, with a small handle on it, has another design cut into its bottom. Once the dough is cut, the pasta disc is transferred to the side of the bottom with the design and pressed with the top part, so it ends up with a design stamped on both sides. If you don't have a wooden corzetti stamp, use a wineglass to cut the rounds, then mark both sides with a fork to create some texture.

Serve with Seaweed-Steamed Fish (page 143) and Tangerine Tart (page 250). Pour a full-bodied Pigato.

Blanch the greens in salted boiling water for 3 to 4 minutes. Drain and, when cool enough to handle, squeeze out as much moisture as possible.

Place the olive oil and onion in a medium saucepan over medium heat and sauté until the onion becomes translucent, about 5 minutes. Add the garlic and marjoram and cook until the marjoram sizzles and the garlic is fragrant, about 3 minutes. Add the fish and blanched greens, cover, and continue to cook, stirring occasionally, until the fish is flaky and falling apart and the ingredients are melting together, about 10 minutes. Let cool.

Puree the fish mixture in a food processor until smooth. Place in a clean dry towel and squeeze dry. Return the mixture to the food processor, add the salt, pepper, nutmeg, and egg, and pulse until the egg is incorporated. Add the flour a little at a time, pulsing with each addition, until a dough forms. The dough will be very soft and sticky.

Lay a large piece of parchment paper on a work surface, spray the paper with a nonstick cooking spray or brush it with olive oil, and place the dough on it. Pat it out with your hands until it is about ½ inch thick. Then roll it out using a lightly floured rolling pin until it is ⅛ inch thick, dusting the dough with a little flour if it sticks to the rolling pin.

Using a corzetti stamp or a cookie cutter, cut out rounds of dough 2 to 3 inches in diameter. Stamp the rounds with the corzetti stamp or press the tines of a fork into both sides of each one to create ridges. The ridges help capture the sauce. Sprinkle with rice flour or all-purpose flour. (Rice flour is preferable, because the dough will not absorb it.) Lay the corzetti on a wire rack to dry slightly.

Bring a large pot of salted water to a boil.

For the Sauce

Melt the butter in a medium saucepan over medium heat. Add the onion and cook until translucent, about 5 minutes. Add the wine, increase the heat to high, and reduce by half. Add the tomato puree and simmer briefly to reduce. Season to taste and keep warm over very low heat while you cook the corzetti.

Coat a warm serving dish with the melted butter. Poach the corzetti in the barely boiling water, 10 to 15 at a time so they do not stick together, until they float to the top, 2 to 3 minutes. As they are cooked, transfer the corzetti to the serving dish. To serve, pour the sauce over the corzetti and stir or toss gently to combine.

Note

If you would like to make the corzetti ahead, they can be frozen. Freeze them in a single layer on a baking sheet. Once frozen, place in an airtight plastic bag and store in the freezer. They may be cooked frozen; give them an extra minute or two.

Lasagnette of Artichokes, Wild Mushrooms, and Hazelnut Pesto

For the Filling

3 tablespoons extra virgin olive oil

12 baby artichokes, trimmed (see page 31) and thinly sliced, or 3 large artichokes trimmed to hearts (see page 31) and thinly sliced

2 tablespoons dry Italian white wine

Kosher or sea salt

1 garlic clove, bruised

1 sprig rosemary (about 3 inches long)

½ pound wild mushrooms, such as porcini, chanterelles, or hedgehogs, cleaned and thinly sliced (or use portobellos, with the black gills and stems trimmed off)

½ cup freshly grated Parmigiano-Reggiano

4 large eggs, beaten

¼ teaspoon freshly cracked black pepper

3 sheets Pasta Dough (page 92), approximately 5 by 20 inches

1 tablespoon olive oil

3 tablespoons unsalted butter, melted

Hazelnut Pesto (page 10), at room temperature

Serves 4 as a first course, 2 as a main course

If the only lasagna you have ever had is that, admittedly sometimes appealing, baked mass of gooey cheese, pasta, and red sauce, you are in for a treat. These small lasagnas are much easier to make, lighter, and more delicate in flavor. The heavy melted cheese is replaced with a sprinkling of Parmesan and the hearty red meat sauce is replaced with artichokes and mushrooms in a light sauce. Fresh pasta, whether homemade or store-bought, is a must for this dish.

The combination of these ingredients brings out the best flavors in each one. The nuttiness of the hazelnuts enhances that same quality in artichokes, and the pleasantly bitter richness of the artichokes, with their faint anise edge, plays delightfully against the woodsy, piney flavor of the wild mushrooms.

A perfect first course for the Roast Chicken with Garlic (page 196). Pour an oaky California Sauvignon Blanc.

For the Filling

Heat 1½ tablespoons of the olive oil in a heavy nonstick skillet over high heat. Add the artichokes and sauté, stirring often, until well browned, 8 to 10 minutes. Splash in the white wine toward the end, scraping the browned bits up from the bottom of the pan. Season to taste with salt and set the artichokes aside in a large bowl.

Put the pan back on the burner over medium-high heat and add the remaining 1½ tablespoons olive oil, the garlic, and rosemary. Sauté until the garlic becomes fragrant. Add the mushrooms and brown, stirring occasionally, about 8 minutes. Discard the garlic and rosemary and add the mushrooms to the artichokes. Set aside to cool.

Bring a large pot of salted water to a boil. Meanwhile, whisk the cheese, eggs, and pepper together in a small bowl. Fold the egg mixture into the artichoke-mushroom mixture and set aside while you cook the pasta.

Cook the noodles, a few at a time, in the boiling water, 1 to 2 minutes. Very carefully remove them with two slotted spoons, dunk them briefly in a large pot of ice water, and pat them dry. Lay them out on a clean work surface so they do not stick together.

Preheat the oven to 500°F.

Lay 1 of the pasta sheets on a baking sheet that has been brushed with the olive oil. Spread half of the artichoke-mushroom filling evenly over the pasta sheet. Place another pasta sheet on top and spread the remaining filling on top of it. Top with the third pasta sheet. Cut the lasagna into 4 equal pieces.

Brush the tops of the lasagnette with the melted butter and cover with foil while you make the pesto.

Bake the lasagnette until warmed through, about 5 minutes. Serve the lasagnette on individual plates with a spoonful of the hazelnut pesto on top of each one.

Note

The lasagnette and pesto can be prepared up to 2 hours in advance and refrigerated.

Seafood Lasagnette

For the Seafood Sauce

2 tablespoons extra virgin olive oil
½ white onion, diced
1 garlic clove, bruised
¼ cup chopped flat-leaf parsley
1 sprig marjoram
6 Manila clams, scrubbed
6 mussels, scrubbed and debearded
¼ pound cooked octopus (see cooking instructions in Grilled Octopus with Broccoli Rabe and White Beans, page 166), cut into ½-inch pieces, optional
¾ pound calamari, cleaned, separated into tubes and tentacles (see page 163), and cut into ½-inch pieces
6 to 8 anchovy fillets, chopped
¼ pound rock shrimp, or medium-sized prawns
¾ cup dry Italian white wine
½ cup reserved pasta water, fish stock, or clam juice diluted with a little water, or tap water
Basilade (page 8), at room temperature

3 sheets Pasta Dough (page 92), approximately 5 by 20 inches, or 6 dried lasagna noodles, approximately 4 by 8 inches
1 tablespoon olive oil

Serves 4 as a first course, 2 as a main course

Shellfish has a different flavor and texture when it is braised until it is tender rather than just barely cooked. Shellfish stews such as this one take on a unified essence of the sea's flavor from long cooking.

The stew can be made with any one or all of the types of seafood listed below, or with fish or scallops as well. Recipes are merely a road map to be applied to ingredients, which are the starting point. You can control the end result by controlling the ingredients you begin with.

Serve as a first course with Roast Guinea Fowl with Pancetta (page 202). As an entrée, it would be good with Fried Artichokes with Parmesan (page 32) as an antipasto and, for dessert, Tangerine Tart (page 250). A California Dolcetto would be wonderful with this dish.

For the Seafood Sauce

Place the olive oil and onion in a medium saucepan over medium heat and sauté until the onion becomes translucent, about 5 minutes. Add the garlic, parsley, and marjoram and cook until the parsley sizzles and the garlic is fragrant, about 3 minutes.

Add the clams, mussels, octopus, if using, the calamari, anchovies, and rock shrimp. Sauté for a few minutes, then add the wine. Cook until the clams and mussels open.

Remove the clams and mussels from the pan, remove them from their shells, and return the meat to the pan. Add the water or stock and continue to cook, stirring occasionally, until the seafood is tender and the liquid is reduced to about ½ cup, about

20 minutes. Let cool, then chop the seafood into ¼- to ½-inch pieces. Meanwhile, prepare the basilade.

Bring a large pot of salted water to a boil.

Return chopped seafood to the liquid and allow to cool.

Preheat the oven to 500°F. Cook the noodles, a few at a time, in the boiling water, 1 to 2 minutes for fresh pasta, or according to the instructions on the box for dried. Very carefully remove them with two slotted spoons, dunk them briefly in a large pot of ice water, and pat dry.

If using fresh pasta, lay 1 of the pasta sheets on a baking sheet that has been brushed with the olive oil. Spread half of the seafood filling evenly over the pasta sheet. Place another pasta sheet on top and spread the remaining filling on top of it. Top with the third pasta sheet. Cut the lasagna into 4 equal pieces.

If using dried pasta, lay 2 of the pasta sheets on a baking sheet that has been brushed with the olive oil. Spread a quarter of the filling evenly over each pasta sheet. Place another pasta sheet on top of each and spread another quarter of the filling on top of each. Top each with the remaining pasta sheets. Cut each of the stacks into 2 equal pieces.

Spread the reserved basilade-seafood liquid over the tops of the lasagnette. Cover the baking sheet with foil and bake the lasagnette until warmed through, about 5 minutes. Serve the lasagnette on individual plates.

Note

The lasagnette can be assembled and refrigerated up to 2 hours in advance.

Trofie with Pesto

- ½ pound Yukon Gold potatoes, unpeeled
- 1½ cups all-purpose flour
- 1 large egg
- ¼ teaspoon kosher or sea salt
- 1 tablespoon extra virgin olive oil

Pesto (page 9)

Serves 4

Properly made pesto is a partial emulsion (like aïoli), thickened with comparatively little oil. Bruising the basil leaves together with coarse salt and garlic releases their oils and at the same time emulsifies their essence into the sauce. The slow, steady addition of the olive oil serves both to prevent the basil from oxidizing and darkening and to thicken the sauce. A properly made pesto should be a light green color, almost fluffy in texture, but thick, with little or no oil seeping out the edges. The olive oil should be a high-quality, delicately flavored, rich, golden oil. Seek out those from Provence and Liguria (see Olive Oil, page 74). The flavors of the cheese and nuts should remain secondary to the basil, enhancing the buttery character of the oil and offsetting the sharpness of the garlic a bit.

Trofie are a sort of gnocchi made with a stiffer dough, each hand-rolled trofie exhibiting a range of textures from chewy to meltingly tender. This dish is time-consuming to make, but well worth the effort.

When it comes to serving the pasta, place some pesto in the middle of each bowl of trofie, bring the bowls to the table, and let your guests toss the trofie themselves to savor the pesto aroma.

Pour a Pinot Noir, Au Bon Climat, Santa Barbara, 1997, and serve with Capponada (page 76) and Bowl of Iced Summer Fruit (page 233).

Place the potatoes in a big pot of cold water, bring the water to a simmer, and cook the potatoes until tender when pierced with a fork. Drain and cool.

Peel the potatoes and pass through a ricer, or mash until fine-textured and fluffy.

Gently knead the flour, egg, salt, and olive oil into the potatoes, mixing well. Form the dough into a large rectangle on a flour-dusted work surface. Cut it into 8 pieces. By hand, roll each piece into a rope 12 to 15 inches long and ¼ inch thick. Cut each rope into ½-inch-long pieces. With your fingers, roll each piece across the floured work surface until it is about ⅛ inch in diameter and 1½ to 2 inches long. If the trofie stick, scrape off any dough sticking to the work surface and your fingers and have at it again. As you make the trofie, arrange them on a baking sheet so they are not touching each other. (The trofie can be frozen for later use; freeze them on the baking sheet, and then transfer them to an airtight bag, tossing them with a little rice flour, and freeze for up to 1 month.)

Bring a large pot of salted water to a boil. Add the trofie, reduce the heat, and simmer until they float to the top and are cooked through, about 4 minutes. Immediately drain the trofie, place in four serving bowls, and put a heaping spoonful of pesto on top of each one.

Silk Handkerchiefs with Two Leftover Sauces

3½ cups (1 pound) all-purpose flour
1 jumbo egg, lightly beaten
½ cup dry Italian white wine
¼ teaspoon kosher or sea salt
¾ cup Pizza Tomato Sauce (page 14), at room temperature
¾ cup Pesto (page 9), at room temperature
2 tablespoons unsalted butter, at room temperature

Serves 4

This dish is a sort of tribute to the notorious frugality of the Genovese, and the North Beach denizens they became. If they didn't have enough leftover pesto or tomato sauce to make dinner, they simply combined the two. The result is extraordinary.

This pasta is named "silk handkerchiefs" because it is extremely light and silky, and it is cut to resemble small handkerchiefs, about six inches square.

Knead together the flour, egg, white wine, and salt on a work surface, adding the flour gradually. Add just enough water to make a firm, elastic dough as you continue to knead. Wrap tightly and let rest for 1 hour in the refrigerator. Divide the dough into 4 balls.

Roll the dough out as directed on page 93, rolling it through the thinnest setting on the pasta machine. Cut the dough into 6-inch squares. Use 12 handkerchiefs for this recipe; freeze the rest of the handkerchiefs for another time. (Lay them on a baking sheet to freeze, then carefully wrap in plastic with a little flour between the layers, and put in a plastic bag.)

Bring a large pot of salted water to a boil. Meanwhile, heat the tomato sauce in a heavy saucepan over medium-high heat until it simmers. Remove from the heat.

Cook the pasta in the boiling water for 1½ minutes. Pasta is done when translucent and limp. Carefully remove the pasta with two large skimmers or a slotted spoon and drain immediately.

Stir the pesto and butter into the tomato sauce. Place 3 handkerchiefs on each of four warm plates, pour the sauce over the top, and serve.

Gnocchi

If you have never tried to make gnocchi, those delicate little potato dumplings, don't be intimidated. They are quite simple and very forgiving. Be careful not to overwork the dough, though, because this might develop the gluten in the flour and make the gnocchi tough. Think of it as like working with biscuit or pie dough rather than bread dough.

Getting the characteristic gnocchi shape using the tines of a fork or a gnocchi board takes some trial and error, but you can simply roll the dough into ropes and cut them into 1-inch lengths. They don't grip the sauce as well, but they are faster and easier to produce—and far superior to packaged gnocchi. Gnocchi are good with many sauces, including Pesto (page 9) or any of the following recipes using gnocchi.

3 pounds Yukon Gold potatoes, unpeeled
2½ cups (¾ pound) all-purpose flour
1 large egg
1½ teaspoons kosher or sea salt
2 tablespoons extra virgin olive oil

Makes about 100 to 125 little dumplings

Place the potatoes in a big pot of cold water, bring the water to a simmer, and cook the potatoes until tender when pierced with a fork. Drain and cool.

Peel the potatoes and pass through a ricer, or mash until fine-textured and fluffy.

Gently knead the flour, egg, salt, and olive oil into the potatoes, mixing well. Form the dough into a large rectangle on a flour-dusted work surface. Pat it down and cut it into 6 pieces. By hand, roll each piece into a rope 12 to 15 inches long and ½ inch thick. Cut each rope into 1-inch-long pieces.

Lightly press and roll each piece of dough on the back of the tines of a fork with your thumb to create a ridged surface. (This ridged surface will allow the dumplings to catch the sauce.) The dumplings will look almost like tiny ridged seashells. Place the dumplings on a lightly floured baking sheet or a sheet lined with waxed paper so that they do not touch one another. (The gnocchi freeze well. Freeze them on a baking sheet, then store in an airtight container.)

To cook the gnocchi, bring a large pot of salted water to a boil. Add the gnocchi. They are done when they float, about 2 minutes if fresh, 3 to 4 minutes if frozen.

Gnocchi with Calamari Bolognese

- ¼ cup extra virgin olive oil
- 1 medium white onion, finely chopped
- 1 garlic clove, bruised
- ¼ cup chopped flat-leaf parsley
- 3 sprigs marjoram (about 4 inches long)
- 2 tablespoons anchovy paste or 6 anchovy fillets, chopped
- 2 teaspoons harissa (see Sources, page 264)
- 1¼ pound calamari, cleaned (see page 163), put through a meat grinder or finely chopped in a food processor
- 1 cup dry Italian white wine
- 2 cups tomato puree (made from processing drained canned peeled whole tomatoes or peeled fresh whole tomatoes)
- 1 cup reserved pasta water (see page 69) or tap water
- ½ recipe Gnocchi (page 119)

Serves 4

To open Rose Pistola, I searched for a dish that summed up the North Beach approach to Italian cooking. One of the things I learned from Rose herself is how the ever-frugal housewives in the area had used plentiful and cheap calamari for the then-more-expensive beef, veal, and pork typical of Italian-American cooking. This is a version of that standby North Beach dish, pasta with ragù, with a twist that recognizes the substitution so often made by the North Beach cooks.

The meat-substitution trick can also be done with wonderful results using geoduck or quahog clams, octopus, or other sturdy shellfish. As with any typical ragù, it's important to allow the "meat" to simmer until it is meltingly tender and the flavors of the sauce marry. This sauce can be used on pasta as well as gnocchi.

Serve with Baby Fava Beans and Pecorino (page 34) and a full-bodied Barbera or an Amador County Zinfandel.

Place the olive oil and onion in a medium saucepan over medium heat and sauté until the onion becomes translucent, about 5 minutes. Add the garlic, parsley, and marjoram and cook until the parsley sizzles and the garlic is fragrant, about 3 min-

utes. Add the anchovy paste and harissa and sauté, pressing on the anchovy paste or anchovies with the tines of a fork, until melted into the oil, about 2 minutes.

Add the calamari, raise the heat to high, and sauté until the calamari is opaque, for another 2 to 3 minutes. Add the wine and cook until reduced by half. Add the tomato puree and pasta water and bring to a simmer. Lower the heat to medium-low and continue to cook, uncovered, until the sauce begins to thicken and the calamari is meltingly tender, 45 minutes to 1 hour. Add a little more pasta water if the liquid evaporates too quickly. (The sauce can be made ahead of time and keeps in the refrigerator for 2 days. It can also be frozen for 2 weeks.)

Bring a large pot of salted water to a boil. Gently reheat the sauce if it was prepared in advance.

Cook the gnocchi; they are done when they float, about 2 minutes if fresh and 3 to 4 minutes if frozen. Drain the gnocchi, transfer them and the sauce to a large sauté pan, and cook over high heat until the sauce thickens and the gnocchi are just coated, 2 to 3 minutes. Serve immediately.

Gnocchi with Shrimp and Peas

1 tablespoon unsalted butter
2 tablespoons extra virgin olive oil
½ small white onion, finely chopped
1 garlic clove, bruised
1 cup English peas (about 1 pound in the pod)
3 medium vine-ripe tomatoes, peeled, seeded, and finely chopped
1 pound peeled and deveined shrimp, such as Santa Barbara prawns
4 basil leaves
1 mint leaf
½ recipe Gnocchi (page 119)
Kosher or sea salt and freshly cracked black pepper

Serves 4

When fresh sweet green peas arrive from a strip of land near Half Moon Bay, it's time to make gnocchi with shrimp and peas, one of our most popular dishes. The ties between the coastal farming area south of San Francisco, North Beach, and Italy are obvious when you visit—even the roadside looks like Italy and the coastal communities and family businesses all bear Italian names. Pomponio Farms, where we get much of our produce, has rich soil right next to the sea. The cold foggy mornings and sunny bright afternoons there make conditions right for the best peas imaginable.

Serve with Shaved Artichokes with Fava Beans and Parmesan (page 30) or with Green Garlic Soup (page 66) and Farmers' Market Peach Ice Cream (page 238). For wine, pour a Ribolla blend from Friuli.

Bring a large pot of salted water to a boil. Heat the butter and 1 tablespoon of the olive oil in a large sauté pan over medium heat. Add the onion and sauté until translucent, about 5 minutes. Add the garlic, peas, and 1 tablespoon water. Reduce the heat to low, cover, and cook for 15 minutes.

Uncover the peas, raise the heat to high, and add the tomatoes, shrimp, basil, and mint. Cook until the tomatoes melt into the peas and the shrimp turn pink and are cooked through, about 3 minutes.

Meanwhile, cook the gnocchi; they are done when they float, about 2 minutes if fresh, 3 to 4 minutes if frozen.

Transfer the gnocchi and the sauce to a large sauté pan, add the remaining 1 tablespoon olive oil, and cook over high heat until the sauce thickens and the gnocchi are just coated, 2 to 3 minutes. Season to taste with salt and pepper. Serve immediately.

Pizza, Farinata, and Focaccia

Here are Ligurian-inspired flat breads—pizza, farinata, and focaccia. While the breadsticks do not fall under the flat category, they surely are crisp and delicious.

Our pizzas are in the traditional style of the early Italian immigrants—thin with a sublime crust and sparingly applied toppings. Farinata is made with chickpea flour and it's similar to a dish called *socca,* which is eaten in and around Nice, in the South of France.

The other flatbread that is indigenous to Liguria is focaccia. The minute guests are seated at Rose Pistola, a plate of freshly made focaccia is brought to the table. We've included the most popular variations.

Flaky yet cloud-like, delicate yet intensely flavored, Stuffed Focaccia bears little resemblance to the focaccia we have become familiar with. Two layers of focaccia dough are filled with cheese, salty prosciutto, bitter radicchio, or woodsy mushrooms. When baked at high heat, the top layer puffs up.

Simona and Dora Franceschi stand in front of Danilo's Bakery, one of the few remaining bakeries in the neighborhood.

Pizza Dough

Scant 1/4 teaspoon active dry yeast
1 cup Biga (page 8)
2 cups unbleached white flour
1 tablespoon extra virgin olive oil

Makes enough for two 8- to 10-inch pizzas

The main difference between American and Italian pizzas is that American pizza is all about the toppings and Italian pizza is all about the crust. If your only experience with pizzas has been gooey, flabby pizza, try this thin, crisp style. Ideally, when a wedge of the pizza is picked up, the crust will not droop.

To achieve that ideal crust, we make our dough with a biga, a fermented starter dough. It requires a little planning ahead, but the results are well worth it. The olive oil helps make the crust crisp and very flavorful.

This recipe works best using a standing mixer with a dough hook. If you don't have one, the dough can be mixed with a wooden spoon and kneaded by hand on a floured surface until smooth and silky.

Place ½ cup lukewarm water (about 100°F) and the yeast in the bowl of a stand mixer fitted with a dough hook. Let stand until foamy, 5 to 10 minutes.

Add the biga and flour and mix on low speed until the dough pulls away from the sides of the bowl and is smooth and elastic, 8 to 10 minutes. The dough will be slightly sticky. Form it into a smooth, round ball.

Rinse the bowl with warm water and coat it with the olive oil. Place the dough in the bowl and turn to coat on all surfaces with the oil. Cover the bowl with a kitchen towel, set the bowl in a warm (not too hot) place, and let the dough rise until 2½ times its original size, 2 to 3 hours.

◎ Pizza Making at Home ◎

If you haven't been successful making pizza at home, don't give up. The method for making this thin, crisp, light pizza is quite simple to master. You need a pizza stone or quarry tiles on a rack in your oven. For my oven at home, I lined a baking sheet with unglazed ceramic floor tiles I bought for a few dollars at the local building supply store and ran through the dishwasher. I leave them in the oven on the lower rack all the time because I found that with the tiles, foods brown more easily and my oven heats at a more constant temperature.

If you have an Atlas or similar pasta machine, you can roll the pizza dough just like pasta dough. If you don't want to go the pasta machine route, just roll out the dough on a lightly floured work surface to an 8- to 10-inch round. Don't worry if you don't get a perfect circle; just tell everyone it's rustic style. Sprinkle a baker's peel or the back of a baking sheet with semolina and put the dough on it. After adding the toppings, slide it into the oven onto the pizza stone. Hand stretching a pizza dough does not give great results—it is very hard to get it thin enough.

Pizza with Roasted Mussels, Green Garlic, and Fontina

½ recipe Pizza Dough (page 124)
1 tablespoon semolina flour
½ cup Pizza Tomato Sauce (page 14)
¼ cup grated Italian Fontina
¼ cup grated mozzarella
10 to 12 mussels, scrubbed and debearded
1 shoot spring garlic, cut into julienne strips, or 1 garlic clove, finely chopped
2 tablespoons extra virgin olive oil
¼ teaspoon crushed red pepper flakes
¼ teaspoon kosher or sea salt

Serves 1 to 2

Here is one of our most popular pizzas. Like most of the pizzas we serve at Rose Pistola, all of the toppings are cooked on top of the pizza so that the high heat of the oven concentrates their flavor. In this case, the mussels steam open as the pizza bakes. We like to mix a bit of Fontina with the mozzarella for flavor and to keep the mozzarella from getting too oily when heated.

Serve with Asparagus, Artichoke, and Poached Lemon Salad (page 81). Enjoy with a nice Italian Merlot or California Charbono.

Preheat the oven and the baking stone to 550°F (or the highest setting).

Roll out the pizza dough as directed on page 125. Sprinkle the semolina over a baker's peel or the back of a baking sheet and put the dough on it. Spread the tomato sauce evenly over the dough and sprinkle with the cheese. Toss the mussels with the garlic, olive oil, red pepper, and salt. Scatter the mussels over the top of the pizza.

Slide the pizza onto the pizza stone. Bake until the crust is golden brown and the pizza rises like a rigid plate when you lift one edge of it with a spatula or pizza peel, 7 to 8 minutes. Remove from the oven and serve at once, discarding any mussels that didn't open. Scoop the mussels out of the shells and eat with the pizza.

Pizza with Calamari and Lemon Aïoli

This pizza respects the old North Beach tradition of using fish on pizza. As you can see by the quantities of ingredients, a small amount of topping goes a long way with this pizza. This is true of all of our other pizzas, in fact, because they follow Italian and North Beach tradition in using a light hand with the topping.

Serve with Tuna Carpaccio with Slivered Artichokes (page 56). Pour a white Cassis wine with this.

- ½ recipe Pizza Dough (page 124)
- 1 tablespoon semolina flour
- 2 tablespoons extra virgin olive oil
- ¼ cup grated Italian Fontina
- ¼ cup grated mozzarella
- ¼ pound cleaned calamari, cut into rings and tentacles (see page 163; about ½ pound uncleaned)
- 1 shoot spring garlic, cut into julienne strips, or 1 garlic clove, finely chopped
- ¼ teaspoon crushed red pepper flakes
- ¼ teaspoon kosher or sea salt
- 6 basil leaves, torn
- ¼ cup Lemon Aïoli (page 165)

Serves 1 to 2

Preheat the oven and the baking stone to 550°F (or the highest setting).

Roll out the pizza dough as directed on page 125. Sprinkle the semolina over a baker's peel or the back of a baking sheet and put the dough on it. Brush 1 tablespoon of the olive oil evenly over the dough and sprinkle with the cheese. Toss the calamari with the remaining 1 tablespoon olive oil, the garlic, red pepper, and salt. Scatter the calamari over the top of the pizza.

Slide the pizza onto the pizza stone. Bake until the crust is golden brown and the pizza rises like a rigid plate when you lift one edge of it with a spatula or pizza peel, 7 to 8 minutes. Remove from the oven, scatter the basil on top, and drizzle with the aïoli. If the aïoli isn't thin enough to drizzle, dab it or thin it with a little more oil.

Pizza with Clams and Pesto

½ recipe Pizza Dough (page 124)
1 tablespoon semolina flour
2 tablespoons extra virgin olive oil
⅓ cup Pesto (page 9)
½ cup chopped raw clams (geoduck if available)
1 shoot spring garlic, cut into julienne strips, or 1 garlic clove, finely chopped
Kosher or sea salt and freshly cracked black pepper

Serves 1 to 2

A geoduck is a fairly obscene-looking mollusk. Geoducks are found mostly in Chinese markets. Where geoducks aren't available, use chopped fresh clams such as quahogs. Or you could shuck a bunch of littlenecks or manilas and use them. Canned clams don't taste the same, so if fresh clams aren't available, use shrimp or scallops instead.

Pour an Arneis wine and serve with Tomato Salad with Bottarga or Anchovies (page 82) and Rustic Nectarine and Berry Tart (page 248).

Preheat the oven and the baking stone to 550°F (or the highest setting).

Roll out the pizza dough as directed on page 125. Sprinkle the semolina over a baker's peel or the back of a baking sheet and put the dough on it. Brush 1 tablespoon of the olive oil evenly over the dough and spread the pesto evenly over it. Toss the clams with the remaining 1 tablespoon olive oil and the garlic. Scatter the clams over the top of the pizza.

Slide the pizza onto the pizza stone. Bake until the crust is golden brown and the pizza rises like a rigid plate when you lift one edge of it with a spatula or pizza peel, 7 to 8 minutes. Season with salt and pepper. Remove from the oven and serve at once.

Pizza in North Beach

Pizza joints come and go, but Tommasso's, an old cave-like pizza and pasta restaurant on Kearny Street, has staying power. Peggy's parents had their first date there. It has been turning out good old-fashioned pizzas for sixty-five years. Unlike many East Coast cities, North Beach is no longer particularly famous for pizza by the slice, so come by Rose Pistola and let us take care of your pizza and focaccia whims—or try a few of these recipes.

Pizza with Broccoli Rabe and Pancetta

At Rose Pistola, as in Liguria, part of what makes a pizza a pizza is the rapid concentration of flavors that happens when ingredients are cooked at high heat. For this pizza, we precook the broccoli rabe for a few minutes in the hot oven to make it more tender, while retaining its nutrients.

This rustic pizza is characterized by a lovely balance of textures and tastes—the crisp crust, the salty, slightly crisp pancetta, the creamy cheese, and the slightly bitter broccoli rabe.

Try a light to medium-bodied red Italian wine such as Valpolicella, Allegrini, Berbera, or Chiarlo. Serve with Pickled Crab (page 40) and Persimmon Pudding (page 244).

½ recipe Pizza Dough (page 124)
1 tablespoon semolina flour
¼ pound broccoli rabe, trimmed of tough stems
2 tablespoons olive oil
1 shoot spring garlic, cut into julienne strips, or 1 garlic clove, finely chopped
¼ teaspoon crushed red pepper flakes
Kosher or sea salt
⅓ cup Pizza Tomato Sauce (page 14)
¼ cup grated Italian Fontina
¼ cup grated mozzarella
2 ounces pancetta, sliced paper-thin

Serves 1 to 2

Preheat the oven and the baking stone to 550°F (or the highest setting).

Roll out the pizza dough as directed on page 125 while you cook the rabe. Sprinkle the semolina over a baker's peel or the back of a baking sheet and put the dough on it.

Toss the broccoli rabe with the olive oil, garlic, red pepper, and salt to taste. Roast on a sheet pan until soft and lightly browned, about 6 minutes.

Brush the tomato sauce evenly over the pizza dough and sprinkle with the cheese. Scatter the roasted broccoli rabe over the top of the pizza and lay the strips of pancetta on top.

Slide the pizza onto the pizza stone. Bake until the crust is golden brown and the pizza rises like a rigid plate when you lift one edge of it with a spatula or pizza peel, 7 to 8 minutes. Serve at once.

Potato and Mushroom Pizza

½ recipe Pizza Dough (page 124)
1 tablespoon semolina flour
2 small Yellow Finn or fingerling potatoes, peeled and thinly sliced
2 tablespoons extra virgin olive oil
1 garlic clove, finely chopped
Kosher or sea salt
½ cup Italian Fontina, Tomme de Savoie, Comté, or other mountain cheese
¼ pound mushrooms, cleaned and sliced about ¼ inch thick
½ teaspoon thyme leaves

Serves 1 to 2

The woodsy combination of shiitake, chanterelle, or other mushrooms is perfectly complemented by the intensely earthy aroma of baked potatoes. On this pizza, the two bake with each other, the potatoes absorbing any juices that run from the mushrooms as they cook.

Preheat the oven and the baking stone to 550°F (or the highest setting).

Roll out the pizza dough as directed on page 125 while the potatoes cook. Sprinkle the semolina over a baker's peel or the back of a baking sheet and put the dough on it.

Toss the potatoes with 1 tablespoon of the olive oil, the garlic, and salt to taste. Roast on a sheet pan until soft and lightly browned, about 10 minutes.

Scatter the cheese over the pizza dough and top with the potato slices. Toss the mushrooms with the remaining 1 tablespoon oil, the thyme, and salt to taste. Arrange on top of the potatoes.

Slide the pizza onto the pizza stone. Bake until the crust is golden brown and the pizza rises like a rigid plate when you lift one edge of it with a spatula or pizza peel, 7 to 8 minutes. Serve at once.

Goat Cheese and Roasted Pepper Pizza

This is a Rose Pistola favorite. The roasted peppers taste as if they were baked by the sun, and the goat cheese and mozzarella go exceptionally well together.

- ½ recipe Pizza Dough (page 124)
- 1 tablespoon semolina flour
- ⅓ cup Pizza Tomato Sauce (page 14)
- ¼ cup shredded mozzarella
- ¼ cup goat cheese
- 1 small red bell pepper, roasted, peeled, cored, seeded, and cut into strips
- 15 Niçoise olives, pitted

Serves 1 to 2

Preheat the oven and the baking stone to 550°F (or the highest setting).

Roll out the pizza dough as directed on page 125. Sprinkle the semolina over a baker's peel or the back of a baking sheet and put the dough on it.

With a large kitchen spoon, spread the pizza sauce evenly over the dough, making sure you get as close to the edge as possible.

Scatter the mozzarella and break up the goat cheese evenly over the mozzarella. Distribute the pepper strips and olives evenly over the pizza.

Slide the pizza onto the pizza stone. Bake until the crust is golden brown and the pizza rises like a rigid plate when you lift one edge of it with a spatula or pizza peel, 7 to 8 minutes. Serve.

Farinata in Liguria

Eaten as snack food in Liguria, *farinata* is typically bought at a food stand or a combination pizza-farinata spot in towns and cities throughout the region. Farinata is a thin, delightfully grainy, savory cross between a crêpe and a tortilla. The same thing is called *socca* in the South of France, but this delectable treat is little known beyond these two areas. It's made with chickpea flour (cheaper in the old days than wheat flour), water, olive oil, and salt. Chickpea flour can be found in Italian, Indian, and Middle Eastern markets or mail-ordered (see Sources, page 264). Farinata is sold with a number of different toppings, but it is the flavor of the farinata itself that is most important. Do not overdo the toppings, or they will overwhelm the grainy, smoky quality of the farinata, even if not cooked in a wood-burning oven.

Farinata

For the Farinata Batter

1 cup chickpea flour

1¼ teaspoons kosher or sea salt

¼ cup plus 2 tablespoons extra virgin olive oil

Toppings of your choice (recipes follow)

Makes 2 to 3

Farinata was joyfully revived in North Beach when Rose Pistola opened. Luciano Repetto of the third-generation, family-owned Graffeo Coffee Company, was particularly delighted, as memories of his childhood came rushing back.

Made with chickpea flour, it can be topped with all sorts of spices, cheeses, vegetables, olives, and tiny fish—and always a liberal sprinkling of ground pepper. With a few olive leaf-like sage leaves scattered randomly over its grainy golden surface and dotted with a liberal sprinkling of olives, farinata looks like a still life under an olive tree. But I found it so hard to describe farinata on the menu that I gave away hundreds of orders in the first few months that Rose Pistola was open to introduce our customers to what has now become one of our most popular dishes.

Cooks love to debate over recipes for farinata, particularly about the proportions of chickpea flour to water. It is made daily in our wood-burning oven and we find that this recipe works best, even in home kitchen ovens. Chickpea flour can be found in Italian, Indian, and Middle Eastern markets or mail-ordered (see Sources, page 264). As when making pancakes, the first one sometimes does not come out perfectly, but don't be discouraged.

Serve farinata by itself, with cocktails, or as a sophisticated accompaniment for roasts or braised meats. Pour an Orvieto white wine or a light lager beer.

For the Farinata

Whisk together the chickpea flour and 2½ cups cold water in a bowl. Add the salt and 2 tablespoons of the olive oil and whisk well again. Let the batter rest for at least 30 minutes. It will be thin, like pancake batter.

Preheat the oven to 550°F (or the hottest setting you have). If you have a pizza stone or an alternative (see Pizza Making at Home, page 125), put it in the oven to preheat.

Place a seasoned 8- to 10-inch cast-iron skillet in the oven, on the pizza stone if you have one, and preheat the skillet for at least 10 minutes. Remove the hot skillet from the oven and pour in ½ tablespoon of the olive oil. Tilt the pan so that the entire bottom is covered with a film of oil.

Working quickly, stir and ladle about ⅞ cup of the batter evenly into the pan (the batter will sizzle and start to set almost immediately). Quickly scatter on the topping and carefully return the pan to the pizza stone. Bake for 15 minutes, turning oven setting to broil for the last 3 to 5 minutes if using an oven with a built-in broiler (or transfer the pan after 15 minutes in an oven to a preheated broiler for 3 to 5 minutes). It should be golden brown and crispy around the edge and appear dry and flecked with golden spots on top.

Slide the farinata onto a cutting board and return the pan to the oven to get it hot for the second farinata. Slice the farinata into roughly 8 rectangular strips. (Traditionally farinata is not cut into wedges.) Prepare a second and third farinata in the same way, and enjoy the first as the second and third bake.

Farinata (a chickpea flour cross between a crepe and a flat bread), made with sage leaves and olives, and baked in a wood-burning oven.

Sage, Niçoise Olives, and Caramelized Onions

15 small or 10 large sage leaves
10 Niçoise olives, pitted
½ white onion, thinly sliced and cooked in 1 teaspoon olive oil until golden and caramelized
Freshly cracked black pepper

Anchovy, Onion, and Peppers

6 anchovy fillets, cut into thin strips
½ white onion, thinly sliced and cooked in 1 teaspoon olive oil until golden and caramelized
1 small red bell pepper, roasted, peeled, cored, seeded, and cut into strips
10 Niçoise olives, pitted

Sardines or Tuna and Tomatoes

1 fresh sardine, filleted and cut into strips, or 2 ounces tuna, cut into thin strips
1 medium tomato, sliced and juices squeezed out
1 teaspoon marjoram leaves

Rosemary and Pancetta

3 sprigs rosemary (about 3 inches long)
1 garlic clove, bruised
¼ pound pancetta, sliced paper-thin

Focaccia

- ½ teaspoon active dry yeast
- ½ cup Biga, at room temperature (see page 8)
- 3 cups all-purpose flour
- 2 tablespoons semolina
- 1 tablespoon powdered milk
- 1½ teaspoons kosher or sea salt
- ¼ cup extra virgin olive oil

- 2 tablespoons extra virgin olive oil
- Topping of your choice (recipes follow), optional
- 2 tablespoons coarse salt

Makes approximately fifteen 2 × 3-inch pieces

At one corner of Washington Square, where Stockton and Filbert Streets meet, a North Beach classic called Liguria Bakery is run today by the third generation. Nothing but focaccia is made there. (Focaccia is practically the regional bread of Liguria, hence the name of the bakery.) The focaccia and the window decorations have not changed for half a century. It's the kind of store-front shop that you pray will not succumb to progress by being replaced by a coffee bar or a fast food joint.

Here is the typical Ligurian focaccia that we serve with every meal at Rose Pistola instead of bread. The easy starter, or biga, as the Italians call it, needs to be made at least twenty-four hours in advance of making the focaccia. It keeps for up to a few weeks if covered and refrigerated; bring it back to room temperature before using. Bigas can be kept "alive" for years. When most of the biga is gone, feed it with another recipe of biga and wait a day before using.

Experiment with the various toppings suggested at the end of the recipe, keeping in mind that they are to be used lightly, just as an accent.

In the bowl of a stand mixer or another large bowl, whisk together 1 cup water, the yeast, and the biga. The biga will dissolve into the warm water. Stir in the flour, semolina, and powdered milk and knead until a smooth, slightly sticky dough is formed, about 5 minutes in a mixer with a dough hook on medium-low speed or about 8 minutes by hand. Add the salt and olive oil and knead until well incorporated, about 2 minutes longer. The dough should slap the sides of the bowl and clean it. Remove the dough and place in an oiled bowl. Brush the top with a little more oil. Place in a warm spot until the dough has doubled in size, about 1½ hours.

Oil a 10½ × 15½-inch baking sheet with the olive oil and press the dough evenly over the sheet. It should just about fill the pan. Turn the dough over. If desired, scatter one of the toppings over the dough. Cover and let rise for 30 minutes.

Preheat the oven to 425°F. If you have a pizza stone or an alternative (see Pizza Making at Home, page125), place it in the oven to preheat.

Poke holes about 1 inch apart all over the dough, using your fingertips. Sprinkle the top of the dough with the coarse salt and the following toppings, if using. Bake until just barely browned, 20 to 25 minutes. Let cool slightly and serve.

Caramelized Onions and Rosemary

- 2 tablespoons extra virgin olive oil
- 1 white onion, very thinly sliced
- 1 tablespoon rosemary leaves, chopped
- ¾ cup cherry tomatoes, halved, optional

Sage and Parmesan

- 5 ounces Parmigiano-Reggiano, shaved with a vegetable peeler
- 20 sage leaves

For the Caramelized Onions and Rosemary

In a large skillet, warm the olive oil over medium-low heat. Add the onion and rosemary. Cook, stirring constantly, until the onion is barely translucent; do not brown. Let the onion and rosemary mixture cool slightly before using.

If using the cherry tomatoes, press them into the dough after you've added the caramelized onions. Cook according to the directions above.

For the Sage and Parmesan

Shave the Parmigiano-Reggiano evenly over the surface of the uncooked focaccia. Scatter the sage leaves randomly and cook according to the directions above.

Stuffed Focaccia

1 package active dry yeast
2 cups bread flour
½ teaspoon kosher or sea salt
¼ cup extra virgin olive oil
1 tablespoon semolina
8 ounces crescenza or teleme cheese
2 tablespoons milk

Serves 2 to 4

This is very different from traditional bread-like focaccia. Two thin layers of flaky dough capture a fragrant layer of crescenza cheese. The focaccia is baked on an oiled pizza pan in a hot pizza oven. The result is heaven—gooey, aromatic, sophisticated, and unlike anything else. It even passes the pizza test—it's good the next day.

The dish originated in the Italian town of Recco, just over the hill from Portofino in Liguria. The best story I have heard about it is that the restaurant that originated it, Manuelina, was Mussolini's favorite stopping place in Northern Italy. When Il Duce was overthrown, Manuelina was burned down. Il Duce was hung—but Manuelina was rebuilt. Italians have their priorities right.

An excellent way to enjoy this dish is with lots of shaved white truffle over the top. Or try one of the variations suggested at the end of the recipe. Barring that, enjoy it simply with friends and a glass of good wine.

Onion focaccia hot from the oven at Rose Pistola.

In a large bowl or the bowl of an electric mixer, mix the yeast with 1½ cups warm water (100° to 110°F). Let stand until foamy, about 10 minutes. Then add the flour, salt, and 2 tablespoons of the olive oil. Mix well with a wooden spoon and then knead by hand for 15 minutes, or until the dough is smooth and glossy. Alternatively, mix on medium-low speed to incorporate the ingredients, then raise the speed to #2 and mix for about 8 minutes.

Oil a bowl with 1 tablespoon of the olive oil. Place the dough in and turn it to coat on all sides. Cover with a kitchen towel and let rise in a warm spot in your kitchen until doubled in size, 1½ to 2 hours.

Punch down the dough and divide it into 4 pieces; shape into balls. Place the dough on a sheet pan oiled with 1 tablespoon olive oil, cover, and refrigerate for 10 to 15 minutes.

Preheat the oven to 550°F (or the highest setting). If you have a pizza stone or an alternative (see Pizza Making at Home, page 125), place it in the oven to preheat.

Roll out 1 piece of the dough on a lightly floured work surface into a 12-inch round. If you have a pasta machine, you can roll the pizza dough like pasta dough. Just tell everyone the weird oblong shape you get is traditional (I'm sure it is somewhere!). Sprinkle a baker's peel or the back of a baking sheet with 1 tablespoon of the semolina and put the dough on it. Spoon walnut-sized pieces of half the cheese about 2 inches apart on top of the dough and brush with the milk.

Roll a second ball of dough out to the same size as the first. Lightly flour your hands. Place the dough on the tops of your fists and gently stretch until it becomes almost transparent. It should be almost as thin as strudel dough. Carefully place the stretched dough over the dough with the cheese on it. Press down on the top of the dough with your fingers to remove any air pockets. Brush the top with olive oil.

Slide the focaccia onto the baking stone and bake until golden brown and crisp, about 8 minutes. Serve hot.

Prosciutto

Cover the top of the focaccia with very thin slices of prosciutto after it comes out of the oven.

Mushrooms

Thinly slice ¼ pound of mushrooms. Scatter half the mushrooms on top of the cheese before adding the top layer of dough to each focaccia. The dough traps their perfume as the mushrooms cook, giving the focaccia a very heady fragrance when it is cut.

Radicchio

Slice ½ head radicchio into julienne strips. Scatter half the radicchio on top of the cheese before adding the second layer of dough to each focaccia.

Focaccia in North Beach

Focaccia has been a North Beach staple since the first Ligurian immigrants came here in the mid-1800s. The memory of children walking home from school eating focaccia in North Beach is a little like the image of French children walking down a street in Paris with a baguette over their shoulder. North Beach kids would have gone to Liguria Bakery or Danilo's Bakery for their squares of focaccia. There, big slabs of tomato, green onion, or raisin focaccia are cut, then wrapped in white butcher paper and tied, the old-fashioned way, with string. Nowadays, on weekend mornings there is a long line of people patiently waiting to get a piece. In keeping with this North Beach tradition, we take it to every table at Rose Pistola as soon as people are settled in.

Spicy Breadsticks

2 teaspoons dry yeast
2½ teaspoons olive oil, plus extra for brushing
3 cups all-purpose flour
½ cup whole-wheat flour
1½ teaspoons kosher or sea salt, plus extra for sprinkling
2 ounces finely grated Parmesan
1 tablespoon freshly cracked black pepper

Makes about 100

These thin, elegant breadsticks are always available on the bar at Rose Pistola. Come by, munch on a few as you sip a drink, and watch the world go by on Columbus Avenue.

Everyone has his or her favorite bakery in North Beach, each with its own particular breadsticks. Italian French Bakery is known for big, handmade, gnarly sticks, while Danilo's makes a paler, more feminine version. A favorite North Beach antipasto is one in which breadsticks are wrapped in prosciutto.

These are good on their own, and you will not be able to eat just one.

This version was inspired by Carol Field in her book The Italian Baker.

Combine the yeast and 1⅓ cups warm water (110°F) and mix to dissolve the yeast. When it starts to activate, after 10 to 15 minutes, add the olive oil and flours. Combine well, then add the salt, Parmesan, and pepper. Mix with a dough hook in an electric mixer for about 5 minutes to develop the gluten.

Lightly flour a work surface and roll the dough into a rectangle. Place the rectangle of dough in a large baking pan dusted with a little flour, brush with a little olive oil, cover with plastic wrap, and place in a warm spot in your kitchen for about an hour.

Again, lightly flour the work surface, roll the dough into a ball, and punch it down. Then roll it out to about ½ inch thick.

Preheat the oven to 400°F.

Lightly flour two baking sheets. Divide the dough in half. If you only want 4 dozen breadsticks, divide the dough and freeze half of it, carefully wrapped in plastic wrap and then in a plastic bag. Bring the frozen dough to room temperature before rolling out.

Cut the dough into thin breadstick strips, about ½ inch wide by 8 inches long. Lift them off the work surface, pulling slightly so that they reach about 10 inches in length. Lay each breadstick carefully on the baking sheets. You can fit quite a few breadsticks on each sheet, since they will not expand much. Do not let

them touch one another. They can bake in slightly irregular shapes; if some twist and turn a bit, it just makes them more interesting. Bake the breadsticks for about 20 minutes, or until golden brown. Watch carefully; if the breadsticks get too brown on one side, turn them with tongs. Remove the breadsticks from the pans and brush off any excess flour. Brush or spray with a little olive oil and sprinkle with the coarse salt.

Store up to a few days in an airtight container.

Spicy breadsticks on the bar at Rose Pistola.

Fish and Seafood

By the turn of the century, a thriving community had grown up around what is now called Fisherman's Wharf, with amateur cooks setting up tables to sell their fresh-caught catch and sourdough bread. A line of caffès and simple restaurants extending up Columbus into the heart of North Beach was established. Many still exist today, selling and serving crab, calamari, clams, oysters, mussels, salmon, and other finfish.

San Francisco Bay and its fishing fleets have always been an integral part of life in North Beach. Rose Pistola's father was a fisherman, and the whole family took refuge from the fire that was the aftermath of the Earthquake of 1906 on his fishing boat in the Bay. Rose remembered watching the city burn while her family was safe.

A small fleet of fishing boats, today a bit more elaborate than Rose's father's, still figure prominently in the bustling harbor just behind the touristy façade of Fisherman's Wharf. Because of pollution in the Bay, however, today most of the fish in local restaurants and fish stores comes from the chilly waters of the Pacific outside the Golden Gate.

It is the fanciful lore of Fisherman's Wharf that has kept it on the tourist path. Its history has seen it through the transition of sail-propelled vessels to marine engines, the time when the Sicilians fought the Genoese for command of the industry, and the rise and fall of the fishing unions against powerful fish brokers in waterfront battles.

But meals of cioppino, roasted fish, crab, braised clams or mussels, and the ever-present calamari dominate the tables of the area with as much vigor today as in the days of the early immigrants. Then as now, the seafood is complemented by the best olive oils, wines, and fresh vegetables and herbs.

Fisherman's Wharf: turn of the century fishing boats.
Courtesy J. B. Monaco Photography.

Roast Fish with Potatoes and Artichokes

There is a chorus of surprising flavors in this straightforward dish. The earthiness of the potatoes and artichokes plays off the salty olives, while the fish brings all the elements in line.

Halibut, sea bass, rock cod, salmon, Arctic char, or ono will all work well in this recipe. You can use individual fillets, one large fillet, or a whole fish. A whole fish will take longer to cook, but the flavors are enhanced because the skin and bone are left intact.

This is one of my favorite ways to cook fish in my own kitchen, because when I'm cooking at home, I don't like timing lots of things on the top of the stove and doing lots of dishes. Instead, this one-dish meal involves simply roasting the fish with potatoes and artichokes. While the fish roasts, make a Salad of Mushrooms, Endive, and Parmesan (page 73). Serve with a medium-bodied Chianti.

1 pound Yellow Finn potatoes, peeled, cut into 1/4-inch-thick slices
1 medium whole fish (approximately 2 1/2 pounds), cleaned and scaled, or 1 1/2 pounds fish fillets with skin (see headnote)
10 baby artichokes or 5 globe artichokes, trimmed and sliced (see page 31)
Kosher or sea salt and freshly cracked black pepper
3 tablespoons extra virgin olive oil, plus extra for drizzling
1 garlic clove, bruised
1 sprig rosemary
1/2 cup dry Italian white wine
Approximately 24 Niçoise olives, optional

Serves 3

In a small pot of salted, boiling water, blanch the potatoes until they are tender. Drain.

Preheat the oven to 550°F (or the highest setting).

Season the fish generously with salt and pepper. Toss the potatoes together with the remaining ingredients and spoon into an oval gratin or baking dish. Nestle the fish in the mixture, turning it to make sure the top is well coated with olive oil, and leaving fillets skin side up, roast until the fish is opaque, the skin brown, and the potatoes have begun to dry out, about 10 minutes per inch of thickness of the fish.

If using a whole fish, lift the top fillet off the fish with a cake server and knife or fish spoon and knife and place on a warm plate. Grab the fish head, tail, and backbone (it will come out in one piece), remove, and discard. Discard the rosemary. Lift the bottom fillet onto the warm plate. Divide the fish, potatoes, and artichokes among three warm plates and serve. Pass additional oil for drizzling.

Fish Roasted in a Salt Crust

3 pounds kosher salt
6 large egg whites, beaten
1 small whole fish, (approximately 2 pounds), cleaned and scaled
½ head red radicchio or radicchio di Treviso, separated into leaves
½ fennel bulb, thinly sliced
¼ pound mushrooms, preferably porcini or portobello, cleaned (trim off black gills if using portobellos) and thinly sliced
2 tablespoons extra virgin olive oil
Kosher or sea salt and freshly cracked black pepper

Serves 4

When you roast a fish in a salt crust, the salt acts as a sealant to keep in all the moisture of the fish. Despite the fact that this recipe uses three pounds of salt, the dish does not, in fact, taste salty, but rather of the perfume of the sea contained in the salt. The fish emerges moist and delicate.

This is one of the most dramatic, elegant but simple, and savory ways to cook fish. Please try it. Once you crack the salt crust, the fish is so perfect on its own it needs only a drizzle of the highest-quality olive oil. A two-pound farmed striped bass or other small whole fish, such as trout, red snapper, or Arctic char, will do nicely. We accompany it with a fragrant salad of shaved fennel and radicchio.

Pour a Tra Vigne, Zamo & Zamo, Collio Orientali, 1997.

Preheat the oven to 500°F.

In a bowl, mix the salt and the egg whites together; the salt will feel like wet sand. Press a ¾-inch-thick layer of salt over the bottom of a heavy oval roasting pan slightly bigger than the fish. Place the fish on top of the salt. Spread the remaining salt on top of the fish and press into place with your hands into an even layer about ¾ inch thick, patting it down so that it completely seals the fish. Place the roasting pan in the oven and bake until the crust turns golden around the edges, 20 to 25 minutes.

Just before the fish is done toss the radicchio, fennel, and mushrooms in a bowl. Drizzle with the olive oil. Season to taste with salt and pepper. Divide the salad among the four plates.

Remove the pan from the oven. Crack the surface of the salt layer and pry it off gently. (It is very dramatic to do this at the table.) Scrape back the skin of the fish. Lift the top fillet off the fish with a cake server and knife or fish spoon and knife and place on a warm plate. Grab the fish head, tail, and backbone (it will come out in one piece), remove, and discard. Carefully brush off any salt adhering to the fish and lift the bottom fillet onto the warm plate. Divide the fish among four plates, with the salad. Serve accompanied by a bottle of the finest-quality olive oil for drizzling.

Seaweed-Steamed Fish

This dish is delicate, simple, and light. Can you think of a more basic way to cook fish than in seaweed? Imagine fishermen pulling up a bunch of seaweed tangled in their nets and throwing it in the pot for flavor as they steam fish. Like the salt crust for Fish Roasted in a Salt Crust (page 142), steaming fish in seaweed heightens its delicate flavor. If you like, add a handful of mussels, clams, or shrimp to add to the complex perfume of the dish.

Lobsters are typically packed in seaweed for shipping, so the easiest way to get your hands on some seaweed would be to ask your favorite restaurant or fishmonger for a few handfuls. Or try Asian markets, which often have fresh seaweed and always have dried seaweed, which you can rehydrate. Rinse the seaweed well before using it and add it to the pot with the water still clinging to it.

This is wonderful accompanied with Roasted Mushroom and White Asparagus or Endive Salad (page 80) and a bottle of a full-bodied California Sauvignon Blanc or a Pigato.

- 3 handfuls seaweed (see headnote), well rinsed
- 2 small whole fish, such as Arctic char or red snapper (approximately 1¼ to 1½ pounds each), cleaned and scaled, or 1½ pounds fish fillets with skin, such as halibut
- Extra virgin olive oil for drizzling
- Kosher or coarse sea salt

Serves 4

Preheat the oven to 500°F.

Put the seaweed in a heavy nonreactive roasting pan or braising dish with a tight-fitting lid. Nestle the fish in the seaweed. Add ¼ cup water to begin cooking it. Cover and heat over high heat on top of the stove until you begin to see steam come out of the pan. Transfer the pan to the oven and bake the fish until it is cooked through, about 8 minutes per inch of thickness.

Remove the fish and a little of the seaweed to a large platter. If using whole fish, lift the top fillet off the fish with a cake server and knife or fish spoon and knife and place on a warm plate. Grab the fish head, tail, and backbone (it will come out in one piece), remove, and discard. Lift the bottom fillet onto the warm plate as well. Divide the fish among four plates, drizzle with olive oil, and sprinkle lightly with coarse salt.

Filleting a fish at Rose Pistola.

Crisp Salmon with Fennel and Tapenade

12 baby, 4 medium, or 2 large fennel bulbs, trimmed (leafy tops reserved for garnish)
Kosher or sea salt and freshly cracked black pepper
¼ cup plus 2 tablespoons extra virgin olive oil
1 garlic clove, crushed
1 sprig rosemary
1 cup dry Italian white wine
1½ pounds salmon fillet with skin, pin bones removed and cut into 4 pieces
2 tablespoons Tuna Tapenade (page 25)
Serves 4

This dish combines two of my favorite local products, bridged by the accent of a salty tapenade. A very hot pan is essential for ensuring that the salmon has a nice crispy skin. Use a heavy skillet for even heating, and heat the pan before adding the oil. This allows the skillet to become sizzling hot without burning the oil. Try this same technique with sea bass, mahi mahi, or Arctic char fillets (skin on).

The fennel can be made ahead of time and reheated, although once you put it in the oven, it takes about the same amount of time to cook as does the fish, so preparing the two together is fairly straightforward.

Serve with Fried Potatoes with Parsley and Garlic (page 215) and pour a Chardonnay or a Pinot Gris from Oregon's Eyrie Vineyard.

If using baby fennel bulbs, leave them whole; cut larger bulbs lengthwise into quarters. Season with salt and pepper.

Preheat the oven to 550°F (or the highest setting).

Heat ¼ cup of the olive oil in an ovenproof sauté pan over medium heat. Add the fennel bulbs and brown well on all sides, turning them with tongs to caramelize evenly, 10 to 15 minutes. Add the garlic and rosemary and cook until fragrant. Add the white wine and reduce by half. Add ½ cup water, place the pan in the oven, and cook, turning several times, until the fennel is easily pierced with a fork or wooden skewer, 10 to 15 minutes. You should have about ½ cup liquid remaining in the pan; if you don't, add a little more water.

Meanwhile, preheat a well-seasoned griddle or nonstick pan over medium-high heat. Toss the fish fillets with the remaining 2 tablespoons oil and a generous amount of salt and pepper. Add the salmon fillets skin side down to the pan and, regulating the heat as necessary, cook until the skin is crisp, fully rendered of its fat, and browned, about 7 minutes. Turn the fish, increase the heat, and continue cooking until well browned on the other side and cooked medium-rare to medium, about 4 more minutes, or to taste.

Transfer the fennel and its braising liquid to a serving platter. Place the salmon on top of the fennel, skin side up. Top each salmon fillet with a spoonful of tapenade and garnish with the reserved leafy green fennel tops.

Braised Sea Bass with Wild Mushrooms

¼ cup extra virgin olive oil
1 garlic clove, bruised
1 sprig rosemary (about 6 inches long)
1 pound mushrooms, such as chanterelle, porcini, morel, crimini, portobello, or button, cleaned (black gills trimmed off if using portobellos)
1 cup dry Italian white wine
Four 6-ounce sea bass fillets
Kosher or sea salt

Serves 4

A variety of mushrooms would work well in this dish, such as chanterelles, crimini, or morels. If you cannot find these mushrooms in your local market, try the dish with portobellos (with the black gills trimmed off) or button mushrooms. Any firm mild fish that will not overpower the flavor of the mushrooms, such as halibut, can be substituted for the sea bass. Begin with Tuna Carpaccio with Slivered Artichokes (page 56) and serve a Pigato or medium-bodied Pinot Noir wine.

Preheat the oven to 500°F. In a flameproof baking dish or ovenproof skillet just large enough to hold the fish, warm 3 tablespoons of the olive oil over medium-high heat. Add the garlic, rosemary, and mushrooms and cook until the mushrooms start to brown, about 10 minutes. Add the white wine and bring to a simmer.

Tuck the fish fillets under the mushrooms and season with salt. Bake the fish until just cooked through, about 10 minutes. Serve with a drizzle of the remaining olive oil.

One of the joys of living in the Bay Area occurs each year at the beginning of salmon season, when I go out to the Farallon Islands, twenty-some miles beyond the Golden Gate, to fish for salmon with our chefs and friends. As we venture out on the roiling seas, we enjoy the stunning views of Northern California's coast on our way to encounter salmon in their wild state.

Then as we come back into San Francisco Bay, in the late spring or early summer, Telegraph Hill, near my house, is covered in wild fennel. Its fragrant wild shoots are always a reminder to me of the fundamental link between Italy and the Bay Area. The first fennel seeds were carried to California by early Italian immigrants, and now the plant grows as a weed in and around San Francisco and Los Angeles. You can harvest these wild fennel shoots when they are young, tender, and still bright green. After careful washing, scatter them over hot coals when grilling fish, lamb, or fowl. They create a great perfume that permeates the air and the flesh of whatever you're cooking.

Fennel growing at Pomponio Creek Farms in Pescadero, California.

Grilled Sea Bass with Lemon and White Beans

For the Lemon and Beans

1 lemon

2 cups cooked cannellini or gigande beans (see page 16)

1 garlic clove, crushed

2 sprigs marjoram (about 5 inches long)

¼ cup extra virgin olive oil

Kosher or sea salt and freshly cracked black pepper

Firm, sweet white sea bass is grilled alongside lemon halves, which caramelize to give the finished dish a distinctive sweet-tart flavor. The creamy marjoram-spiked beans round out the dish.

Look for one of the many terrific varieties of organically raised large dried beans available now in many markets for this recipe. We list cannellini beans or gigande beans here, which are large white dried beans, sometimes called emergo beans. If you have trouble finding good dried beans in your area, contact Phipps Farm (see Sources, page 264), which offers a wide selection of beans. If fresh shell beans are available, by all means, use them instead of dried. Use your best olive oil to drizzle over the beans.

This recipe can be made with a wide variety of full-flavored fish, such as fresh sardines or anchovies, mackerel, salmon, striped bass, salmon, swordfish, or grouper.

Serve the grilled fish and beans with Artichoke, Fennel, and Mushroom Salad (page78) and a Barbera wine.

Prepare a fire in a charcoal grill.

For the Lemon and Beans

Cover the lemon with water in a small saucepan, bring to a boil, reduce the heat slightly, and cook, uncovered, until tender, about 15 minutes. Drain and let cool, then thinly slice.

While the fish cooks, heat the beans in a saucepan with the lemon slices, garlic, marjoram, and olive oil. Heat together gently until most of the olive oil is absorbed, about 5 minutes. Season with salt and pepper. Keep the beans warm while you grill the fish.

For the Fish

In a mortar or a mini food processor or blender, pound together or puree the marjoram, olive oil, garlic, salt, and pepper. Rub this mixture onto the fish fillets. Place the lemon halves alongside the fish and grill, cut side down, until the fish is opaque halfway through (it will just begin to turn white around the edges), about 3 minutes. Turn the fish—don't move it too early, or it will stick; if it resists, leave it on the fire a little longer—and continue to cook until nearly opaque at the center, 3 to 5 minutes longer. (Total grilling time depends on the thickness of the fish and the heat of the grill.) The lemons should be nicely caramelized by this point.

Pour the warm beans onto a warm platter. Arrange the fish and lemons on top and serve.

For the Fish

1 tablespoon marjoram leaves

2 tablespoons extra virgin olive oil

1 garlic clove

¼ teaspoon kosher or sea salt

½ teaspoon freshly cracked black pepper

Four 6-ounce sea bass fillets

2 or 3 lemons, halved

Serves 4

Farm-raised striped sea bass from California.

Braised Halibut with Tagliarini

6 ounces fresh tagliarini (see page 92) or dried tagliarini
2 tablespoons extra virgin olive oil
2 garlic cloves, chopped, or 1 tablespoon chopped green garlic when available
1/3 cup chopped flat-leaf parsley
6 anchovy fillets
2 halibut steaks or fillets (approximately 3/4 pound), skin on
1/2 cup dry Italian white wine
Kosher or sea salt and freshly cracked black pepper
A few drops of fresh lemon juice, optional

Serves 2

The wonderful flavor for the halibut comes from sautéing it with anchovies, parsley, and garlic and then finishing it in the oven along with the tagliarini and its creamy cooking water. Shellfish such as clams, mussels, or prawns are also all delicious prepared in this parsley, garlic, and anchovy sauce.

To make your own tagliarini, see the directions for making the pasta dough and cutting the noodles on page 92. Or buy a fresh egg tagliarini for this dish; or buy a good-quality dried egg pasta.

Serve with a dry reserve Riesling, such as Oregon's Argyle Vineyards, 1996.

Preheat the oven to 500°F.

Bring a large pot of salted water to a boil. Add the tagliarini and cook until about half-done, about 1 minute for fresh and 4 minutes for dried. (They will finish cooking in the braising liquid.) Drain, reserving ½ cup of the cooking water, and set aside.

Warm the olive oil in a flameproof gratin dish or heavy ovenproof skillet over medium-high heat. Add the garlic and sauté until fragrant. Add the parsley and anchovies, pressing the anchovies with the tines of a fork. Continue to sauté until the parsley sizzles and the anchovies melt into the oil, about 3 minutes.

Add the fish and sauté it briefly on both sides until the edges of the fish are opaque, about 1 minute on each side. Add the wine, increase the heat to high, and boil rapidly until reduced by half, about 2 minutes. Add the reserved pasta water and the noodles, distributing them around and under the fish. Season to taste with salt and pepper.

Place in the oven and bake until the fish is cooked through and the pasta has begun to absorb the liquid, 6 to 7 minutes. Remove from the oven and serve at once, directly from the dish. Sprinkle with a few drops of lemon juice, if desired.

Note

Cooking fish with skin and bone attached results in a much better texture and flavor.

Salt-Roasted Prawns with Lemon Aïoli

We don't often think of salt as having a scent, but good sea salt actually does have the aroma of the ocean. Roasting prawns on a bed of sea salt brings out their briny sweetness. Such a simple dish really needs very little else. The Lemon Aïoli works well, as would a few potatoes roasted in the salt alongside the prawns. Start small potatoes about 20 minutes before you start the prawns and cook them the same way. If sea salt is unavailable, use kosher salt.

Serve with Grilled Corn with Red Pepper Butter (page 214) and a full-bodied Pinot Noir.

3 cups kosher or sea salt

1½ pounds prawns or shrimp, preferably with heads

Lemon Aïoli (page 165)

Serves 4

Preheat the oven to 550°F (or the highest setting).

Spread the salt over the bottom of a 10-inch (approximately) gratin dish or other shallow ovenproof dish. The salt should be about ½ inch thick. Place the prawns in one layer directly on the salt, pushing them down slightly to partially bury them in the salt. Roast the prawns until pink, 5 to 7 minutes. Remove the baking dish from the oven.

Place the aïoli in a small bowl and nestle it into the center of the baking dish, with the prawns on the salt around it. Bring it to the table as is. Guests can use their fingers to remove the shells and dip the prawns into the aïoli. Have a bowl for the shells and finger bowls for guests.

Frank Damarco, crab fisherman extraordinaire, on his boat, the *Lionelda*.

As Indian summer gives way to brisk, clear November skies, Frank Damarco is about to embark on his fifty-seventh crabbing season. On opening day, he and two fellow fishermen will shove off on the Lionelda, *a handsome forty-six-foot-long wood-trimmed crabber, stacked high with two hundred crab traps, neatly bound and ready to be dropped outside of the Golden Gate, at Frank's special spot. "Crabs don't migrate like fish," explains Damarco. "If they're there, they'll be attracted to the pots." Every day or two, the crabbers will replenish the bait and collect the crabs, which will be sold to wholesalers at a previously agreed upon price per pound.*

Damarco is one of the few third-generation crabbers left on Fisherman's Wharf. In the mid-1880s, his grandfather, Fred, fled unspeakably hard times in Sicily and became a fisherman. Grandson Frank carries on the tradition. After a long stretch of salmon fishing in Alaska, Frank finally saved enough money to buy his own boat.

"My boat, one of only twenty-five to thirty remaining on Fisherman's Wharf, was considered big in the early days. Today, it's a toy," he laments. "Bigger boats, from up north, most eighty to ninety feet long, and each with a thousand crab pots aboard, move into our territory with huge crews and spotlights that illuminate the crabbing waters at night." The fact that they can work around the clock disturbs Frank and local fishermen, who only go out, as they always have, every couple of days.

"There was a ten-year stretch in the fifties and the sixties when I was hauling in four hundred dollars a day, five days a week. I thought it was all the money in the world," he says. "I was still living at home and giving money to my parents," he adds proudly. "One day I decided what I needed was a car, so I went out and bought a Pontiac Catalina. The money came from one week's work. But due to overfishing, we don't make that kind of money anymore, and that's why you don't see young men fishing today. They want nice cars too."

Cold Cracked Crab with Crab Sauce

One of the most enduring San Francisco treats is cold, cracked Dungeness crab. It's best if you start with a live crab for this dish, although most San Franciscans buy their crab already cooked and chilled from a reputable fish market.

One of the things that I've learned from my old-time Italian neighbors and the cooks and fishmongers in the adjacent Chinese community in San Francisco is that the most spectacularly flavorful part of the crab is the fat. It's the thick yellow matter in the back of the shell, which you only get if you buy whole uncleaned crabs.

We make a sort of mayonnaise using the crab fat, olive oil, lemon juice, cognac, and cayenne. It is the only thing I can really think of to eat with chilled Dungeness crab, since it does not interfere with, but rather enhances, the "crabness."

All you will need with this is crusty bread and a good green salad or the Salad of Mushrooms, Endive, and Parmesan (page 73). Consider serving a bottle of great Champagne such as Salon 1983.

- 1 live Dungeness crab (2 to 2½ pounds), cooked
- 1 tablespoon salt
- Reserved crab butter (see Step 4, page 157), strained through a fine-mesh sieve
- 1 large egg, cooked in boiling water for 5 minutes, cooled, and peeled
- 2 tablespoons extra virgin olive oil
- ¼ cup mild olive oil
- A few drops of fresh lemon juice
- A few drops of Cognac
- Dash of cayenne pepper

Serves 1 to 4, depending upon greed and the occasion

Bring a large pot of water to a boil. Add the salt and then add the crab, completely submerging it. Bring the water back to a boil and cook the crab for about 10 minutes, until the shell is bright orange and the legs and claws curl up against the body.

Remove the crab with tongs to a work surface. Let cool. Clean, section, and crack as directed on page 157. Reserve the crab butter for the sauce. Cover the crab and refrigerate until serving. Refrigerate for up to 2 days, under ice, well covered.

Push the crab butter through a fine sieve and put it and the egg in a food processor. Pulse to combine. With the motor running, pour in the olive oil in a slow steady stream and process until the mixture begins to thicken. Stop the motor and scrape down the sides of the work bowl. Then, with the motor running, add the lemon juice and Cognac, a little at a time, and finally add the cayenne. Pulse for a few seconds. The sauce will be a little runny.

Serve the cold cracked crab on a cold plate with the dipping sauce on the side.

Whole Roasted Crab Crusted with Garlic and Red Pepper

- 1 tablespoon salt
- 2 live Dungeness crabs (about 2 pounds each)
- ⅓ cup extra virgin olive oil
- 2 tablespoons finely chopped spring garlic or 4 garlic cloves, chopped
- 2 tablespoons chopped thyme
- 1 teaspoon fennel seeds, crushed
- 1 teaspoon kosher or sea salt
- 1 teaspoon crushed red pepper flakes
- 8 tablespoons (1 stick) unsalted butter, melted

Serves 2 as a main course, 4 as a first course

Eating crab out of the shell is always messy business. The good thing about Dungeness crab is that the shells are relatively soft and easy to split open with your fingers. So rather than fight the inherent messiness of all of this, here's a dish that has an extra reward for all of the shelling and digging out of the crabmeat. The red pepper flakes, thyme, fennel, and garlic mixture that is tossed with the crab is powerful, but it doesn't penetrate the shell. Instead, it clings to your fingers while you are eating the crab, flavoring the meat as you free it from its crevices.

Serve with a loaf of crusty bread to sop up the juices, a good green salad, and a medium-bodied Dolcetto d'Alba, Mauro Molino, 1997, from the Piedmont.

Bring a large pot of salted water to a boil. Add the crabs, submerging them completely. Return to a boil and boil for 3 minutes. Drain the crabs, discarding the liquid.

When cool enough to handle, place the crabs on a work surface and clean, section, and crack them (see page 157). Place the crabs in a large bowl.

In a mortar or in a mini food processor or blender, pound together or puree the olive oil, garlic, thyme, fennel seeds, salt, and crushed red pepper. Toss the crabs with this marinade, coating them well. Place the coated crabs side by side on a metal baking dish and let them sit while the oven preheats.

Preheat the oven to 550°F (or the highest setting).

Roast the crabs until golden brown and bubbling, 8 to 10 minutes. Transfer to a warmed platter and serve with the melted butter for dipping.

Where and How Dungeness Crabs Are Caught

Dungeness crabs proliferate in the 50° to 57°F waters from Santa Barbara to the Aleutian Islands. They prefer sandy bottoms, at a depth of three hundred feet.

The crab industry is regulated by the California, Oregon, Washington, and Alaskan departments of fish and game. Only males at least 6½ inches across the shell may be caught. The strictly enforced season varies from state to state, but in California, it is November 15 to June 30. Because the season tends to peak early, often in its first month, in order to stay in business most crab boats have had to diversify their catch and are outfitted to catch a variety of fish in other seasons.

Game wardens make sure that each 60- to 120-pound circular steel trap, or crab pot, has two escape hatches so small crabs can swim free. All pots must also be equipped with a self-destruction device that allows the trapped shellfish to escape should the pot get lost in stormy weather.

- 1 live Dungeness crab (2 to 2 1/2 pounds)
- 1/4 cup extra virgin olive oil, plus extra for drizzling
- 1 white onion, chopped
- 1/2 cup thinly sliced leeks (white part only)
- 2 garlic cloves, crushed
- 4 sprigs marjoram
- 6 anchovy fillets or 2 tablespoons anchovy paste
- 1/3 cup chopped flat-leaf parsley
- 1 teaspoon harissa or 1/2 teaspoon crushed red pepper flakes
- 1/2 pound lingcod or other white fish fillets, cut into small pieces
- 1 cup dry Italian white wine
- 1 cup pasta water (see page 69), or tap water
- 1 3/4 cups tomato puree (made from processing drained canned peeled whole tomatoes or peeled fresh whole tomatoes)
- 1/2 pound mussels, scrubbed and debearded
- 1/2 pound prawns, or large shrimp, peeled and deveined
- 1/2 pound calamari, cleaned and cut into rings and tentacles (see page 163)
- Kosher or sea salt

Serves 4

No San Francisco dish is more famous than cioppino. The name comes from the Genoese fish stew ciuppin, *a traditional fisherman's dish made from small whole fish. San Francisco's early immigrants translated the spirit of that fisherman's stew into cioppino, which they made from the surplus of their local catch, including the then-plentiful Dungeness crab. Archives describe fishermen's wives cooking great kettles of cioppino over wood fires on the slopes of Telegraph Hill.*

This recipe revives the spirit of the early cioppinos. Its texture is light and fresh, achieved by adding a bit of pasta water, that frugal traditional housewife's broth (see Save the Waters, page 69), white wine, and a bright tomato puree. I use harissa to add heat to the stew rather than traditional dried chilies, because I love its broad, robust heat. Harissa is available in specialty food shops and Middle Eastern markets (see Sources, page 264).

Use whatever fish is available in your area, but aim for a balance of shellfish and meaty white fish. If you cannot get Dungeness crab, try lobster or Alaskan king crab in its place.

Serve with a green salad and toasted country bread. Even though the stew includes white wine, instead of red, a break with tradition, one of my favorite things to drink with it is a slightly chilled Charbono from California, since the acidic tomatoes blend nicely with the fruit in the red wine and the spice in the Charbono goes especially well with the rich crab and the fish.

Kill, clean, and section the crab as directed on the next page, reserving the crab fat.

Warm the olive oil in a large heavy nonreactive pot over medium-high heat. Add the onion, leeks, and garlic and sauté until the garlic is golden. Add the marjoram, anchovies, parsley, and harissa and stir to mix, mashing the anchovies with the tines of a fork. Add the crab and the fish and cook until the fish begins to fall apart, 7 to 10 minutes. Add the white wine and reduce by one-third.

Mix the reserved crab fat, the pasta water or tap water, and tomato puree in a small bowl. Add to the pot, raise the heat to high, and bring to a boil. Add the mussels and shrimp and continue to boil until the mussel shells begin to open and the shrimp turns pink, about 3 minutes. Add the calamari and cook until stiffened, about 1 minute. Season to taste with salt. Stir well. Ladle into a soup tureen and drizzle olive oil over the top. Serve at once with grilled bread.

Preparing Dungeness Crab for Cooking

It is always best to buy live crabs for the finest flavor and texture. You also are assured that the crab is fresh. For some of these recipes, the crabs are killed by immersing them in boiling water. They are then cleaned and sectioned. For others, they are killed and then cleaned and sectioned before cooking, as described here. If you kill the crab by immersion, skip to Step 4 for cleaning and cracking only.

1. Refrigerate the live crab until you're ready to cook it.
2. Wearing heavy gloves, if you wish, pick up the crab from behind to avoid being pinched. Grab all four legs and the claws on each side and hold them close to the body.
3. To kill the crab, using the edge of a heavy cutting board or the sink, crack the underside of the crab shell down the middle with one sharp blow. Alternatively, quickly puncture the area between the eyes with a sharp knife or ice pick.
4. With one hand, gather both sets of legs together. Grasp the back shell with the other hand and pull the back shell off. A lot of whitish or yellowish fat, also known as crab butter, will be visible in the back shell. Remove it and any additional fat hiding in the corners of the shell and set aside for later use.
5. Remove and discard the mouth parts, gills, and intestine.
6. Split the crab lengthwise through the body and cut each half into sections, with a leg attached to each section.
7. To crack the crab, after it has been cooked lay a clean kitchen towel over the crab pieces to avoid spattering and strike each leg and claw with a hammer or mallet.

Dungeness Crab and Artichokes Meunière

- 2 tablespoons extra virgin olive oil
- 8 baby artichokes, trimmed (see page 31) and quartered, or 4 medium artichokes, trimmed (see page 31) and quartered, held in lemon water
- 2 tablespoons unsalted butter
- 1 garlic clove, bruised
- Pinch of cayenne pepper
- 1 pound fresh crabmeat (about 2 cups), picked over for shells and cartilage
- 1 tablespoon minced chives
- 2 tablespoons Cognac

Serves 4

San Francisco has been home to a number of Italian restaurants called Joe's: old New Joe's in the Marina District and in North Beach on Broadway; Original Joe's on Taylor Street; and Little Joe's on Broadway, formerly on Columbus Avenue. It is not clear whether these "Joe's" were related, but they were the first to feature the now-common California-style open kitchen. Half the fun at a Joe's was watching the sauté chef toss items into a pan and then dramatically flambé the entire dish. Many of these flaming creations featured crab in one form or another.

This is one of those old-fashioned North Beach dishes that contrasts the deep earthy taste of caramelized artichokes with the delicate richness of great crabmeat. You'd be hard-pressed to order a more San Franciscan dish than this. It is luxuriously rich and delicate at the same time. Unlike the recipe for Cioppino (page 156), you need not start with a live crab.

Serve this as the main course in a dinner with Salad of Bay Shrimp and Belgium Endive (page 84) to start and Persimmon Pudding (page 244) as dessert. This works wonderfully with a Pinot Grigio, Venica & Venica, 1997, Collio.

Heat the olive oil in a large sauté pan over medium-high heat. Meanwhile, drain and pat dry the artichokes.

Sauté the artichokes in the hot olive oil until lightly browned and just tender, about 5 minutes. Add the butter and garlic and cook until the butter turns a rich hazelnut color, about 3 minutes. Remove and discard the garlic and add the cayenne and crabmeat. Stir until just heated through. Add the chives and Cognac and cook about 1 minute more. Serve directly from the sauté pan onto warm plates.

Crab in North Beach Feasts and Holidays

Dungeness crab is to San Francisco what lobster is to Maine. It's our celebration food, our Christmas lunch, our Chinese New Year's dinner, our Thanksgiving hors d'oeuvre. It's what we serve when good cooks and friends come to town and we want to impress them. Crab feed dinners are annual favorites with many Italian-American organizations in San Francisco at places such as the Italian Athletic Club and the Dolphin Swimming and Rowing Club.

Alaskan king crab also lurks in West Coast waters; any San Franciscan will tell you, however, that Dungeness crab is by far the better of the two—smaller, sweeter, much more flavorful, and never as chewy. Furthermore, while conservation is always a concern of ours and any crustacean must be respected because of its dwindling numbers, Dungeness crab is less in danger of being fished to below sustainable levels than Alaskan King crab is.

The most logical spot to shop for cooked hard-shelled crab would be, of course, Fisherman's Wharf, but it's not where most San Franciscans shop. They heed the rumors, rife each season, that the frozen remainder of last year's catch is sold off there as "fresh." Locals go to Chinatown or to a trusted vendor, such as Swan Oyster Depot.

Braised Clams with Coteghino and Salsa Verde

1 coteghino sausage (about 3/4 pound)
2 cups Homemade Kitchen Broth (page 70)

1 cup chopped flat-leaf parsley
2 garlic cloves
12 anchovy fillets
Pinch of crushed red pepper flakes
1 tablespoon capers
1/4 cup extra virgin olive oil

1/4 cup dry Italian white wine
1 pound Manila clams, scrubbed
4 slices country bread, grilled or toasted, optional

Serves 4

You could serve this as an antipasto, a pasta sauce, or a hearty main course stew, but however you serve it, it is packed with wonderful briny flavors of the sea and the earthy taste of sausage.

This is a great dish to make the day after you've made Hazelnut Coteghino with Lentils (page 190), combining the leftover fresh sausage with the clams. Or buy coteghino, a mild Italian boiling sausage made from pork, from an Italian market. Molinari Meats on Columbus Avenue has a long tradition in San Francisco of making great sausages; coteghino is just one of many.

You might want to toast some crusty bread, place it in a shallow bowl, and pour the stew over it. If this is your main course, consider starting with Crostini of Asparagus, Prosciutto, and Teleme (page 26). Pour a Sauvignon Blanc, Voss Vineyard, Napa Valley, 1997.

Place the coteghino in a pot that just holds it, add the broth, and poach until a thermometer inserted into the center of the sausage reads 160°F, about 20 minutes. Slice the coteghino into thin discs and return to the broth.

To make the salsa verde, place the parsley, garlic, anchovies, red pepper, capers, and olive oil in a blender and blend until smooth. Set aside.

In a tightly covered pot, over high heat, heat the white wine. Steam open the clams in the white wine over high heat, about 5 minutes. Remove from the heat and add the coteghino, its broth, and the salsa verde to the pot of clams. Simmer briefly and serve in bowls over the toasted bread if desired.

Braised Calamari with Polenta

Next to crab, calamari is the seafood most associated with North Beach. Rose Pistola used it more than any other ingredient, except for the always-present leaf of basil that she liked to stick in her cleavage to attract the men. Calamari is inexpensive, spiked with the flavor of the sea, and very simple to prepare once cleaned. Many fish stores sell already-cleaned calamari.

Summer in San Francisco can be famously cold, so I sometimes find myself cooking cold-weather food with hot-weather produce. Variations of this hearty stew can be made throughout the year, but it is particularly good made with fresh tomatoes and fava beans or peas. Serve it with soft polenta or, in the height of summer, Fresh Corn Polenta.

Pour a Fiano del Avellino or Arneis, Seghesio Family Vineyard, 1997.

- 2 tablespoons extra virgin olive oil
- 1 medium white onion, finely diced
- 1 garlic clove, bruised
- ¼ cup flat-leaf parsley leaves, chopped
- 4 sprigs marjoram (about 4 inches long)
- 1 tablespoon harissa (see Sources, page 264), or ½ teaspoon crushed red pepper flakes
- 3 anchovy fillets, chopped, or 1 tablespoon anchovy paste
- 1 cup dry Italian white wine
- 2 pounds calamari, cleaned and cut into rings and tentacles (see page 163)
- 2 cups fresh tomato puree (made from processing drained canned peeled whole tomatoes or peeled fresh whole tomatoes)
- Kosher or sea salt
- 1 cup fava beans, peeled (about 1 pound in the pod), or 1 cup English peas (about 1 pound in the pod)
- Polenta (page 15) or Fresh Corn Polenta (page 211)

Serves 4

Warm the olive oil in a heavy skillet over medium heat. Sauté the onion until soft. Add the garlic and cook until fragrant, about 5 minutes. Add the parsley, marjoram, harissa, and anchovy fillets and sauté until the anchovy fillets melt into the oil and the parsley sizzles. Add the wine and reduce by half.

Add the calamari and tomato puree and braise over low heat until the sauce is thickened and the squid is tender, about 45 minutes. Season with salt. About 10 minutes before the calamari is done, add the favas or peas.

Mound the polenta in the center of a large warm platter, ring it with the braised calamari, and serve at once.

Grilled Calamari with Potatoes, Peas, and Spring Onions

- ½ pound tiny potatoes (no more than ¾ inch in diameter), preferably Yellow Finn or fingerling (if only large potatoes are available, peel and quarter them)
- 2 strips lemon zest, each about 3 inches long and 1 inch wide
- 8 spring onions or 4 small white onions, halved, with roots left on
- 1½ cups English peas (about 1½ pounds in the pod)
- 3 basil leaves
- ½ teaspoon kosher or sea salt
- 4 tablespoons extra virgin olive oil
- 1 garlic clove
- ½ teaspoon crushed red pepper flakes
- 1 pound calamari, cleaned and cut into tubes and tentacles (see page 163)

Wooden skewers, soaked in water for 30 minutes

Serves 2 as a main course, 4 as an antipasto

This combination of springtime vegetables and charred briny calamari has become a favorite on Rose Pistola's menu. As with most of our green vegetable dishes, we do not blanch or boil the peas. Instead, we gently braise them with a tiny bit of water and a little olive oil to allow their grassiness to meld with the other ingredients and intensify their flavors.

Serve with Farinata with Sage, Niçoise Olives, and Caramelized Onions (page 132) and a Verdicchio or Single Vineyard "La Monacesca," 1995.

If using a charcoal or gas grill, start the fire.

Put the potatoes, lemon zest, onions, peas, basil, ¼ teaspoon of the salt, 2 tablespoons of the olive oil, and 1 tablespoon water in a heavy casserole with a tight-fitting lid. Cook over medium-low heat, covered, without stirring until the potatoes are tender, about 25 minutes.

Meanwhile, put the garlic, the remaining ¼ teaspoon salt, the red pepper, and the remaining 2 tablespoons olive oil in a mortar or a blender or mini food processor and pound or puree. Toss the calamari with this marinade and thread the calamari onto four skewers.

Grill the calamari over a wood fire or gas grill, or cook in a preheated ribbed grill pan over high heat, turning until browned and crusty on all sides, about 6 minutes. (Charring the calamari makes the calamari more tender, so it's important that it grill over high heat.)

Place the pea and potato mixture on a serving platter and let cool slightly. Top with the grilled calamari and serve.

Blessing of the Fleet mass and celebration at Rose's church (Saints Peter and Paul Church), around the time of the Columbus Day Parade.

Cleaning Calamari

1. Cut the tentacles off the calamari just above the eyes and reserve them.
2. Just above the spot where the tentacles were attached is the mouth (it looks like a pea). Squeeze it out between your forefinger and thumb; discard the head and mouth.
3. Pull out the translucent bone from inside the body and discard.
4. Rinse the body inside and out, pulling out and discarding any remaining innards.
5. If the recipe calls for "rings and tentacles," cut the body into rings and leave the tentacles whole, or cut them in half if they are long or too big for your taste.

Calamari and Artichoke Cakes

- ¼ cup extra virgin olive oil
- ½ large white onion, finely chopped
- 2 tablespoons chopped flat-leaf parsley
- 1 teaspoon chopped marjoram
- 1 tablespoon anchovy paste
- Pinch of crushed red pepper flakes
- 1 large artichoke
- 1 pound calamari, cleaned, cut into rings and tentacles (see page 163), and finely chopped in the food processor
- 1 cup fresh Bread Crumbs (page 9)
- 5 large eggs, beaten
- ½ teaspoon kosher or sea salt

The idea to use ground calamari came from Rose herself, who explained that when calamari was truly cheap and plentiful, frugal housewives in the neighborhood substituted ground calamari for more expensive ground meat. It is one of the most appreciated ingredients in North Beach. We use ground calamari in that way in both our Spaghetti with Calamari Meatballs (page 100) and Gnocchi with Calamari Bolognese (page 120), but this dish is a little different. It is an Italian take on a combination of a crab cake and a Chinese fish cake.

The aïoli is wonderfully creamy and tart. Serve this dish as a light entrée or a substantial antipasto. Serve with a mixed green salad or with Polenta (page 15) if it is the entrée. A simple, crisp white wine such as a Vermentino or Pinot Grigio would be nice with this.

Heat 2 tablespoons of the olive oil in a heavy skillet over medium-high heat. Sauté the onion until it is translucent, about 5 minutes. Add the parsley, marjoram, anchovy paste, and red pepper and sauté until the parsley sizzles and the anchovy paste melts into the oil, about 3 minutes. Remove from the heat and allow to cool.

Trim the artichoke of its leaves and choke and cut the heart into ⅜-inch chunks. Bring a small pot of water to a boil and drop in the chunks. Reduce the water to a simmer and cook the chunks until tender, 10 to 15 minutes. Drain.

In a bowl, stir together the calamari, bread crumbs, artichokes, and eggs. Stir in the onion mixture and the salt. Refrigerate while you make the aïoli.

For the Lemon Aïoli

Place the egg yolk, the juice of 2 lemons, garlic, and salt in a food processor. Process until well blended. With the machine running, pour in the olive oil in a slow steady stream and process until the mixture thickens. Scrape into a bowl, squeeze a few more drops of lemon juice over the top, stir, and set aside.

For the Lemon Aïoli

1 large egg yolk

Juice of 2 lemons, plus a few drops

1 garlic clove

½ teaspoon kosher or sea salt

¾ cup extra virgin olive oil

Serves 6 to 8

Heat the remaining 2 tablespoons oil in a large nonstick sauté pan over medium-high heat. For each calamari cake, spoon a heaping tablespoon of the calamari mixture into the oil; you can cook several cakes at a time, but do not crowd them, as they can be tricky to turn. Sauté the cakes until browned on one side, turn, and cook until cooked through, about 4 minutes more. As the cakes are cooked, remove them to a warm platter and keep them warm while you finish the remaining cakes. Serve with the aïoli spooned on top.

Grilled Octopus with Broccoli Rabe and White Beans

For the Octopus

2 tablespoons extra virgin olive oil
2 garlic cloves, bruised
¼ cup diced white onion
1 carrot, diced
1 bay leaf
3 sprigs flat-leaf parsley
1 cup dry Italian white wine
1 octopus (about 1½ pounds)

Kosher or sea salt
¼ cup plus 2 tablespoons extra virgin olive oil
2 garlic cloves, chopped
¼ teaspoon kosher or sea salt
¼ teaspoon crushed red pepper flakes
1 bunch broccoli rabe, trimmed to about 5-inch lengths, blanched in boiling salted water until tender, and drained
2 cups cooked cannellini beans (see page 16; omit the Parmesan rind)
Juice of ½ lemon

Serves 2 as a main course, 4 as a first course

When Rose Pistola first opened, I was nervous about cooking Italian food for the Italians in the neighborhood who were scrutinizing my take on "their" food. One day at lunch, Mrs. Azzolini, whose family owns Café Roma, a famous roastery and coffee shop next door and who is the heartbeat of gossip central for the entire neighborhood, came in. She asked the waiter to have me come over to her table. After exchanging pleasantries, her dining companion somewhat heatedly asked me how I had gotten her recipe for grilled octopus and rabe. I burst out laughing and told her how flattered I was. I somehow felt then that while I might still be under suspicion, the kitchen at Rose Pistola was definitely on the right track and in tune with the tradition of the neighborhood.

Pour a Sauvignon Blanc or a 1997 Fumé Blanc, Ferrari-Carano, from Sonoma County.

For the Octopus

Heat the olive oil in a heavy nonreactive saucepan over medium heat. Add the garlic, onion, carrot, bay leaf, and parsley and sauté over medium-high heat until fragrant, 6 to 8 minutes. Add the white wine and reduce by half.

Add the octopus and enough water to barely cover it. Bring to a simmer and season to taste with salt. Put a plate or lid slightly smaller than the diameter of the pot on the octopus to keep it submerged. Lower the heat to just below a simmer and cook for 1 hour.

Place the pot on a heat diffuser or on a skillet and cook over the lowest heat possible until the octopus is tender, adding more water, if necessary, about 2 more hours. The octopus should have the texture of cooked lobster, tender with a little "bite." Remove from the heat and let the octopus cool in the broth.

Clean the octopus, discarding the beak. Separate the octopus into individual tentacles and cut the head lengthwise in half. (See instructions at right.)

If using a charcoal or gas grill, start the fire.

In a mortar or a mini food processor or blender, pound or puree 3 tablespoons of the olive oil, the garlic, salt, and crushed red pepper. Toss the octopus and cooked broccoli rabe with this marinade.

Either place the octopus and broccoli rabe in a sauté pan over a charcoal or gas grill or put directly on a ribbed grill pan over high heat until brown and crusty on all sides, about 6 minutes. (Charring the octopus actually makes it more tender, so it is important that it grill over high heat.)

Meanwhile, heat the beans with the remaining 3 tablespoons olive oil.

Spoon the beans onto a warm platter and serve the grilled octopus and broccoli rabe on top of the beans, drizzled generously with lemon juice.

Cleaning and Cutting Octopus

Remove the octopus from the saucepan. Cut off the tentacles and remove the eyes from the head and discard them. Invert the hood and discard the viscera. Cut the octopus into bite-sized pieces. Keep warm.

Meat and Fowl

With its precipitous wooded hills that drop dramatically to the Mediterranean, Liguria has been inhabited by fishermen and sailors, foragers, and farmers, who worked its steep terraces for centuries. These and their regional neighbors are the people who first populated North Beach. Since the land in the Old Country did not support a heavily carnivorous diet, Ligurians took a different approach to cooking with meat and fowl than we are traditionally familiar with.

Meat in Liguria was often from smaller animals like lambs and rabbits. Beef, a rare treat, was stretched as far as possible when it was available, typically in sauces and stews. Fowl usually came from wild game birds.

Meat and fowl were both prepared with vegetables and often included mushrooms or nuts gathered from the woods. Seafarers longed to be welcomed home from journeys around the Mediterranean with such earthy combinations. This cooking style, reflected in the following recipes, came with the immigrants to Northern California, where they adapted it to the bountifulness of their new home.

A new lamb at Bellwether Farms.

Terrorized Steak

Ex-mayor of Nice, felon, prison escapee, and all-around-interesting fellow Jacques Médecin wrote an opinionated book on Niçoise cooking that has a recipe for "Terrorized Steak" with a vinegar and shallot sauce. I adored the name. Applying Médecin's own version of the golden rule (beg, borrow, and steal whatever you can) I figured it was okay to appropriate the name.

This is a recipe in the tradition of the Italian-American steak house. It is a charred steak, made unique by its spicy seasonings, rather than by Médecin's vinegar and shallot sauce. Its flavor is so distinct it is best served as suggested here, with a simple watercress salad and a few lemon wedges. A little herb butter is nice with it if you are so inclined.

A nice starter is Griddled Artichokes and Potatoes (page 207). Pour a classic Napa Valley Cabernet Sauvignon such as the Grgich-Hills 1995.

For the Terror

Leaves from 6 sprigs marjoram (about 5 inches long)
Leaves from 6 sprigs rosemary (about 5 inches long)
8 garlic cloves
1 teaspoon kosher or sea salt
1 teaspoon crushed red pepper flakes
2 tablespoons Cognac
2 tablespoons extra virgin olive oil
1 tablespoon freshly cracked black pepper

4 bone-in New York (strip) steaks, each about 1½ inches thick and about 1½ pounds
Herb Butter (page 11)
2 cups watercress sprigs
Red Wine Vinaigrette (page 79)
1 lemon, cut into wedges

Serves 4

For the Terror

In a mortar or mini food processor, pound or process the marjoram, rosemary, garlic, salt, red pepper flakes, Cognac, olive oil, and black pepper until a coarse paste is formed. Rub the paste evenly on both sides of the steaks. Allow the steaks to rest at room temperature for at least 30 minutes and up to 1½ hours before grilling.

Prepare a medium-hot fire in a charcoal grill.

Grill the steaks, turning occasionally, until crusty on the outside, about 5 minutes on each side for medium rare. Transfer the steaks to a warmed platter, spread evenly with the Herb Butter, and let rest briefly. Toss the watercress with the vinaigrette. Serve the meat accompanied with the watercress and lemon wedges.

Boiled Beef with Winter Vegetables and Two Sauces

- 1 two-pound New York (strip) steak, boneless
- 1 garlic clove, slivered, plus 1 garlic clove, bruised
- 2 anchovy fillets, cut into small pieces
- ¼ cup extra virgin olive oil
- 1 sprig rosemary (about 4 inches long)
- 2 small carrots
- 1 large or 6 small parsnips, cut into small pieces
- 1 medium or 6 small turnips, cut into small pieces
- 12 cipollini (flat Italian sweet onions) or small white onions
- 2 cups dry Italian white wine
- 2 cups Homemade Kitchen Broth (page 70) or good beef stock
- 2 dried porcini
- 3 celery leaves
- Kosher or sea salt

Serves 4 to 6

Saturday night was traditionally boiled beef night for many Italian families in North Beach. The broth in which the meat was cooked was usually served as a first course, with a few handfuls of pastina thrown in. The boiled meat was customarily accompanied with a traditional Italian green sauce, or salsa verde. Like most North Beach cooking, it was very practical—when the family returned from church the next day, leftovers for lunch awaited them.

In thinking of this dish, long-cooked bollito misto may come to mind. Instead of strictly following tradition, whereby an inexpensive cut of beef turns gray as it boils for a long time, buy a thick chunk of New York strip and poach it lightly in an aromatic broth with winter vegetables. The rare poached beef is accompanied here with an absolutely fitting hazelnut sauce alongside the more traditional salsa verde. Even old-timers in the neighborhood have become converts.

Enjoy with a medium-bodied Rosso di Montalcino.

Using a sharp knife, make ½-inch slits every couple of inches in the surface of the meat. Insert the garlic slivers and anchovy pieces in alternating slits. Set aside.

Heat the olive oil in a large heavy pot over medium heat. Add the bruised garlic clove and the rosemary and cook until fragrant. Add the vegetables and sauté until golden. Add the white wine and reduce by one-third. Add the broth or stock, bring to a simmer, add the porcini and celery leaves, and season to taste with salt.

Place the meat in the sauce and poach over medium-low heat for about 5 minutes per inch of thickness, or until the internal temperature reads 105°F on a meat thermometer. Allow the meat to rest for 5 minutes before carving, keeping it warm.

While the meat cooks, prepare the sauces, or prepare them ahead of time.

Remove the meat from the broth and slice it into thin strips.

Arrange it on a serving platter, spoon out the vegetables with a slotted spoon, and scatter them around the meat. Put the sauces in small bowls and serve them alongside.

For the Salsa Verde

Place the parsley, garlic, anchovies, capers, and vinegar in a blender and process for about 30 seconds, until blended. Pour in the olive oil and blend again. Transfer to a bowl, and stir in the egg. Season with salt and pepper to taste. Set aside.

For the Hazelnut Sauce

In a mortar or a mini food processor, pound or process the rosemary leaves, salt, garlic, pepper to taste, and olive oil until smooth. Add the hazelnuts and pound or pulse until broken and coarse. Stir in the shallot and set aside.

For the Salsa Verde

- 1 cup chopped flat-leaf parsley
- 2 garlic cloves, bruised
- 12 anchovy fillets
- 1 tablespoon capers, rinsed
- 2 tablespoons red wine vinegar
- 1/3 cup extra virgin olive oil
- 2 hard-boiled eggs, peeled and sieved or chopped
- 1/4 teaspoon kosher or sea salt
- 1/4 teaspoon freshly cracked black pepper

For the Hazelnut Sauce

- 1 sprig rosemary, leaves removed
- 1/2 teaspoon kosher or sea salt
- 1 garlic clove
- Freshly cracked black pepper
- 3/4 cup extra virgin olive oil
- 1/2 cup hazelnuts, toasted and peeled (see page 191)
- 1 medium shallot, chopped

A behind-the-scenes look at the grill cart at the Rose Pistola booth at the Ferry Plaza Farmers' Market.

Braised Oxtails with Asparagus

4 pounds oxtails
1 bottle dry Italian white wine
1 medium white onion, ½ chopped, ½ diced
2 garlic cloves, bruised
Kosher or sea salt and freshly cracked black pepper
¼ cup extra virgin olive oil
4 carrots, diced
5 celery leaves
1 dried porcini, soaked in warm water for 20 minutes
¼ cup Niçoise olives
8 anchovy fillets, chopped
12 asparagus spears, trimmed and peeled
1 tablespoon unsalted butter
3 tablespoons Basilade (page 8)
Polenta (page 15), optional

Serves 4

While oxtails rarely come from oxen these days, beef tails are very meaty for long-cooked, hearty stews, braises, and soups. Here the rich taste of the long-cooked beef contrasts nicely with the bright, fresh flavors of the briefly cooked asparagus, lemon, and basil.

After an overnight marinade, this will take about six hours to cook. The oxtails practically cook themselves once they go in the oven. We braise this meaty and satisfying dish in one of those great-looking clay pots, often available in Asian markets, but a Dutch oven will do the job as well.

Since oxtails are hard to find in some areas, you could substitute beef short ribs. But try an Asian butcher, as we do in nearby Chinatown for ours, or an Italian butcher.

Serve on a bed of Polenta (page 15), with a Dolceacqua or California Cabernet.

Combine the oxtails, white wine, chopped onion, and 1 garlic clove in a large bowl and marinate in the refrigerator overnight.

About 6½ hours before serving, preheat the oven to 325°F.

Remove the oxtails from the marinade, reserving the marinade, and pat dry. Season with salt and pepper. Heat 2 tablespoons of the olive oil in a large heavy skillet. Brown the meat in batches over medium-high heat on all sides, about 10 minutes. Remove the meat from the pan and pour off the fat.

Heat the remaining 2 tablespoons oil in the pan. Add the diced onion, the carrots, celery leaves, the remaining garlic clove, and the porcini. Cook until the onion becomes translucent, scraping the pan often, about 5 minutes. Add the olives and anchovies and stir well. Strain the marinade and add to the pan. Bring to a boil, then place the browned oxtails, in one layer, on top of the vegetables.

Braise in the oven in a large heavy covered skillet for about 6 hours, or until the meat is practically falling off the bone. Turn the meat every 30 minutes.

When the oxtails are done, remove them from the braising liquid and set aside. Pour the liquid into a large measuring cup. Refrigerate it for a few minutes or put it in the freezer. This will make it easy to see the fat so you can remove it. Skim off the fat and discard it. Strain the liquid.

Return the braising liquid to the pan, add the oxtails, and cover and return to the oven for 10 minutes so that the flavors meld.

Meanwhile, combine the asparagus, butter, ¼ teaspoon salt, and ½ cup water in a large sauté pan and cook over medium-high heat until almost all the water has evaporated.

Add the asparagus to the oxtails, bring to a simmer over heat, and stir in the basilade.

To serve, if using polenta, pour the polenta into the middle of a platter and place the oxtails and sauce on top.

There are as many bars in North Beach as there are stars in the sky. Every sort of music imaginable spills out of its saloon doors—jazz, folk music, opera, Dixieland, even old Beatles tunes. Barkers on Broadway contend with horns, sirens, and screeching brakes. Girls, barely out of high school, dressed in scanty, cheap attire do their best to lure passersby. But there is a quieter neighborhood drinking cult that is still steeped in tradition.

If you comb the bars of North Beach, you'll find some of the country's most determined drinkers. Poets, garbagemen, journalists, sports figures, socialites, and cooks all pass through the neighborhood's saloon doors. Neighborhood drinkers make visiting a series of bars on a daily basis their job—their duty, really. In a wake of good humor or boisterous malcontent, a serious drinker may pass through five or six bars on a given day. He or she might start one of those days at 10:00 A.M. with a Rolling Rock beer handed over by Bobby the bartender at Moose's on Stockton Street. This first chilled beer starts the chain in motion, a way to whet one's whistle en route to the post office.

Drinking is an episodic pursuit that unapologetically accommodates specific patterns, but by nature of the substance, serious drinking respects fluid regimens. A pattern starts to develop for our neighborhood drinker—unable to keep from stopping in at Tony Nic's, a classic bar with its faded, peeling black-and-white neon sign. The bar is decorated with economy—Venetian blinds, several bar stools, and an ancient TV tuned in only to golf matches and W. C. Fields movies. It's not a bar that beckons the unfamiliar visitor. Opposite the back door of Rose Pistola on Stockton Street, near Union Street, Tony Nic's is the quietest bar in the neighborhood. Bartender Butch is the most senior barkeep in North Beach. A jukebox and modern refrigeration would be totally out of place there. Beers are kept in an antediluvian icebox at the rear of the bar; old Italian men play cards by the window to the drone of garbage trucks grinding their pickup and the din of deliveries being made to Rose Pistola and other restaurants.

One's blood pressure seems to drop on entering Tony Nic's, which is why so many neighborhood waiters and waitresses cool down there after hectic shifts. Butch, a war hero who bought the unpretentious spot in 1945, serves a North Beach drink called a Picon Punch. It was Rose Pistola's favorite drink. It's made with Picon, a brandy float, and the option of a twist of lemon. "But," according to well-known neighborhood drinker Tony Dingman, "most people wouldn't want that extra frill; it just displaces the liquor." The secret to Butch's Picon is the beautiful beveled glass in which it is served. There are only five left—you really go for the glass. It's got class.

A small group waits by the doors of Gino and Carlo's Cocktail Lounge on Green Street every morning at 6:00, anxious to start drinking and stop the hangover shakes that woke them in the first place. Sometimes there'll be a few off-duty cops or other people ending their night shifts, like garbagemen or taxi drivers, at that ungodly hour. Another group comes in a little later for Fernet Branca with soda, no ice. And what a North Beach drink it is. It's actually three drinks in one—a digestive, an apéritif on the way to lunch, and a drink sometimes consumed with a brandy float.

Gino and Carlo's is a serious Italian-owned neighborhood bar. It's called a "cocktail lounge" in the telephone book and is frequented by all the usual suspects—restaurant people, electricians, artists, gamblers, pool players, and sports fans. It's no longer quite the same as in years gone by, when poets and columnists, such as the late Charles McCabe, came in to celebrate having written a column or a poem before noon.

Enrico's is another not-to-be missed stop on the bar path in North Beach: a well-known sidewalk caffè and bar on Broadway since the Beat days, where Ward, longtime bartender and rowdy storyteller, holds court with a huge spiritual and physical presence. When business slows and customers dwindle, Ward can be seen, head tilted, patiently practicing calligraphy.

Tosca is arguably one of the best bars in this city of great bars, filled with celebrities

A beerwagon on Montgomery Street, after deliveries to Buon Gusto Restaurant and Toscano Hotel. *Courtesy J. B. Monaco Photography.*

both local and international, drinking to the sounds of an opera-playing jukebox. It has the oldest cappuccino machine in town, which spews forth boozy after-dinner drinks. The place is owned by one of the most fun-loving, sassy proprietors in the neighborhood, Jeanette Etheredge. Her back room with its pool table is the discreet domain for stars of film, sports, and politics.

In the heart of North Beach, Capp's Corner, a raucous, fun-loving corner bar is the place to have a drink with the second-most-senior bartender in the quarter, Sam White. While family-style red-checkered-tablecloth Italian dining has been a neighborhood tradition there for years, it's really the bar that makes it with serious drinking locals of a certain age. Just across the street and another old-time Italian bar, North Star is popular with the younger crowd, who hang out and pick up dates. A jazzy place that falls on the epicenter of North Beach and Fisherman's Wharf called Sweeties is owned by another lively restaurateur and barkeep, artist Flicka McGurrin, also of Pier 23. Her place, now overseen by her kids, is a no-nonsense bar with an old-fashioned pool table. On Francisco Street near Powell, Sweeties serves great slabs of local cheese, pizzas, and onion soup.

"Bars," to Dingman, a poet of some note, "are really language labs. Dictionaries are written by the way people talk, you know. And what better place to hear the drawl of humanity than at a bar." James Joyce said, "God is a noise from the street." But hang out in bars and you'll hear more than noise; you'll get jokes, gossip, restaurant tips, Bay Bridge traffic news, and a lot of language.

By the time the neighborhood drinkers have retreated home, the lawyers, stockbrokers, yuppies, and bridge-and-tunnel types come out. They come to lose themselves for a night or to disappear for a weekend. They find a balance of just enough light by which to be seen and darkness in which to hide. There are all kinds of illegal and promiscuous doings that go on in North Beach alleys at night, keeping up the same mystery that has prevailed since the bawdy Barbary Coast days.

Rose's Cures-What-Ails-You Tripe

For many, tripe is an acquired taste, but, once familiar, you will find it absolutely delicious—meltingly tender, hearty, and soothing when it is cooked "low and slow," as it is here. It does take a long time to cook, but it is cheap, nourishing, and a reputed miracle cure for hangovers and other ailments of human weakness, according to Rose herself.

Serve it over polenta with lots of grated Parmigiano cheese. Start with Capponada (page 76) and pour a Vermentino wine from Corsica or Sardegna.

- 2 tablespoons white vinegar
- 2½ pounds honeycomb tripe, cut into ½ × 2-inch pieces
- 2 tablespoons extra virgin olive oil
- 2 large white onions, thinly sliced
- 2 garlic cloves, bruised
- 1 sprig rosemary (about 4 inches long)
- 6 sprigs thyme
- 2 small dried hot chilies or ¼ teaspoon crushed red pepper flakes
- 2 cups (½ bottle) dry Italian white wine
- ½ cup tomato puree (made from processing drained canned peeled whole tomatoes or peeled fresh whole tomatoes)
- Kosher or sea salt
- Polenta (page 15)
- Freshly grated Parmigiano-Reggiano

Serves 4 to 6

Preheat the oven to 275°F.

Bring 2 quarts water and the vinegar to a boil in a large pot. Blanch the tripe for 5 minutes, then drain.

Heat the olive oil in a heavy flameproof casserole over medium-high heat. Sauté the onions until they are translucent, about 5 minutes. Add the garlic, rosemary, thyme, and chilies and cook until fragrant and sizzling, about 5 minutes. Add the white wine and reduce by half. Add the tomato puree and the tripe, bring to a simmer, and season to taste with salt. Cover and braise in the oven 6 to 8 hours (or overnight), stirring occasionally. Let cool.

Place the pot in the freezer to make it easy to skim off any fat from the tripe. Put the pot on the stovetop, return it to a simmer, taste for seasoning, and serve over the polenta, with plenty of grated Parmigiano-Reggiano alongside.

Roast Leg of Lamb with Braised Artichokes

6 medium artichokes, trimmed (see page 31), stems peeled, and quartered lengthwise, chokes removed
Juice of 2 lemons
¼ cup extra virgin olive oil
1 small white onion, chopped
4 garlic cloves, crushed, plus 4 garlic cloves, each cut into 5 slivers
3 ounces prosciutto ends (see headnote), julienned (1 inch by ⅛ inch)
8 sprigs thyme
½ cup chopped flat-leaf parsley
1 cup dry Italian white wine
1½ cups tomato puree (made from processing drained canned peeled whole tomatoes or peeled fresh whole tomatoes)
Kosher or sea salt and freshly cracked black pepper
1 leg of lamb (4 to 5 pounds, bone-in), preferably spring lamb

Serves 6 to 8

One of the great joys every spring is the first call from Cindy Callahan, letting us know that she is ready to take orders for spring lamb. You might have a farmer in your area who raises special lamb. If so, try to get some. If not, this dish is still remarkable with any leg or shoulder of lamb and young artichokes—an amazing combination and a North Beach tradition.

Ask your butcher to save you the end of a prosciutto ham for this dish. Leave the stems on the artichokes; they provide an extra hit of artichoke flavor and look elegant.

This lamb is perfect served by itself. Start a great meal with Fava Bean Puree Crostini (page 27) and finish with Panna Cotta with Berries (page 251). Pour a medium-bodied Cabernet Sauvignon from the Russian River area.

Preheat the oven to 425°F.

Place the artichokes in a bowl of 4 cups water mixed with the lemon juice until ready to use.

Heat 2 tablespoons of the olive oil in a large sauté pan over medium-high heat. Add the onion and sauté until translucent, about 5 minutes. Add the crushed garlic, the prosciutto, thyme, and parsley and sauté until fragrant and sizzling, about 5 min utes. Add the wine, raise the heat to high, and reduce by half, about 5 minutes. Add the tomato puree. Drain the artichokes and add them. Bring to a simmer. Season to taste with salt and pepper and pour into a large roasting pan.

With a boning knife or other thin sharp knife, make 20 slits about 1 inch deep by ¼ inch wide evenly spaced over the whole leg of lamb. Rub the lamb with the remaining 2 tablespoons olive oil and season generously with salt and pepper, rubbing it into the meat. Stick a garlic sliver into each slit. Place the lamb on top of the artichokes and roast, basting occasionally with the liquid in the pan, until the meat is crisp and brown on top and a meat thermometer reads 120°F for rare and 125°F for medium rare, about 1¼ hours, depending upon the size of the leg of lamb.

To serve, remove the meat from the oven and let rest for 15 minutes.

Skim off any accumulated fat from the top of the artichokes. If the artichokes have begun to dry out and the braising liquid is thick, add a little more water to thin it out. Taste the artichokes for seasoning, adding salt and pepper if necessary, and slice the lamb directly on top of the artichokes in the roasting pan. Serve from the pan.

To Market, To Market

The most important thing to remember is that the cooking process begins when you're at the market. Go see what is fresh, is in season, and catches your fancy. Buying local organic produce is often the best way to ensure that you are buying high-quality ingredients that are in rhythm with the season. Then go home, look up how to prepare your purchases, and use the recipes as guides, improvising based on what you bought.

Roast Loin of Lamb with Early Summer Vegetables

4 heads garlic, unpeeled, plus 3 garlic cloves, cut into slivers, or 8 whole shoots spring garlic, plus 2 shoots cut into slivers
2 carrots, cut into 2-inch lengths
8 cipollini or small white onions
2 sprigs rosemary (about 4 inches long)
1 cup dry Italian white wine
Kosher or sea salt and freshly cracked black pepper
1 loin of lamb (2½ to 3 pounds) or 1 full rack and loin spring lamb (approximately the same weight)
2 tablespoons extra virgin olive oil
¼ pound pancetta, cut into ½-inch dice
¾ pound jumbo asparagus spears, trimmed to 4 inches and peeled
2 small zucchini, cut into 1-inch-thick slices
8 baby artichokes, trimmed (see page 31), stems peeled, and halved
½ cup peeled fava beans (see page 195)
1 strip lemon peel, about 1 inch by 2 inches
2 mint leaves

Serves 4

I never seem to make this dish exactly the same way twice, because it is so dependent upon which vegetables are in season. Some years in the Bay Area, summer comes early, with the hot sun forcing zucchini to flower and tomatoes to ripen in late June. Other years, the fog hangs heavy off the coast, threatening to roll in with each nightfall. Sweet peas, fava beans, and asparagus seem as if they will last forever. Then one day, without much warning, the season changes—and so does the menu at Rose Pistola.

This is one of many dishes that adapt to whatever vegetables look great at the market. If cippolini or small white onions are not available, use big ones. If spring garlic is a rarity in your area, use regular garlic. The asparagus, fava beans, and baby artichokes are hard to beat for taste and presentation, but you could use root vegetables in the colder months.

Start with Octopus with Potatoes and Baby Green Beans (page 47), then finish with a Bowl of Iced Summer Fruit (page 233).

Preheat the oven to 500°F.

If you are using head garlic, cut the pointed tops off the 4 garlic heads to expose the tops of the cloves. If using spring garlic, cut the roots off the 8 shoots and clean them if necessary. Place the garlic in a roasting pan large enough to hold the lamb. Add the carrots, onions, rosemary, wine, and salt and pepper to taste and stir.

With a boning knife or other sharp thin knife, make 12 slits about 1 inch deep by ¼ inch wide evenly spaced over the whole loin of lamb. Rub the lamb with the olive oil and season generously with salt and pepper, rubbing it into the meat. Stick a garlic sliver (from either the remaining 3 garlic cloves or 2 shoots spring garlic) into each slit. Place the meat on top of the vegetables. Place the pan in the oven for 10 minutes.

Meanwhile, put the pancetta in a saucepan over medium-high heat and cook, stirring occasionally, to render the fat and crisp slightly, about 6 minutes. Transfer the pancetta and rendered fat to a bowl, add the asparagus, and toss well. Add the zucchini, artichokes, fava beans, lemon peel, and mint and toss together.

Remove the roasting pan from the oven. Carefully lift the lamb out of the pan and skim any fat off the lamb juices in the pan. Add the rest of the vegetables to the pan and stir to coat with the lamb juices. Place the lamb on top of the vegetables and roast until a meat thermometer registers 120°F for rare or 125°F for medium rare, another 12 to 15 minutes.

Take the pan out of the oven and let the meat rest for about 5 minutes on top of the vegetables. Slice the meat on top of the vegetables and serve from the roasting pan.

Lamb Shanks with Peas and Potatoes

4 lamb shanks (10 to 12 ounces each)
Kosher or sea salt and freshly cracked black pepper
¼ cup plus 1 tablespoon extra virgin olive oil
1 white onion, chopped
6 garlic cloves, bruised
1 sprig rosemary
2 cups (½ bottle) dry Italian white wine
12 small fingerling, Yellow Finn, or other small potatoes
2 pounds English peas, shelled (2 to 2½ cups)
2 tablespoons unsalted butter
1 bunch basil, stems removed

Serves 4

This is a classic North Beach/Italian combination of long-cooked lamb shanks with peas and potatoes. Once the meat is browned and the peas are shelled, the whole thing goes in the oven, and the shanks need only an occasional turning and basting. It is a great company dish; it will keep in the oven until you are all ready to sit down, rather than dictating when everyone must sit and eat. The meat is even better the second day, reheated—or remove the bones and serve the sauce over pasta.

While lamb shanks are a relatively inexpensive cut of lamb, you may need to order them ahead of time from your butcher. Ask the butcher to leave the shanks whole rather than cutting them in half lengthwise as they often do.

Serve with Pickled Crab (page 40) and Warm, Soft Chestnut Pudding (page 243) for dessert. Pour a Dolceacqua or medium-bodied California Cabernet.

Preheat the oven to 400°F.

Sprinkle the shanks with salt and pepper. In a heavy braising pan in which the shanks will just fit, heat 2 tablespoons of the olive oil over medium-high heat. Brown the shanks, turning them so they brown all over, about 15 minutes. Remove the shanks and set aside and pour off the fat from the pan.

Add the onion, 1 tablespoon of the olive oil, 5 of the garlic cloves, and the rosemary to the pan and cook over medium-high heat until the onions become translucent, about 5 minutes.

Place the shanks back in the pan and pour the wine over the meat. When it boils, transfer the pan to the oven and cook, uncovered, for 1½ to 2 hours, or until the meat can be pierced with a wooden skewer or the tip of a knife with no resistance. Turn the shanks every 10 to 15 minutes so that they cook evenly. If the pan begins to dry out, add water or broth so there is about ½ inch of liquid in the bottom of the pan.

Meanwhile, after the shanks have cooked for an hour, place the potatoes, peas, butter, and ¼ teaspoon of salt in a large heavy flameproof casserole, add 2 tablespoons water, and cook, tightly covered, over low heat for about 30 minutes. Remove from the heat and keep warm, on top of the stove until the potatoes are tender.

While the potatoes and peas are cooking, in a mortar or mini food processor, pound together or process the remaining 1 garlic clove and salt, adding the basil a few leaves at a time. When all of the leaves are incorporated, add the remaining 2 tablespoons olive oil and pound or process again.

When the lamb is done, remove it from the oven. Transfer the meat to a large plate. Pour the braising juices into a large measuring cup, let the solids settle, or place in the freezer until the fat solidifies, and skim off the fat from the top; do not strain. Stir the basil paste into the braising juices.

To serve, put the peas and potatoes on a platter, pour the basil sauce over them, and arrange the meat on top.

Spring Lamb Sugo

- 1 carrot, cut into 1-inch chunks
- 1/4 cup chopped celery (pale inner stalks and leaves)
- 1 small white onion, chopped
- 2 cups dry Italian white wine
- 1 sprig rosemary (about 4 inches long)
- 5 sprigs thyme (about 4 inches long)
- 6 garlic cloves
- 2 pounds boneless lamb stew meat, preferably from the neck, shoulder, shank, and/or breast, cut into 1 1/2-inch pieces
- 2 tablespoons all-purpose flour
- Kosher or sea salt and freshly cracked black pepper
- 1/4 cup extra virgin olive oil
- 6 anchovy fillets
- 1 cup tomato puree (made from processing drained canned peeled whole tomatoes or peeled fresh whole tomatoes)
- 3 cups Homemade Kitchen Broth (page 70) or unsalted beef or chicken stock
- 1 1/2 cups English peas (about 1 1/2 pounds in the pod) or 1 1/2 cups chopped asparagus spears
- Polenta (page 15)

Serves 4 as a main course, 8 to 10 as a first course

We call this lamb sugo *(sauce in Italian), but it is so rich and hearty that it is almost a stew. It's best when made with the tougher cuts of lamb because, during the braising, the tendons and sinew melt down, leaving silky, gelatinous meat. Using these cuts, which are sometimes considered undesirable, is also economical, and consistent with the way frugal Italian cooks always make the most of everything. White wine is used for braising rather than the traditional red, since the young spring lamb we use is more a white meat than a red meat.*

Present the sugo as an entrée on top of polenta with fresh green vegetables. This sauce could also be tossed with pappardelle or other pasta.

For a springtime dinner, start with Shaved Artichokes with Fava Beans and Parmesan (page 30). A good finish would be Rustic Nectarine and Berry Tart (page 248). Serve with a medium-bodied Zinfandel wine.

Place the carrots, celery, onion, meat, wine, rosemary, thyme, and garlic in a bowl large enough to hold the lamb pieces. Nestle the lamb into the marinade. Cover and refrigerate for at least 2 hours, or overnight.

Preheat the oven to 300°F.

Remove the lamb from the marinade. Strain the marinade through a sieve and reserve the liquid and the vegetables separately.

Toss the lamb with the flour to coat and season generously with salt and pepper. Heat 2 tablespoons of the olive oil in a large heavy ovenproof skillet or a Dutch oven over medium-high heat until it just begins to smoke. Add the lamb and brown on all sides, about 5 minutes on each side. Remove the lamb from the pan and set aside. Pour off the fat.

Add the remaining 2 tablespoons olive oil and the reserved vegetables to the pan, lower the heat to medium, and cook until the vegetables start to brown slightly, about 15 minutes. Add the anchovies, stirring until the anchovies melt into the vegetables. Add the reserved marinade, increase the heat to high, and reduce by half. Add the tomato puree and broth and bring to a simmer. Return the lamb to the pan and stir well. Taste for seasoning.

Place in the oven and cook, uncovered, until the meat is tender and beginning to fall apart, about 2 hours. Stir occasionally to make sure the meat is cooking evenly.

Remove the pan from the oven. Skim off any visible fat from the sauce. Check for seasoning. Add the peas or asparagus and simmer over medium heat on top of the stove until the vegetables are meltingly tender, about 15 minutes. Serve over the polenta.

Roasted Pork Loin with White Beans, Artichokes, and Salsa Verde

For the Brine

½ gallon whole milk

¼ cup plus 2 tablespoons kosher or sea salt

1 white onion, sliced into ½-inch-thick rings

1 bunch sage

1 teaspoon freshly cracked black pepper

Pinch of ground allspice

One 4-pound pork loin roast, boned

¼ cup extra virgin olive oil

6 medium artichokes, trimmed (see page 31)

1 garlic clove, crushed

4 sprigs thyme

1 cup dry Italian white wine

7½ cups cooked White Beans (page 16)

Kosher or sea salt and freshly cracked black pepper

Double recipe salsa verde (page 49)

Serves 8 to 10

This is a great party dish, since most of the ingredients can be prepared ahead of time. Brining, or soaking the meat in a seasoned liquid, is an age-old preserving and flavoring technique. It brings out the intrinsic goodness of meats. Ever since pork became the "other white meat," it has needed a boost in the flavor department. Brining does just that.

If you would like to serve the pork with something other than the beans, artichokes, and salsa described here, please do. Make the beans before you cook the pork. Start with Crostini of Figs, Crescenza, and Prosciutto (page 28). Pour a Chianti Classico from the '97 vintage or a Riserva from the '95.

For the Brine

Combine the milk, salt, onion, sage, pepper, and allspice in a large glass or ceramic bowl and mix well. Add the pork loin, weight it down with a smaller heavy bowl so it stays submerged, cover, and refrigerate for 2 to 4 days, turning once a day.

Preheat the oven to 375°F. Remove the pork from the brine, pat dry, and place in a roasting pan. Roast for 45 minutes or until the thermometer reads 140°F when inserted in the thickest spot on the loin.

Meanwhile, heat the olive oil in a heavy skillet over medium heat. Add the artichokes, garlic, thyme, wine, and ½ cup water. Bring to a simmer and cook until the artichokes are tender when pierced with a fork, about 35 minutes. If the liquid evaporates, add more water. Remove the artichokes from the skillet and keep warm. Pour the beans into a roasting pan large enough to hold them, the artichokes, and the meat. Season with salt and pepper to taste. Swirl in half of the salsa verde and fold in the artichokes.

When the meat has cooked for 45 minutes, remove it from the oven and place it on top of the beans and artichokes. Pour about ¼ cup of the roasting juices over the meat and beans. Roast the meat for 30 minutes longer. The meat is done when the meat thermometer reads 160° to 170°F. Remove it from the oven and let it rest for about 10 minutes before carving. Carve the meat into ½- to 1-inch slices. Pour the beans and the artichokes into a warm serving platter and arrange the sliced meat on top. Spoon the remaining salsa verde on top and serve.

Brining

I love to brine fowl, rabbit, and pork. Somewhere along the line the great taste of these meats has slipped away. They all need help in the flavor department. Brining is just the thing to restore it. Brining is a technique that is really paying off at Rose Pistola and at our caffè called Rose. We get the most amazing compliments on all our dishes that are brined. Guests have been asking since we opened, "Why does this simple meat or chicken taste so good?"

Brining is an age-old preserving technique. In the case of meat and poultry, it imparts improved flavor to the final dish, bringing out the intrinsic goodness of the meat or fowl. Ever since pork became "the other white meat," it really has little meaty taste at all. Brining brings out the good taste of meats and makes them taste like they are supposed to.

Start the brining process two hours to two or three days before you plan to cook the pork, chicken, or rabbit. It takes a little getting used to—mainly to planning ahead. I guarantee that your guests will be absolutely amazed at the spectacular taste of the brined product.

See specific recipes for brining techniques. Basically, with chicken and other fowl use this simple ratio of salt to water. One tablespoon salt to one cup water. The water should be warm so that the salt will dissolve, but the water should be cooled when the bird is submerged in it. If you buy a chicken or a few breasts and find that you are not going to use them right away, throw them in a brine and refrigerate it for up to four days. Brining will preserve them and improve their flavor.

We brine absolutely all our pork at Rose Pistola, because it makes all the difference in the world to the end product. The possibilities of milk brine such as we use for Roasted Pork Loin with White Beans, Artichokes, and Salsa Verde (page 186) are appealing in several ways. Here, as the milk brine soaks and marinates the meat, it actually transforms the flavor of the pork. It does the same with lean, delectable rabbit. In both cases the flavor of the milk enhances the meat's delicacy, while its lactic acid tenderizes the flesh. The salt acts as a conductor in the brine, bringing the milk into the flesh, all the while keeping the meat from drying out when it is cooked.

The same type of brine is used to marinate and brine our Fried Milk-Brined Rabbit and Roasted Morel Salad (page 194). The milk does wonders to the fried morsels, caramelizing them in the sweet milk residue as they fry.

For decades, Bruno Iacopi's butcher shop was the culinary heart of North Beach. Six days a week, Mr. Iacopi stood below dangling branches of fresh rosemary, hanging prosciuttos, and fresh and dried sausages. There, moving as gracefully as an operatic tenor, he aged his meats, painstakingly prepared roasts, and dispensed such precise cooking instructions that chefs and housewives lived and cooked by his words.

In Italian villages even today, the butcher's role is ambassadorial. He is often one of the community's most powerful citizens, the one who keeps track of the comings and goings of the villagers and rewards the most worthy with the best meat. If you want to eat well, you'd better be nice to the butcher—and to everyone else for that matter, for he'll hear of your deeds.

North Beach is really just a village, and Bruno Iacopi was its culinary godfather from 1940 to 1978. His heart was warm and his eminence imposing; he had a special soft spot in his big heart for the women of the neighborhood. In the store, at the corner of Union Street and Grant Avenue, he filled orders, chatted up clients, and let the best-looking women watch him make sausages on Friday mornings.

Before the advent of cooking schools, many housewives and other cooks came to Mr. Iacopi for recipes and techniques that their own mothers had failed to pass on. They would not dream of giving a dinner party without consulting him first. Those were the days when meat was at the center of every plate. And nobody knew meat like Bruno Iacopi.

No order was too big for him. He did not blink an eye if an order came in for capretto *(baby goat) for two thousand (as it often did from Francis Ford Coppola). He would explain to you exactly how to barbecue it, basting it with olive oil, wine vinegar, lemon juice, garlic, and rosemary just before it came off the grill. He'd give you simple directions for cooking sausage and polenta, roasting a stuffed shoulder of veal, or preparing vitello tonnato—that is, if he liked you. One of his favorite customers had a vegetarian boyfriend, whom Mr. Iacopi loathed. He did not trust people who did not eat meat.*

He was rhapsodic about California cheeses, especially Monterey Jack. He always had a big ripe square of soft teleme on the edge of his counter next to big wheels of dried Jack, their rinds crusted with a mixture of powdered chocolate, black pepper, and olive oil.

And what would he do with his favorite cheese? "Well," according to North Beach food archivist and restaurateur Mary Etta Moose, "he made golden sandwiches. His favorite time of the year was May," she explains, "because that was when the flavor of the teleme peaked. This was due, he'd explain, to a certain flower that the cows eat only in the late spring. When the season was right, Bruno would split a sheet of hot-from-the-oven focaccia, wedge a softened slab of ripe teleme inside, wrap the whole thing in foil, and press it to his ample chest for a few minutes while the cheese melted. All the while, his eyes would shine as if he were concealing a surprise."

Hazelnut Coteghino with Lentils

For the Coteghino

1 small white onion, finely diced
2 tablespoons extra virgin olive oil
2 large eggs, lightly beaten
1¼ teaspoons kosher or sea salt
¼ teaspoon freshly ground white pepper
2 teaspoons chopped fresh sage, or 1 teaspoon dried
Pinch of ground cloves
1 small garlic clove, finely chopped
1¼ pounds pork shoulder butt, cut into ½-inch cubes
⅓ pound pancetta, cut into ½-inch cubes
½ cup hazelnuts, toasted and peeled (see Note)

Serves 4 (makes 1 large sausage, about 10 inches long and 3 inches in diameter)

I love to make sausages, and North Beach has a tradition of making some of the world's great dried sausages, including salami and coppa. But that sort of sausage making is too involved and complicated to be much fun for home cooks. This coteghino, or boiling sausage, on the other hand, is just the sort of dish that you can shop for, prepare, cook, and serve in the course of a few hours. If you've never made sausage, please try this. It is quite easy, as you do all of the grinding in a food processor, without a sausage grinder and stuffer or sausage skins. The trick is to add small batches of the meat mixture to the food processor. This sausage is fresh, as opposed to dried or smoked or aged. If you choose to make it a day or so before serving, that's fine; in fact, its flavor will only deepen in the refrigerator.

Lentils and sausage are a traditional North Beach dish—delicious, inexpensive, and comforting. We use French lentilles du Puy, or green lentils, because they are the best, but use what is available if you cannot find them. The flavors of pork, lentils, and hazelnuts seem to have been made for each other. Hazelnuts bring out a wonderful, rich nuttiness in pork. The lentils bring the dish together. If you choose not to make the coteghino, buy a 1½- to 2-pound coteghino from an Italian market and proceed with the recipe.

Serve this with Salad of Mushrooms, Endive, and Parmesan (page 73) and some good crusty bread. Pour a medium-bodied Valpolicella wine.

For the Coteghino

In a small sauté pan or saucepan, sauté the onion in the olive oil over medium-high heat until translucent, about 5 minutes. Transfer to a bowl and chill in the refrigerator while you assemble the other ingredients.

Beat together the eggs, salt, white pepper, sage, cloves, and garlic in a large bowl. Add the cooled onions. Add the meat, pancetta, and hazelnuts and toss together until the ingredients are evenly distributed.

Pulse the mixture in the food processor, a small handful at a time, until coarsely chopped (about ⅙-inch pieces). The mixture will roughly form a ball in the processor. Work quickly to keep the mixture as cold as possible, and as you finish each batch, transfer it to a bowl in the refrigerator. When all the mixture is chopped, fold the batches together so the ingredients are evenly distributed.

Lay a piece of aluminum foil about 12 inches by 23 inches on a work surface. Place the sausage mixture along one long side of the foil and flatten it into a rectangle about 6 inches by 16 inches. Using the foil to help shape the sausage, roll it up into a log shape; it should look like a long salami. Twist the ends of the foil like a Tootsie Roll to seal them. (At this point, you can refrigerate the foil-wrapped sausage for up to 2 days. The flavor develops considerably if allowed to mellow for at least 24 hours.)

Place the foil-wrapped sausage in a pot and fill with water. Bring the water to a boil, reduce the heat to barely simmering, and poach the sausage for about 1½ hours, until it reaches an internal temperature of 150°F. (A quick way to test for doneness is to insert a thin knife into the center of the meat, through the foil, let the knife remain in the meat for about 30 seconds, and then remove the knife and immediately touch the flat side of the tip to the inside of your wrist or your upper lip; if the knife feels hot, the sausage is done.)

For the Lentils

- 2 tablespoons extra virgin olive oil
- 1 small white onion, chopped
- 1 small garlic clove, chopped
- 1 sprig rosemary
- 1 carrot, chopped
- 3 cups lentils, picked over and rinsed
- 2 dried porcini, soaked in water for 30 minutes
- 1 cup red wine
- Kosher or sea salt

For the Lentils

Heat the olive oil in a large saucepan over medium heat. Add the onion, garlic, rosemary, and carrot. When the onion becomes translucent, add the lentils, porcini, red wine, and just enough water to cover the lentils. Bring to a simmer, add salt to taste, and simmer gently until the lentils are tender but still firm, about 20 minutes.

To serve, spread the lentils on a warm platter. Remove the coteghino from the foil, slice into ½-inch slices, and arrange on top of the lentils.

Note

To peel hazelnuts with ease, toast them for a minute or two on top of the stove in a dry hot pan. Put them into a clean kitchen towel and rub them abrasively with another kitchen towel placed on top of them to loosen the skins. Pour the nuts into a metal colander and shake them around. Most of the skin will come off and the hazelnuts will be ready to use.

Braised Rabbit with Artichokes and Beans

1 rabbit (about 2½ pounds), cut into 8 pieces
2 cups (½ bottle) dry Italian white wine
2 tablespoons extra virgin olive oil
Kosher or sea salt and freshly cracked black pepper
1 large white onion, finely chopped
2 garlic cloves, bruised
¼ cup chopped flat-leaf parsley
4 sprigs marjoram
2 tablespoons anchovy paste
4 cups cooked beans, such as Christmas limas, cranberry beans, or cannellini beans (see page 16; save some of the cooking water), or 3 cups fresh shell beans
2 large artichokes, trimmed to hearts and stems (see page 31)
Dash of Agruamato (lemon olive oil), or "O" lemon oil, optional

Serves 4

Since rabbit is low in cholesterol and fat, it's surprising that it isn't more popular with home cooks. It is delicious, good for you, easy to cook, and quite versatile, as it both braises and fries well. Give it a try if you have not already. This one-pot meal requires little attention once it's put together, which makes it perfect dinner party fare.

This simple dish is at its best when fresh shell beans are in season (see page 85 on shell beans). Save the bean cooking water for use in braising. Artichokes are also at their peak then, and plump rabbits are readily available.

Serve with Crostini of Figs, Crescenza, and Prosciutto (page 28) as an antipasto and Farmers' Market Peach Ice Cream (page 238) for dessert. A medium-style Valpolicella or a full-flavored Amarone wine is nice with this.

Marinate the rabbit in the wine for at least an hour in a bowl in the refrigerator. (You can do this while you are cooking dried beans, if you are using them.)

Preheat the oven to 325°F.

Heat the olive oil in a large heavy ovenproof skillet over medium-high heat. Remove the rabbit from the wine (reserve the wine) and pat the rabbit pieces dry. Season the rabbit generously with salt and pepper, add to the pan, and brown thoroughly on both sides, about 10 minutes. Remove the rabbit and set aside.

Add the onion to the skillet and sauté over medium heat until it becomes translucent, about 5 minutes. Add the garlic, parsley, marjoram, and anchovy paste and cook until the parsley sizzles and the garlic is fragrant, about 3 minutes. Gently toss in the beans, the artichoke hearts, and the wine used to marinate the rabbit. Place the rabbit on top of the bean and artichoke mixture and push the pieces down into the beans so they braise evenly.

Cover the pan and place it in the oven to braise until the rabbit is meltingly tender, 1½ to 2 hours. Turn the rabbit pieces from time to time. Should the beans begin to dry out, add some water, reserved bean cooking liquid, or Homemade Kitchen Broth (page 70).

Remove the rabbit from the oven and sprinkle a few drops of lemon olive oil over the top if desired. Taste for seasoning and serve.

Since 1895, Molinari Delicatessen has served great salami, coteghino, olive oils, cheeses, and pastas.

Fried Milk-Brined Rabbit and Roasted Morel Salad

For Brining the Rabbit

1 white onion, sliced into ½-inch-thick rings
1 quart whole milk
3 tablespoons kosher or sea salt
1 teaspoon freshly cracked black pepper
¼ teaspoon ground allspice
1 bunch sage
1 medium rabbit (about 2½ pounds), meat cut from the bones into roughly 1½-inch chunks (the pieces will be irregularly shaped)

3 tablespoons extra virgin olive oil
5 shallots, cut lengthwise in half
½ pound morels, rinsed and halved lengthwise if large, or other wild or flavorful fresh mushrooms, cleaned
1 garlic clove, crushed
1 sprig rosemary
Kosher or sea salt and freshly cracked black pepper
1½ cups fava beans (see page 195)
2 tablespoons red wine vinegar
4 cups olive oil, for deep-frying
2 bunches baby dandelion greens or assorted bitter and sweet greens (about 4 cups)
½ cup herb sprigs, such as flat-leaf parsley, chopped chives, chervil, and/or borage

Serves 4 as a main course, 6 as a first course

The rabbit is marinated in a milk brine to achieve a succulent, flavorful dish. The flavor of the milk itself enhances the meat's delicacy, while its lactic acid tenderizes the flesh. The milk that is absorbed by the flesh during the brining process also keeps the lean meat from drying out when it is cooked. And finally, as the rabbit is fried, the milk brine caramelizes on the surface of the rabbit, creating a nutty, rich crust. If morels are unavailable, use other mushrooms of your choice.

Start with Swordfish Brochettes with Salsa Verde (page 49). Serve with a Dolcetto wine.

For Brining the Rabbit

Lay the onion slices in a large dry nonstick sauté pan and cook over medium-high heat until a deep caramel brown on one side, 6 to 8 minutes. Turn and brown on the other side, another 6 to 8 minutes. Transfer the onions to a large bowl and stir in the milk, salt, pepper, allspice, and sage. Add the rabbit, cover, and refrigerate for at least 2 hours, or overnight.

Preheat the oven to 550°F (or the highest setting).

Combine 1 tablespoon of the olive oil, the shallots, morels, garlic, and rosemary in a small baking pan. Season with salt and pepper to taste and toss to coat evenly. Roast until the morels and shallots are slightly caramelized, about 20 minutes. (The amount of roasting time will depend on the moisture in the mushrooms.) Remove the garlic and rosemary, place the shallots and morels in a salad bowl, and let cool.

Add the fava beans to the salad bowl. Add the vinegar and toss, adding the remaining 2 tablespoons olive oil. Season to taste with salt and pepper. Set aside.

To fry the rabbit, lift the rabbit pieces from the brine, discard the brine, and pat the rabbit dry. Heat the 4 cups olive oil to 350°F in a deep heavy pot. Carefully add the rabbit pieces to the hot oil and fry until golden brown and cooked through, about 5 minutes. Remove with a slotted spoon to paper towels to drain briefly.

To serve, add the rabbit to the salad. Toss, add the salad greens and herbs, and toss again. Divide among four plates.

Preparing Fava Beans

One pound of fresh favas in the shell will render about one cup of peeled fava beans. Choose firm, bright green pods. Remove the beans as you would peas from a pod. Drop them into a pot of boiling water for one minute. Drain and plunge them into ice water to stop the cooking, to keep them bright green, and to aid in the peeling of the skins. After draining again, use your thumb and forefinger to carefully slip the skin off each fava bean. If the beans are very small and tender, you need not peel them.

Roast Chicken with Garlic

¼ cup plus 2 tablespoons kosher or sea salt
1 chicken (3 to 3½ pounds)
1 large bunch thyme
1 lemon, washed and pierced all over with a knife
1 to 2 tablespoons unsalted butter
1 tablespoon extra virgin olive oil
8 bulbs spring garlic, including tops, or 4 garlic bulbs, pointed tops cut off
¼ cup Cognac
Freshly cracked black pepper

Serves 4

Nothing is better than a great roast chicken, and the presence of young, green garlic makes it even better. Use whole garlic heads when spring garlic is unavailable.

Most of the United States' crop of garlic comes from near the Bay Area. When you shop for garlic, look for firm, tight heads, preferably with small cloves. Smell the garlic—it should smell clean and fresh. Beware, because there is quite a bit of inferior garlic from China on the market.

Serve with Tuna Carpaccio with Slivered Artichokes (page 56) and Asparagus Bread Pudding (page 210), and pour a full-bodied Pinot Noir.

Mix together the salt and 6 cups warm water in a bowl large enough to hold the chicken, stirring until the salt dissolves. Refrigerate or let the water cool completely at room temperature.

Remove any excess fat from the chicken. Place the chicken in the cooled salted water and place another water-filled bowl on top to keep the chicken submerged in the brine. If more liquid is needed to cover the chicken, add more water and salt at a ratio of 1 tablespoon salt to 1 cup water. Cover and refrigerate for at least 2 hours, overnight, or up to 2 days.

Preheat the oven to 425°F. Remove the chicken from the brine and pat completely dry. Put the thyme and lemon inside the cavity of the bird. Heat a large heavy ovenproof skillet over medium-high heat. Add 1 tablespoon butter and the olive oil. When the butter stops sizzling and turns brown, place the chicken in the skillet, breast side down, and sauté, shaking the skillet gently back and forth so that the skin does not stick, until the breast side of the chicken is well browned. Turn the bird on one side and brown well, then turn and brown on the opposite side.

Turn the bird breast side up, scatter the garlic around the chicken, and put it in the oven. Roast for 20 minutes, then turn breast side down and continue roasting for another 15 minutes, or until the juices that run clear when the thigh is pierced. Transfer the chicken to a warmed serving platter, remove and set aside the lemon, and cut the chicken into quarters.

Pour any fat out of the skillet. Cut the lemon in half, squeeze the juice into the skillet, and add any juices that have run off the chicken and the Cognac, scraping any brown bits from the bottom of the skillet. Reduce the liquid in the pan by half and swirl in 1 tablespoon butter if desired. Pour the sauce over the chicken and serve with cracked pepper.

Chicken Under a Brick

¼ cup plus 2 tablespoons kosher or sea salt
1 chicken (2½ to 3 pounds), cut in half and preferably boned, or 1 pound boneless, skin-on chicken breasts and/or thighs
3 tablespoons extra virgin olive oil
Freshly cracked black pepper
3 garlic cloves, thinly sliced
2 large sprigs rosemary
Lemon wedges

Serves 4

Perfectly cooked chicken is all about crisp brown skin and juicy meat. Cooking chicken under a weight is one of the easiest ways to attain that, particularly if the chicken has been brined, which lets you cook it until the juices run clear without drying the meat out. At Rose Pistola, we do this dish on a cast-iron griddle over a charcoal fire, so it picks up a slight smoky flavor. At home, prepare the chicken on the stove in a cast-iron skillet, or outdoors over a charcoal fire.

I like to make this recipe with a boneless half-chicken. If you're not comfortable boning a half-chicken yourself, ask your butcher to do it for you. You also can use bone-in half-chickens, or boneless skin-on chicken breasts or thighs.

While we use a ceramic fire brick to do this at the restaurant, I don't have a brick lying around my kitchen at home, so I use another heavy skillet or even a pot partially filled with water as a weight. You could also use a building brick or a large flat stone wrapped in foil.

Serve the chicken with Fried Potatoes with Parsley and Garlic (page 215) and Tomato Salad with Bottarga or Anchovies (page 82), with a Barbera, Michelle Chiarlo, 1997, wine.

Mix together the salt and 6 cups warm water in a bowl large enough to hold the chicken, stirring until the salt dissolves. Refrigerate or let cool completely at room temperature.

Remove any excess fat from the chicken. Place the chicken in the cooled salted water and place another water-filled bowl on top to keep the chicken submerged in the brine. If more liquid is needed to cover the chicken, add more water and salt at a ratio of 1 tablespoon salt to 1 cup water. Cover and refrigerate for at least 2 hours, overnight, or up to 2 days. Remove the chicken from the brine and pat completely dry.

If using a charcoal or wood fire, build a hot fire. When the coals are hot, put a cast-iron griddle or skillet on the grill to preheat. Or use a gas grill or a heavy skillet on the stovetop. If using the stovetop, preheat a cast-iron griddle or skillet over medium-high heat until drops of water dance on the surface.

Brush the chicken with the olive oil and season generously on the skin side with pepper. Press the garlic slices and rosemary sprigs on the skin. Carefully flip the chicken and place it, skin and rosemary side down, on the griddle and place a weight on top of the meat. If using the stovetop, lower the heat to medium. Cook until the skin is a deep golden brown and all of its fat is rendered out, about 6 minutes (you want the skin to crisp and brown just like a piece of bacon would). When the skin is sufficiently cooked, remove the weight, pour off any fat from the griddle, and turn the chicken cut side down. Replace the weight and continue to cook the chicken until the juices run clear, about 5 minutes more. Remove the weight and turn the chicken skin side down for 1 minute more. If you are using a bone-in chicken part, allow it to cook for 2 to 3 additional minutes. Serve the chicken with lemon wedges.

Braised Chicken with Turnips, Potatoes, and Carrots

- 2 ounces pancetta, cut into ¼ by 1-inch strips
- 1 tablespoon extra virgin olive oil
- 1 garlic clove, bruised
- 1 sprig rosemary (about 6 inches long)
- 1 bunch kale, trimmed and coarsely chopped
- 1 bunch baby turnips, greens removed and chopped, turnips halved
- 2 large carrots, peeled and cut into chunks
- 4 Yellow Finn potatoes, peeled and quartered
- Kosher or sea salt
- 1 large chicken (3 to 4 pounds), quartered
- Freshly cracked black pepper
- 2 cups (½ bottle) dry red or white wine

Serves 4

This is one of those dishes that evolved as a result of a trip to the market when I was very hungry and in the mood to cook something easy and all in one pot. It was the dead of winter and the produce section was not terribly inspiring, but there were beautiful baby turnips with their greens, potatoes, kale, and dark orange carrots. While this recipe should be enough for four, it was so good that two of us ate it all up that night. For the cooking wine, in the spirit of frugal North Beach cooks, you can use half a bottle of leftover wine—red or white, whatever you have.

In a large heavy casserole, cook the pancetta in the olive oil over medium-high heat until it renders its fat. Add the garlic and rosemary and cook until fragrant. Add the kale, turnips, turnip greens, carrots, and potatoes. Season with salt to taste and sauté for about 5 minutes.

Generously season the chicken with salt and pepper. Pour the wine over the vegetables and reduce by one-third. Put the chicken legs and thigh quarters on top of the vegetables, reduce the heat to low, tightly cover, and cook for 5 minutes. Add the chicken breasts, cover, and continue to cook until the chicken is tender and the juices run clear, about 35 minutes more.

Pour the broth off the vegetables and retain. Skim off any fat. Season to taste. With a slotted spoon, arrange the vegetables on a serving platter and place the chicken on top. Spoon the broth (without the fat) over all.

Roast Sage-Stuffed Quail with Walnut Sauce

Nothing says fall to me quite like game birds. If the sauce here sounds heavy, don't be fooled. It is based on an old Italian sauce technique where bread and nuts are pounded together and boiled in a broth. The result is light, aromatic, and perfect for delicate quail. You could cook chicken in the same way, just varying the cooking time accordingly. And, of course, the recipe can be doubled.

Serve on top of Polenta (page15) or with a green salad. Pour a Carneros Pinot Noir, Saintsbury, 1997.

4 quail
12 sage leaves
Kosher or sea salt and freshly cracked black pepper
2 tablespoons extra virgin olive oil, plus extra for rubbing the quail
1 white onion, cut lengthwise in half and then into thin half-moon slices
1 sprig rosemary
1 teaspoon kosher or coarse sea salt
1 garlic clove
¼ cup walnuts
¼ cup Bread Crumbs (page 9)
1 cup dry Italian white wine
1 cup Homemade Kitchen Broth (page 70) or chicken broth
½ recipe Polenta, if using

Serves 2

Preheat the oven to 500°F.

Gently pull up the skin on the wing end of either side of the breast of each quail and stuff a sage leaf under the skin. Season each quail with salt and pepper and rub with olive oil. For each quail, make a tiny slit in the tendon of one of the legs and stick the other leg into it so the legs will be self-trussed.

In a heavy ovenproof skillet, heat the olive oil over high heat. Add the quail breast side down and brown well. Remove from the heat.

Scatter the onion and rosemary in the browning skillet. Place the quail breast side up and roast for about 15 minutes, or until the breasts are firm to the touch.

Meanwhile, make the walnut sauce: In a mortar or a food processor, pound or pulse the 1 teaspoon salt, the remaining 4 sage leaves, the garlic, walnuts, and bread crumbs.

Pour the wine into a medium saucepan and reduce over high heat to ¼ cup. Add the broth and bring it to a rolling simmer. Stir in the walnut mixture and whisk as it thickens. Simmer for 5 minutes. Grind a generous amount of black pepper into the sauce.

To serve, put the quail and onions on top of the polenta or on a platter and pour the sauce over.

Roast Guinea Fowl with Pancetta

1 guinea fowl or chicken (2½ to 3 pounds) with giblets, neck, liver, and heart
4 tablespoons extra virgin olive oil
2 ounces pancetta, diced, plus 4 slices pancetta
1 medium carrot, diced
1 celery stalk, diced
1 small sprig rosemary, plus a few leaves
1 cup dry Italian white wine
Homemade Kitchen Broth (page 70), optional
Kosher or sea salt and freshly cracked black pepper
3 tablespoons unsalted butter
12 baby carrots, peeled
12 baby turnips, halved
½ large fennel bulb, sliced
12 chestnuts, roasted, shelled, and peeled (see page 218)
⅓ pound mushrooms, preferably chanterelles, washed and trimmed
1 sprig thyme
1 teaspoon thyme
1 garlic clove
2 tablespoons Cognac
2 tablespoons fresh Bread Crumbs (page 9)

Serves 4

The combination of roast chestnuts, caramelized vegetables, and the deep, concentrated sauce made from the trimmings, giblets, and neck of the guinea fowl, a game bird, makes for a spectacular cold-weather dish.

Commercially raised guinea fowl are becoming increasingly available, and they have both a richer flavor and a denser, meatier texture than chicken. If guinea fowl is unavailable, a chicken of the same size will do nicely. In either case, make sure your butcher gives you the giblets and the neck.

For a great fall or winter meal, start with Pappardelle with Broccoli Rabe and Mushrooms (page 101) and serve Caramelized Pear and Almond Tart (page 246) for dessert. A medium-bodied Zinfandel or Merlot would be good with this.

Cut the wing tips off the bird. Chop the wing tips, neck, and gizzards into ½-inch pieces. Combine 1 tablespoon of the olive oil with the diced pancetta in a medium saucepan over medium-high heat. Add the chopped trimmings, carrot, celery, and rosemary. Cook for 10 minutes, stirring occasionally, until the juices from the meat reduce to a deep golden brown glaze on the bottom of the pan. Add the wine and increase the heat to high. Scrape up any browned bits from the bottom of the pan and reduce until about 2 tablespoons of wine remain, 5 to 10 minutes. Add water or broth to cover. Lower the heat to a bare simmer, skim off any fat, and very slowly let the sauce reduce by one-half, about 45 minutes, over low heat.

Strain the resulting broth through a fine-mesh sieve, pushing on the solids to extract as much liquid as possible. Pour the broth into a large glass measuring cup, let it settle, and skim off the fat. Add more water as needed to make 1¼ cups. Transfer to a saucepan and set aside.

Preheat the oven to 400°F.

Season the guinea fowl generously with salt and pepper inside and out. Heat a large heavy ovenproof skillet over medium-high heat. Add 1 tablespoon of the butter and 1 tablespoon olive oil. When the butter stops sizzling and turns brown, add the guinea fowl, breast side down, and sauté, shaking the skillet gently back and forth so that the skin does not stick, until the breast side of the fowl is well browned. Turn the bird on its side and brown well. Then turn and brown on the opposite side.

Turn the bird (browned breast side is up), and put it in the oven. Roast for 20 minutes. Turn breast side down and continue roasting for another 15 minutes, or until the juices run clear when the thigh is pierced with a skewer. When you turn the bird the final time, put the remaining pancetta slices on a baking sheet and bake in the oven alongside the bird until they are crisp, about 10 minutes. Remove the pancetta slices and pat dry.

Meanwhile, cook the vegetables: Heat the remaining 2 tablespoons butter in a heavy skillet over medium-high heat. Add the carrots, turnips (cut side down), fennel, and chestnuts. Cook until the vegetables start to brown, about 7 minutes, then add ¼ cup water. As the water evaporates and the vegetables caramelize, splash in more as necessary to keep the vegetables from burning. After a few more minutes, throw in the mushrooms and the thyme sprig. Add another splash of water and cook until all the vegetables are golden and tender. Season with salt and pepper. Set aside and keep warm.

To finish the sauce, combine the guinea fowl liver, heart, ½ teaspoon salt, the garlic, rosemary leaves, thyme, Cognac, and bread crumbs in a food processor to make a paste. Bring the reserved broth to a boil in the saucepan and stir in the paste. Simmer for 5 to 8 minutes.

When the fowl is done, remove it from the oven and cut it into quarters. Pour off any accumulated fat from the roasting pan and add the sauce to the roasting pan, scraping up any brown bits off the bottom of the pan. Place the vegetables on a serving platter with the quartered bird, pour the sauce over it, and place the pancetta slices on top.

Roasted Squab with Vegetable Ragout

Serves 4

4 squab (about 1 pound each), with livers, gizzards, and heart
⅓ pound pancetta, coarsely chopped
1 small carrot, chopped
1 inner celery stalk with leaves, chopped
2 garlic cloves, bruised
1 sprig rosemary (about 6 inches long)
1 cup dry Italian white wine
¼ cup tomato puree (made from processing drained canned peeled whole tomatoes or peeled fresh whole tomatoes)
1 tablespoon extra virgin olive oil
Kosher or sea salt and freshly cracked black pepper

Squab, a slightly livery, gamy, commercially raised fowl, is a good alternative to the usual chicken or duck. In this dish, using the frugal techniques of the North Beach home cook, we coax out the maximum flavor from the squab trimmings and the vegetables to make the sauce. The technique is a home alternative for what takes hours to achieve with restaurant demi-glace sauces, and the result is even better.

Make every effort to get fresh squab for this dish; frozen squab tends to be tough. As an alternative, use Cornish game hens or poussin. Cook squab to medium-rare so that the juices are still pink, and the meat rosy.

Start with Sautéed Penne with Mussels (page 102) and finish with Zuppa Inglese with Fresh Cherries (page 240). Pour a young or mature Barbaresco or a full-bodied Nebbiolo from the Langhe.

Preheat the oven to 500°F.

To prepare the squab, trim off the wing tips and the neck and feet if still attached. Coarsely chop the trimmings, livers, gizzards, and hearts into about ½-inch pieces. Combine the chopped trimmings, the pancetta, carrot, celery, garlic, and rosemary in a medium sauté pan and cook over medium heat until the trimmings and the vegetables release their juices and a bubbling liquid develops, about 15 minutes. Increase the heat to medium-high and boil, stirring occasionally, until the juices have completely evaporated and a medium-brown glaze develops on the bottom of the pan, about 15 minutes longer.

Pour off any fat and add the wine, scraping up the brown bits from the bottom of the pan. Reduce the wine by half. Add the tomato puree and enough water to cover and bring to a simmer. Let simmer gently until reduced by half, about 40 minutes. By this time, the carrots should be falling apart and the meat from the squab trimmings should have loosened from the bones.

Strain the mixture through a fine-mesh sieve, pressing on the solids to extract as much juice as possible. Skim any fat off the top and set aside.

Meanwhile, rub the squab with the olive oil and season with salt and pepper.

For the Ragout

Place the pancetta, potatoes, garlic cloves, onions, carrots, artichoke, and rosemary in a medium oval roasting pan, add 1 tablespoon of the olive oil, and toss to coat evenly with the olive oil. Place the squab on top of the vegetables, breast side up, and roast until the skin is crusty and brown but the meat is still pink, about 35 minutes.

While the squab roast, in a small heavy casserole with a tight-fitting lid, combine the asparagus, fava beans, peas, a pinch of salt, 1 tablespoon water, and the remaining 1 tablespoon olive oil. Cook, tightly covered, over low heat for about 20 minutes. Add the mushrooms and cook for 10 more minutes. Remove from the heat, uncover, and set aside.

To serve, remove the roasting pan from the oven. Lift the vegetables out with a slotted spoon and lift out the squab. Set aside. Spoon off any fat. Pour the reserved squab sauce into the pan and scrape up any brown crusty bits on the bottom of the pan. Then add the roasted vegetables and the asparagus mixture to the pan and warm briefly on top of the stove. Season to taste with salt and pepper. Cut the squab in half lengthwise and pour the sauce and vegetables around the bird. Serve from the roasting pan.

For the Ragout

2 ounces pancetta, cut into 1½ by ½-inch-thick batons
½ pound small Yellow Finn or fingerling potatoes
6 garlic cloves, unpeeled
8 small white onions or spring onions
4 small carrots, cut into 2-inch lengths
1 medium artichoke, trimmed (see page 31) and quartered lengthwise
1 sprig rosemary (about 3 inches long)
2 tablespoons extra virgin olive oil
½ cup trimmed asparagus (about ½ pound untrimmed)
½ cup fava beans (see page 195)
½ cup English peas (about ½ pound in the pod)
Kosher or sea salt
¼ pound wild mushrooms, such as hedgehog or chanterelle, cleaned
Freshly cracked black pepper

Using Anchovy for Backbone Flavor

Please don't be surprised or put off by the amount of anchovies in many of the dishes in this book, such as Braised Rabbit with Artichokes and Beans (page 192). The anchovy is used to provide a backbone flavor, a nice round nuance that goes so well with many main ingredients. It is not identifiable as anchovy in the finished dish. Using salted fish in this way goes back to Roman times in Italy.

Vegetables

When the immigrants first settled in San Francisco, they felt as if they had arrived in the Garden of Eden. Everything that grew well in Italy grew even better in California, because the soil and climate were perfectly suited to small- and grand-scale agriculture.

Many vegetables that are considered "fancy" today were actually once commonplace in North Beach. Fava beans, fennel, cardoons, baby artichokes, arugula, cavolo nero (black Tuscan kale), and others all grew in profusion in and around the Bay Area. The diaspora of wild fennel seed is evident everywhere. Feathery green shoots grow out of cracks in the sidewalk and in parks and overgrown backyards all over the Bay Area.

The Italians' early respect for vegetables came through loud and clear in the cooking of North Beach. Traditional cured meats such as prosciutto or pancetta are often added to enhance flavors, but the true star is always the vegetable itself, often perfumed with olive oil, garlic, and onions.

Fisherman's Wharf: Teamsters at the foot of Hyde Street haul rubble from the earthquake of 1906 to Aquatic Park. In the background are tall ships on San Francisco Bay. *Courtesy J. B. Monaco Photography.*

Griddled Artichokes and Potatoes

Cooking foods under a weight on a griddle is an effective way to get them crisp, brown, and cooked through very quickly. If you are not used to cooking on a griddle, you might want to begin with a non-stick griddle or grill pan.

This dish is great with Terrorized Steak (page 169). You could also try this alongside Chicken Under a Brick (page 198).

- 4 artichokes
- ¼ cup plus 2 tablespoons extra virgin olive oil
- 6 Yukon Gold, Yellow Finn, or small russet potatoes
- Kosher or sea salt and freshly cracked black pepper
- 2 garlic cloves, bruised
- 4 sprigs rosemary (3 to 4 inches long)
- 1 lemon, cut into wedges, optional

Serves 4

Trim the artichokes as directed on page 31, cutting off the stem even with the base and peeling the bottom with a small sharp knife. Pull open the leaves to reveal the center and pull out and discard the inner leaves. If the choke is prickly, scoop it out with a spoon. Immediately rub the artichokes with 2 tablespoons of the olive oil to prevent them from turning brown and bitter.

Have ready a foil-wrapped brick or bricks or a clean heavy weight such as a pan filled with water. They will be used to keep the artichokes flattened during cooking, so be sure your weight(s) will cover all of the flattened artichokes.

Working with one at a time, place each artichoke on a work surface and press down on the trimmed stem side with the palm of your hand so that the leaves will flatten out as much as possible.

Preheat a heavy griddle over medium heat. Cut the potatoes into rounds as thick as the flattened artichokes. Toss them both with the remaining ¼ cup olive oil and season them generously with salt and pepper. Arrange them on the griddle, clustering the artichokes as close together as possible so that the weight you have chosen will effectively keep them all flattened while they brown and become crisp.

Place the brick(s) or heavy weight(s) on the flattened artichokes and cook until both they and the potatoes are crisp and brown on one side. Remove the weight or weights from the cluster of artichokes and turn them and the potatoes, distributing the garlic and rosemary sprigs under most of the vegetables. Replace the weight(s) and continue to cook until the vegetables are soft throughout, 15 to 20 minutes. Serve. This rustic dish is good served with lemon wedges.

The first Italians in San Francisco arrived from northern Italy in the 1840s. They came with one of two intentions, to settle down and start a new life, or to earn money and return home. Once here, they relied on the work they knew best: farming and fishing. Some entered through Ellis Island, and early documents indicate that immigration officers tried to relocate the newcomers to a landscape that echoed that of their homeland. Since Genoa was strikingly similar to San Francisco (both hilly port towns with a mild climate and a raucous and bold sensibility), the Genovese farmers were directed to North Beach, while Tuscan farmers often ended up in nearby Sonoma County, with its Mediterranean-like agricultural conditions.

Many sections of San Francisco were suited to raising spinach, cauliflower, broccoli, brussels sprouts, and artichokes, and the newly arrived Italians were soon putting under the plow vast fields where today's Civic Center, Noe Valley, the Excelsior District, and outer Market Street now stand. The diet of all San Franciscans quickly felt the influence of the farmers' labor, and even Italian herbs such as fennel, rosemary, oregano, basil, marjoram, and thyme were swiftly adopted by local cooks. A cookbook of the era illustrates just how widely the Italian pantry was embraced: Written in Chinese for cooks who prepared food in the homes of the city's well-to-do, it includes information on Italian ingredients and recipes.

A rigid, Old Country regional hierarchy governed the growing and selling of the produce, and the Genovese were clearly in charge. The Lucchesi and other Tuscans ran most of the retail distribution, as well as the nearby boardinghouses and stables that were established expressly for the Genovese growers from the outlying farm regions.

In order to maintain control, the Genovese allowed the Tuscans to sell produce, but not to grow it. The one exception was fennel, used as both a vegetable and an herb.

Today, evidence of the Tuscans' early crops remains visible in the wild fennel that sprouts from cracks in the city pavement, in the parks, and in vacant lots. Horse beans, now known as fava or broad beans, were introduced to the local diet at the same time, acquiring their name because they were fed to the horses that pulled the produce wagons from the garden plots to the city center.

By the early 1870s, the hierarchy had crumbled and the giardinieri, *or farmers, were from a mix of regions. (Just ten years later, twelve hundred Genovese truck gardens were in operation.) They clustered on Sansome Street near the Embarcadero to sell their produce to the neighborhood housewives, the nearby ships' stewards, and restaurant and hotel proprietors. Today, the Ferry Plaza Farmers' Market, held on Saturdays on the Embarcadero, carries on that early tradition.*

Asparagus Bread Pudding

- 1 pound asparagus, trimmed and cut into 3-inch-long pieces
- ½ cup morels or other wild mushrooms, cleaned, optional
- Zest of 1 lemon, removed with a vegetable peeler and cut into thin strips
- ¼ teaspoon kosher or sea salt
- 2 tablespoons unsalted butter
- 1 leek (white part only), sliced lengthwise in half and cut into half-moons
- 1 garlic clove, bruised
- ½ loaf country bread, crust removed and cut into 1-inch cubes (about 3 cups)
- 8 basil leaves
- 2 tablespoons chopped flat-leaf parsley
- 1 tablespoon minced chives
- ½ cup cubed Italian Fontina
- Freshly cracked black pepper
- ¼ cup freshly grated Parmigiano-Reggiano

Serves 4

We bake bread every day at our restaurants and there are almost always some leftovers around. When that happens, I do as I learned from my frugal North Beach neighbors—I make bread pudding. This recipe displays one of the basic methods of vegetable cooking we use at Rose Pistola. We cook the asparagus in highly seasoned water and then use that water to moisten the leftover bread. The better the bread (even from leftovers), the better the pudding.

Vary this recipe throughout the year as different vegetables become available in your area. Try it with artichokes, peas, tomatoes, squash, greens, or mushrooms.

Serve with Roast Chicken with Garlic (page 196), followed by Zabaglione with Strawberries in Red Wine (page 232).

Preheat the oven to 450°F.

Place a large sauté pan over high heat. Add the asparagus, mushrooms, if using, the lemon zest, ¼ teaspoon salt, the butter, leek, and 1 cup water. Cook until the asparagus spears are tender, about 7 minutes. You should have about ½ cup liquid left in the pan.

Rub a wooden bowl with the garlic clove. Add the asparagus mixture, including the liquid, and toss together with the bread, basil, parsley, chives, and Fontina. Season to taste with salt and pepper. Put the mixture in a large gratin pan and sprinkle with the Parmigiano cheese.

Brown in the oven until the top is golden and crunchy, 10 to 15 minutes. Serve.

Fresh Corn Polenta

This fresh creamy corn dish can be used almost anywhere you use polenta. It is very simply made with fresh corn, cheese, and butter and is an ideal accompaniment for roasted, grilled, or stewed meats or seafood dishes.

8 ears very fresh sweet corn, shucked
1 sprig marjoram
3 tablespoons unsalted butter, cut into cubes
3 tablespoons freshly grated Parmigiano-Reggiano
Kosher or sea salt and freshly cracked black pepper

Serves 4

Cut the kernels off the corn, but do not cut too close to the cob. Working over a bowl, scrape each cob with the dull side of the blade of the knife to extract as much of the corn milk as possible.

Place the corn kernels and corn milk in a small heavy saucepan. Mix well and add the marjoram. Bring to a simmer and cook until the mixture thickens. Add the butter, cheese, and salt and pepper to taste. Remove from the heat and serve at once.

In 1874, the United Vegetable Dealers Association and the San Francisco Gardeners and Ranchers Association organized a Covent Garden-like district and named it Colombo Market. Located on Davis between Front and Pacific Street, the land was rented from the city for $750 a month. By the early 1880s, Colombo Market was the epicenter of the city's produce industry, an industry dominated by the Genovese and the Tuscans. Indeed, the relationship of these two regional groups became so symbiotic that the Genovese shoveled up the manure from the horses that pulled Tuscan truck farmers and then sold it back to them as fertilizer. (Not long afterward, the Genovese started the city's first scavenger company, and to this day a celebration is held at the Scavengers' Hall every September to choose the queen of the Columbus Day Parade. It is not uncommon for the choice to be an offspring of one of the original scavenger company families.)

With the establishment of the central produce market, local truck gardening flourished. Whole families got into the act. Children and mothers harvested, washed, and packed the produce that the fathers then took to market in horse-drawn wagons, and later trucks. The Colombo was described in the daily Morning Call *as "an Italian Colony in the center of a California city" and "the Greatest Vegetable Market in the World." It resembled the public market in Florence, Italy, occupying a full roofed block, and wagonloads of produce reached it by a roadway lined with gaslights to illuminate the early morning hours. Bars and caffès rimmed the area, providing meeting and drinking spots for the hardworking Italians. A reporter of the day described how language patterns mirrored the market schedule: The Genovese dialect filled the space up until 5:00 A.M., reflecting the control the Genovese had over all the activities. After that hour, the Tuscans would be heard speaking*

Florentine dialect as they distributed the Genovese produce, while the Genovese were well on their way back to their farms.

As each farmer approached the market, his horse knew to turn into his appointed stall without guidance. When the horses' work was done, they were led to a nearby stable and fed horse beans (fava beans) while their owners unloaded and stacked their wares.

The buyers from the big stores arrived earliest in the morning, to secure the pick of the crop. Later, hotel and restaurant wagons pulled in, followed by Lucchesi pushcart peddlers and greengrocers, who would one day become some of the area's leading independent grocery owners. Then the housewives appeared, looking for bargains to nourish their families.

The Genovese were soon supplying produce to local canners, the forerunners of California's world-renowned canning industry. Rose Pistola worked as a young girl at a red-brick cannery built near Fisherman's Wharf (today the Cannery, a well-known retail complex). "I quit school and went to work for the Del Monte peach-canning factory that used to be just down the block," Rose recalled. "I'd get in terrible fights with the other girls there over the best spot to stand, and one day I knocked the hell out of a big blond," she continued, raising her fist to emphasize the point. "Every day after that, the other workers would bet on who'd win between us. I always did."

By the 1930s, the population of North Beach was about thirty thousand, half of whom worked in agriculture in the Bay Area. Today, top Bay Area agricultural products include grapes, milk, mushrooms, tomatoes, and cattle, and their gross annual value is $1.5 billion. The city's many farm plots are long gone, of course, and only one acre remains under cultivation, tended by a single organic farmer.

Grilled Corn with Red Pepper Butter

1 red bell pepper, roasted, cored, seeded, and peeled
8 basil leaves
Grated zest of 1 lemon
Kosher or sea salt
¼ teaspoon freshly cracked black pepper
1 garlic clove, sautéed in a few drops of olive oil until soft
4 tablespoons (½ stick) unsalted butter, at room temperature
4 ears corn, shucked
2 tablespoons extra virgin olive oil

Serves 4

We run a booth every Saturday at the Ferry Plaza Farmers' Market, not far from the location of the old Colombo Market (see page 212). We are often very busy, but never busier than when corn and peppers are in season. Summer has arrived when you can see children munching, typewriter-style, on the red pepper-flecked ears of our sweet grilled corn. This is one of the easiest, tastiest ways to prepare great fresh corn. If you are not using a charcoal fire, you can do this on top of the stove on a griddle or in a grill pan.

Serve with Salt-Roasted Prawns with Lemon Aïoli (page 151).

Prepare a fire in a charcoal grill or preheat a stovetop griddle or grill pan.

In a mortar or a mini food processor, pound or puree the roasted pepper, basil, lemon zest, ¼ teaspoon salt, the pepper, and garlic until a rough paste is formed. Add the butter and continue to pound or process until the butter turns orange.

Brush the corn with the olive oil and season generously with salt. Grill the ears, turning as they brown and blister, until browned all over, about 8 minutes. Spread with the red pepper butter and enjoy summer.

Note

For a dramatic presentation, as well as a handle, I pull the shucks back from the ears, but do not pull them off the cob. They are beautiful if they brown slightly—just watch out, as they burn easily.

Fried Potatoes with Parsley and Garlic

Good fried potatoes are hard to make without a commercial fryer, but these are the exception. They are tender, flavorful, and very crisp on the outside, an effect achieved by the double-frying. Try them with any grilled or roasted foods.

1½ pounds Yukon Gold potatoes
2 cups olive oil, for deep-frying
1 tablespoon salt
2 tablespoons chopped flat-leaf parsley
1 garlic clove, bruised, or 1 stalk green garlic, chopped
Kosher or sea salt and freshly cracked black pepper

Serves 4

Peel the potatoes and cut into ½-inch-thick wedges. Place them in a pot of cold water so they do not darken.

Put a metal basket in a large pot, add a gallon of water and one tablespoon salt, and bring to a boil. Drain the potatoes from the cold water and add them to the boiling water. Lower the heat and simmer them until they are crisp/tender, a few minutes. Lift the basket from the water and let the potatoes drain and cool in the basket. A few might have broken; don't worry, they will just brown a little more quickly than the whole wedges. Pat them dry.

Alternatively, you may drop the potatoes into a pot of salted boiling water, simmer as directed above, and when they are crisp/tender simply drain them in a colander. Pat them dry.

In a deep pot heat the oil to 350° to 365°F. Drop the potatoes into the oil in batches and fry them until their edges just begin to turn golden, about 10 minutes. Any bits that might have broken up will brown more quickly and should be skimmed out of the oil before the rest are done. Remove the potatoes with tongs or a metal skimmer. Drain them on a wire rack with paper towels placed underneath and set aside. The potatoes can be prepared up to this point, a few hours ahead, but do not refrigerate or they will change flavor.

Reheat the oil to 350° to 365°F and refry the potatoes, in batches, until crisp and golden brown, about 5 minutes. Do not crowd the potatoes or the temperature of the oil will drop and they will not crisp effectively. Drain and toss with the parsley and garlic. Season with salt and pepper and serve.

Note

If you fry the potatoes between 350° and 365°F, they will absorb little oil.

Fried Morels with Fennel and Shaved Parmesan

½ pound morels or other mushrooms, cleaned and cut in half if small, into quarters if large
1 fennel bulb, very thinly sliced crosswise
2 cups whole milk
½ cup flour, preferably 00 *farina di grano tenero* from Pastiticio (see Sources, page 264) or a flour such as Wondra
Kosher or sea salt and freshly cracked black pepper
2 cups olive oil, for deep-frying
2 tablespoons chopped flat-leaf parsley
1 garlic clove, minced
2 to 3 ounces Parmigiano-Reggiano

Serves 4

A great way of concentrating flavors in foods is to lightly flour and fry them. The heat of the oil boils away the vegetables' water, leaving them with their own intensified flavor. In order for this to work, you need a clean, light-tasting oil and a light dusting of flour. You can use this technique with lots of different vegetables.

For this dish, use whatever mushrooms are available in your area, although it is really outstanding during the short period each year when morels are in season. When the mushrooms are combined with paper-thin slices of fried fennel and shaved Parmesan cheese, the flavors are similar to those in the Salad of Mushrooms, Endive, and Parmesan (page 73), but made distinctive by their different preparation methods.

Serve with Roast Leg of Lamb with Braised Artichokes (page 178), and Strawberry Ice Cream (page 235).

In a bowl, soak the morels and fennel slices in the milk. Season the flour with salt and pepper.

Heat the oil in a large heavy pot to 350°F. Drain the morels and fennel and pat dry. A few at a time, dredge them lightly in the seasoned flour, tapping off the excess, and carefully lower them into the hot oil. Fry until crisp and brown, about 5 minutes. Remove from the oil with a strainer to drain on a wire rack with paper towels set under them.

Toss in a bowl with the parsley and garlic. Season with salt and pepper. With a vegetable peeler, shave the Parmigiano over the top and serve at once.

Green Beans with Potatoes and Pancetta

These beans are soft, soothing, and redolent with pork flavor. I love to use Romano beans, but Kentucky Wonder beans are good too. Serve as a side dish or an antipasto. These days, using high-quality vegetables turns them into the stars and satisfies our concerns over having a healthy diet.

¼ cup extra virgin olive oil
¼ pound pancetta, cut into matchstick pieces
1 garlic clove, bruised
1 sprig rosemary (about 4 inches long)
1 pound fingerling potatoes
1 pound large green beans, such as Romano or Kentucky Wonder
Kosher or sea salt and freshly cracked black pepper

Serves 4

Heat the oil in a large heavy pot over medium-high heat and sauté the pancetta until it renders its fat and begins to brown, about 5 minutes. Add the garlic and rosemary and sauté until the rosemary sizzles and the garlic is fragrant, about 3 minutes. Add the potatoes, beans, and enough water to almost cover. Bring to a boil, cover tightly, and let simmer until the potatoes are cooked through, about 20 minutes. Season with salt and pepper to taste. Serve the vegetables in their broth.

Ultra Baby Fennel (3 for $1.00) at Ferry Plaza Farmers' Market.

Caramelized Fall Vegetables

2 tablespoons unsalted butter
12 baby carrots
12 baby turnips
8 baby fennel bulbs or 1 large fennel bulb, cut into 8 wedges
12 chestnuts, roasted, shelled, and peeled (see box below)
¼ teaspoon kosher or sea salt
⅓ pound mushrooms, preferably chanterelles, cleaned
1 sprig rosemary
1 garlic clove, bruised

Serves 4

This easy yet unusual method of cooking vegetables works for a wide range of starchy root vegetables, such as carrots, turnips, parsnips, and rutabagas—but not potatoes. All of the natural juices that come out of the vegetables are preserved, reduced, and browned to produce a fine caramel savor.

Perfect with Roast Guinea Fowl with Pancetta (page 202) or other roasted or grilled meat.

Place the butter, carrots, turnips, fennel, chestnuts, ⅓ cup water, and the salt in a large nonstick sauté pan. Cook over high heat, stirring or tossing (if you're daring) occasionally, until the water evaporates and the butter begins to sizzle, about 7 minutes. Add the mushrooms, rosemary, garlic, and ¼ cup more water and let evaporate again, stirring or tossing occasionally, until the butter sizzles, about 3 minutes more. Continue to sauté over medium-high heat, stirring or tossing occasionally, until the vegetables are a deep caramel brown all over, 5 to 8 minutes longer.

Preparing Chestnuts

Prepare the chestnuts by cutting an X with a small sharp knife in the flat side of each one. Heat a heavy skillet over high heat. When it is very hot, add the chestnuts and roast them, shaking them continuously, until the shells crack, about 15 minutes. Remove from the heat. When cool enough to handle, peel off the shell and the inner skin.

If fresh chestnuts are unavailable in your area, buy a packaged brand, such as Compagnie du Mont Lozère at a specialty store and proceed without roasting them.

Brussels Sprouts with Pancetta and Lemon

I rarely hear anyone rave about brussels sprouts in the way they do about asparagus or artichokes, but this preparation will win you some converts who have only eaten overcooked, cabbagey sprouts. The rich pancetta in combination with the brussels sprouts' intense, leafy green vegetable flavor tastes amazing, and the bits of thinly sliced lemon keep the dish bright and clean-flavored.

You can roast these alongside other foods in the oven. The temperature for cooking is not critical. Higher heat means more caramelization, but it's not crucial.

Much of the nation's crop of brussels sprouts is grown south of San Francisco, near Half Moon Bay. The brussels sprouts grow off the sturdy central stalk and, just like cabbage or broccoli, they have a sweet flavor when fresh that can turn a little skunky when old. Look for stalks at farmers' markets and take one home.

1 pound brussels sprouts, trimmed and halved

1 tablespoon extra virgin olive oil

2 ounces pancetta, cut into ½-inch pieces

1 lemon, cut into quarters and then into paper-thin slices

Kosher or sea salt and freshly cracked black pepper

Serves 4

Preheat the oven to 500°F.

Toss the brussels sprouts, olive oil, pancetta, lemon, and salt and pepper to taste in a medium baking dish. Roast on a baking sheet until the sprouts are brown and tender, about 15 minutes.

Decked out in rubber boots and shorts on a chilly San Francisco fall day, George Gutekunst looks as if he could have sprung from the pages of a Smith and Hawken catalog. He bends to adjust the snowy-white mesh, called agro fabric, that covers a dozen beds of greens in the secret urban garden he has created just thirty-two blocks from the ocean in San Francisco's Richmond District, the city's foggiest neighborhood.

Fog does wonders for Gutekunst's quarter-acre of edible greens. Agro fabric produces a mild greenhouse effect that enhances seed germination and warms the soil in the winter months, nurturing his varied assortment of greens, or prebog-gion, *as the early Ligurian settlers of North Beach would have called them. He cultivates radicchio, dandelion, escarole, endive, and other greens and herbs for braising, salad blends, pizza toppings, and ravioli fillings at Rose Pistola.*

In 1991, Gutekunst started with just three pots on a window ledge, then transplanted those plants into his backyard. A few years later, his neighbor, an elderly Frenchwoman who was delighted to see his backyard transformed, offered him her backyard as well. Restaurants learned of his green thumb and his greens and began buying as much produce as he could grow.

Many of Gutekunst's Asian, Russian, and French neighbors in this middle-class neighborhood would be surprised to learn of the thriving agricultural enterprise he has created in the midst of their community. Gutekunst stands out in his neighborhood as a bright stripe of local color. "The herbs thrive on denial," George says. "Thirsty plants fight for their lives and sprout great flavor." He believes that small plants are not necessarily the tastiest. "The bigger the plant, the more mineral content and flavor. Trendy tiny plants that some people find stylish tend to have rather insipid flavor."

If it hadn't been for an article in a local paper, the activities of Summer Fog Gardens might have remained a neighborhood phenomenon. But one of the sous-chefs at Rose Pistola happened to see the article and called to ask for samples. Rose Pistola is now this urban farm's only customer; we buy its entire harvest. The chefs call George and ask what's available, then write their menus accordingly. "Restaurant Rose Pistola and I have the perfect agricultural relationship," says Gutekunst, who loves getting organic fruit and vegetable trimmings from Rose Pistola. "Their leftovers make for diversity when added to bonemeal, rock phosphates, and my own compost. It makes the whole process biodynamic.

"Most people have got it backward," Gutekunst says. "They demand a specific vegetable instead of what is growing best at any given time. That's why my collaboration with Reed and Scott is so satisfying to all of us—and to their customers."

Grower George Gutekunst checks his greens at Summer Fog Gardens, a small inner-city garden in the foggiest part of town. George grows radicchio, dandelion, escarole, endive, and braising greens, used for preboggion and stuffing of ravioli. Rose Pistola is his exclusive customer.

Braised Greens with Pancetta

1 large white onion, cut lengthwise in half and then into half-moons
1 garlic clove, bruised
1 sprig rosemary
½ pound pancetta, cut into batons
1 tablespoon extra virgin olive oil
2 cups mixed greens (see headnote), coarsely chopped
Kosher or sea salt

Serves 4

A simple pot of nutritious braised greens is one of the most deeply satisfying dishes I know. The greens are wonderful alone, ladled over polenta, or swirled into a soup or a bowl of beans.

Your choice of the greens can change with the seasons. Martin at Pomponio Creek Farm (see page 226) sells us beet greens, dandelions, arugula, and broccoli rabe in the spring; mature lettuces, borage, spinach, and pea leaves in the summer; and chard, cavalo nero (black kale), beet and turnip greens, nettles, and thistles in the fall and winter. These mixtures of greens form the basis of our ravioli fillings, fish stuffings, soups, and dozens of other dishes.

Try these with a simple roast chicken and a bottle of very good red wine.

Sauté the onions, garlic, rosemary, and pancetta in the olive oil in a skillet over medium-high heat until the onions are tender and the pancetta has rendered its fat. Pour off most of the fat and add the greens and 1 cup water. Braise over low heat until the flavors have melded and the greens are tender, anywhere from 5 to about 30 minutes, depending on the type of greens. Season to taste with salt.

Preboggion

Preboggion refers to a Ligurian mixture of wild greens, the name of which derives from the Italian phrase *per bollire,* meaning either "parboiling" or "for boiling." Because they're wild, the greens have the scent and flavor of the soils from which they come. In the past, sailors returned home to Genoa from spice-trading expeditions craving their native plants, with tastes so distant from the spices they had smelled constantly during their long voyages. In Liguria, as in other parts of Italy, foraging for wild greens and herbs is a favorite pastime, almost as popular as mushroom hunting. City-dwelling Ligurians often maintain a vegetable patch, or terraced plot, on the outskirts of town, where they might grow olives, figs, and the preboggion that could be mistaken for weeds by the untrained eye. For many Ligurians, a meal is not complete without a mixture of a few of these wild greens.

Early Italian settlers in Northern California, longing to rekindle the culinary traditions of their homeland, sowed greens on small plots of land. Many of those plots later became what were known as truck gardens—the gardeners would truck their goods to market. Old-timers in North Beach still extol the curative powers of the greens, believed to be good for everything from thinning the blood to enlivening one's mood.

In the early days, as now, preboggion was a sensory link between North Beach and the soil and the soul of Liguria. The combination of wild and domestic greens is an integral part of the cuisine at Rose Pistola. My chefs and I, anxious to keep "wild" greens a part of the North Beach dining table, have nurtured relationships with local Northern California growers. Summer Fog Gardens in San Francisco, Pomponio Creek Farm in Pescadero, and Star Route Farms in Bolinas supply cultivated versions of beloved Italian wild greens such as stinging nettles, borage, arugula, milkweed, mint, marjoram, thyme, rosemary, and various chicories.

Chard Stems with Sage and Hazelnuts

- 2 pounds Swiss chard, white part only
- 3 tablespoons extra virgin olive oil
- ½ white onion, finely diced
- 4 large sage leaves
- 1 ounce prosciutto, sliced paper-thin and cut into julienne strips
- Kosher or sea salt
- 3 tablespoons toasted, peeled, and chopped (see page 191) hazelnuts
- Freshly cracked black pepper

Serves 4

Most chard recipes call for the leafy part of chard. This one offers a delicious use for the stems. The recipe is very much in the spirit of North Beach home cooking and Rose Pistola restaurant cooking in which nothing is wasted—the frugal housewife syndrome. The green leaf can be used for Braised Greens with Pancetta (page 222) or in the filling for Ravioli of Mixed Greens with Mushrooms (page 104).

Here, Swiss chard stems are trimmed and combined with hazelnuts. Their flavor is reminiscent of other white vegetables such as endive, celery hearts, fennel, and white asparagus. Since it is not our custom to blanch vegetables, we braise the chard stems in their own juices.

Serve this as a vegetable side dish with any roast meat or fowl.

Peel away any stringy outside parts from the chard stems with a sharp knife, trimming them in much the same way you trim celery. Cut the stems into 4-inch lengths.

Heat the olive oil in a large skillet over medium heat. Add the onions, sage, and prosciutto and sauté until the onions are translucent, about 5 minutes. Add the chard stems, salt to taste, and 2 tablespoons water and cover tightly. Braise over low heat until the chard is meltingly tender, about 25 minutes.

Raise the heat to high, add the hazelnuts, and cook for 1 minute. Season to taste with salt and pepper. Serve the chard on a warm platter with the braising liquid, and spoon the nuts over the top.

Sautéed Arugula with Pancetta and Garlic

Nothing could be more simple or elegant than this Rose Pistola favorite. Save small arugula leaves for salads and use the big ones for this dish. If you would prefer a vegetarian dish, substitute ½ cup diced onions for the pancetta, and omit the garlic.

Serve this quick sauté with fowl, fish, or meat.

- 1 garlic clove, crushed
- 2 ounces pancetta, diced
- 1 tablespoon extra virgin olive oil, if needed
- 4 cups loosely packed large-leafed arugula (about 2 bunches), rinsed, drained, but not dried
- Kosher or sea salt and freshly cracked black pepper

Serves 4

Sauté the garlic and pancetta in a large skillet over medium-high heat until they begin to crisp and turn golden. If the pancetta is lean and renders little fat, add the olive oil. Add the arugula and cook, turning occasionally, until the leaves wilt, 3 to 5 minutes. Season to taste with salt and pepper and serve.

On a brisk fall day after a long rainy spell, the wavy rows of vegetables at Pomponio Creek Farm look like flags fluttering above the soil. Visitors are serenaded by Mexican music issuing from the boombox set to the favorite station of the twelve semimigratory farm workers who tend the land. We are handed a pair of rubber boots to put on, and off into the dewy fields we go.

Sixteen-acre Pomponio Creek Farm is the brainstorm of Martin Bournhonesque, a former political science student and restaurant worker who gave up politics for farming after years of tending backyard gardens around the Bay Area.

Bournhonesque has farming in his genes. His family has farmed in Southern France for centuries and his Incan relatives passed down their ancient agricultural practices. So in 1990, when he saw this property on the fog-drenched San Mateo coast, nestled up against an oak-and-mushroom-studded hillside and bisected by Pomponio Creek, he knew he'd found his dream.

The farm is located halfway between the California Portuguese fishing and farming villages of San Gregorio and Pescadero, just one hour south of San Francisco. It is there that Bournhonesque started planting a wide variety of greens and vegetables, joining an energetic group of young local farmers who were doing the same thing. Older, more established farmers, taking note of the trend, have recently started supplementing their standby crops of pumpkins, artichokes, brussels sprouts, and flowers with leeks, fennel, and radicchio.

"On the coast, we can grow green crops, golden and striped Italian beets, green beans, six kinds of potatoes, four kinds of summer squash, leeks, and spring onions all summer long, while the rest of California is baking," says Bournhonesque.

Four miles inland from the Pacific, we are discussing and planning what is to be grown for Rose Pistola. Bournhonesque is delighted to have a dialogue between farmer and chef. "The more you tell me what your thoughts are, the better I am able to accommodate your specific needs," Martin explains.

I say I don't want anything too fancy or too small. Although many people have become accustomed to baby produce, we agree that vegetables and lettuces taste best when they've had a chance to mature and develop flavor. As I pick a purple radish and pop it into my mouth, I tell Martin, "It's a win-win situation with the weeds such as milkweed thistle. They grow all by themselves and we pay for them." Bournhonesque reminds me that they are prickly and do take time to harvest. I examine, and approve of, the tight-headed radicchio. I like to use the whole plant: the inner part of the head for salads, the stalk and outer leaves for braising.

Bournhonesque shows me how he puts rubber bands around the frisée and plants them very close together so they become self-blanching. (By placing them close together, no sun gets through, and they don't turn green like endive that is grown in darkness or underground.) In keeping with Italian and French farming practices, many chefs favor the delicacy in flavor that blanching achieves. I put in a request for the creamiest escarole, and Bournhonesque has a request of his own. He asks if he can have the shrimp shells discarded by the restaurant. "I'll use them in my compost," he says, "to keep the worms away from my big honking onions."

Chef Scott Warner (far left), grower Martin Bournhonesque, Reed Hearon, and Peggy Knickerbocker at Pomponio Creek Farm in Pescadero. Pomponio Creek Farm is one of the region's foremost farms, supplying Rose Pistola with beets, green beans, white chard, potatoes, fennel, brussels sprouts, and radicchio.

Dandelion Greens with Dried Fava Bean Puree

- 1 cup dried peeled fava beans (see page 195)
- ¼ cup plus 1 teaspoon extra virgin olive oil
- 2 ounces pancetta, diced
- 2 garlic cloves, bruised
- 2 bunches dandelion greens, rinsed but not dried (about 4 cups)
- 1 sprig rosemary (about 4 inches long)
- Kosher or sea salt

Serves 4

Dandelion greens still grow wild around the outskirts of North Beach. In the early days, immigrants went foraging for greens on the slopes of Telegraph and Russian hills. Look for dandelions at the market that are not too large, or they will be tough and bitter. The greens are best for cooking when they are about eight inches long.

The cooked puréed beans serve as a base for the braised dandelion greens. You could use polenta, or a purée of another bean. If you cannot find already shelled dried fava beans, soak the dried fava beans overnight and then peel off the skins. If you would like to make this a vegetarian dish, omit the pancetta. You can even make a soup out of the dish by loosening the beans with a cup or so of water and then swirling in the greens.

Serve with Braised Sea Bass with Wild Mushrooms (page 146) and Tangerine Tart (page 250).

Combine the dried fava beans and about 3 cups of water in a saucepan and simmer for 45 minutes or until tender. Drain.

Heat 1 teaspoon of the olive oil in a heavy skillet over medium heat. Add the pancetta and 1 garlic clove. When the garlic begins to turn color, add the dandelion greens, turn the heat to high, and cook until they become tender and wilted. Set aside and keep warm.

Meanwhile, heat the remaining ¼ cup olive oil in a small pot over medium heat. Add the remaining garlic clove and the rosemary and cook until the rosemary sizzles and the garlic is fragrant. Add the fava beans and heat through. Puree the fava bean mixture in a food processor and season with salt.

To serve, pour the puree into a serving dish and spoon the warm dandelion greens around and on top of it. Remove the rosemary sprig before serving.

Broiled Radicchio with Gorgonzola

Snack on this quick dish while waiting for the pasta water to boil. Or think of it as a side dish or a first course, or serve on toast as crostini. Any way, it is very easy, quick, and absolutely packed with flavor and style.

Radicchio di Treviso *is the lovely elongated version of the more familiar, tight round radicchio* di Verona*—the flavor is similar but more delicate. Its name derives from the town in the Veneto, in Northern Italy, from which it comes. If you can't get it, the more conventional radicchio may be substituted.*

Serve with the Roast Guinea Fowl with Pancetta (page 202), or as an antipasto, with your favorite red wine.

2 heads radicchio di Treviso, or other radicchio, cut into eighths
2 tablespoons good balsamic vinegar
2 tablespoons extra virgin olive oil
Kosher or sea salt and freshly cracked black pepper
¼ pound Gorgonzola

Serves 4

Preheat the broiler. Place the radicchio in a small gratin dish. Toss with the balsamic vinegar, olive oil, and salt and pepper to taste. Place under the broiler for 3 to 5 minutes, until the cheese is melted and brown. Remove from the broiler and dot with small pieces of the Gorgonzola. Put the dish back under the broiler for 1 minute, or until the cheese melts. Serve either as is or on toast.

Broccoli Braised with Anchovy and Garlic

2 tablespoons extra virgin olive oil
1 garlic clove, chopped
2 anchovy fillets, or 1 teaspoon anchovy paste
Pinch of crushed red pepper flakes
1 large or 2 small bunches broccoli (1½ to 2 pounds), cut into small florets, stalks reserved for another use
Kosher or sea salt
1 lemon, halved

Serves 4

Many vegetables are good raw or just blanched, but broccoli is not one of them. When broccoli is gently cooked in its own moisture, absorbing this mixture of garlic, anchovy, red pepper, and lemon, it is so good that it has become a favorite at Rose Pistola. Using this method, the broccoli does not lose flavor and vitamins to the water, as in the more usual blanching method. It keeps well, can be made a few hours ahead, and is delicious at room temperature as a side dish.

Serve with Braised Sea Bass with Wild Mushrooms (page 146) and Persimmon Pudding (page 244).

Heat the olive oil in a large skillet over medium heat. Add the garlic and sauté for a minute or so, until it perfumes the oil. Add the anchovies and pepper flakes and cook, pressing down on the anchovies with the tines of a fork until they melt into the oil, for another minute.

Add the broccoli and salt to taste and toss until coated with the sauce. Reduce the heat to low, add 1 tablespoon water, and cover the pan. Cook until the broccoli is tender, about 8 minutes. Squeeze the lemon juice over, check for seasoning, and serve.

Farinata with Sage, Niçoise Olives, and Caramelized Onions

(page 133)

Stuffed Focaccia

(page 136)

Roast Fish

with Potatoes

and Artichokes

(page 141)

Cioppino

(page 156)

Terrorized Steak

(page 169)

Rustic Nectarine

and Berry Tart

(page 248)

Sacripantina

(page 256)

Gorgonzola
with Honey
and Hazelnuts
(page 255)

Desserts

North Beach, full of its Italian immigrants, has a strong tradition of indulging in desserts. Whenever there's a birthday or an anniversary to be celebrated, one of two cakes is traditionally ordered. A St.-Honoré cake from Victoria Pastry, the pristine bakery on the edge of Chinatown, has long been a favorite. The St.-Honoré cake is a sort of *putti* cake with a rum-soaked sponge cake center covered with lots of whipped cream. It has an unbelievably flaky base and is decorated with custard-filled puff pastry balls around the edges. The alternate cake of celebration is the sacripantina, a dome-shaped sponge cake soaked in rum, rich with zabaglione, marsala, and whipped cream, from Stella Pastry, down the block on Columbus Avenue.

While we love the St.-Honoré cake, we leave it to Victoria. We do make the sacripantina. Our version is inspired by the cake made famous at Stella Pastry and by one from Harry's Bar in Venice, where the baroque, cloud-like, génoise cake has airy white meringues encircling it.

Other desserts are simpler and reflect the immigrants' closeness to the land, with their heavy reliance on fruit, used in puddings, soufflés, tarts, and ice creams.

Workers fill in cobblestones (basalt blocks) between cable car rails on Hyde Street, between Chestnut and Bay Streets, circa 1911. (Peggy Knickerbocker's house is the first on the left.) *Courtesy J. B. Monaco Photography.*

Zabaglione with Strawberries in Red Wine

2 pints ripe strawberries, hulled
1 cup light red wine, such as a California Charbono or a Chianti
½ cup plus 2 tablespoons sugar
8 large egg yolks
Finely grated zest of 1 orange
⅓ cup Moscato or other sparkling wine
Large bunch of mint

Serves 4

Serve a cluster of mint sprigs in the bowl along with this dessert, which itself is perfumed with ripe strawberries and young, fresh red wine. The combination of scents is wonderful. The dish has the added virtue of letting your wine-loving friends keep going through the dessert course.

Put the strawberries in a pretty glass bowl, add the red wine and 2 tablespoons of the sugar up to 2 hours before serving, and stir from time to time to dissolve the sugar. (This is best done at the beginning of dinner.)

Put the egg yolks in a large heatproof bowl, add the remaining ½ cup sugar, and whisk until light and fluffy.

Bring a large pot of water to a boil over high heat. Whisk the orange zest and Moscato into the egg yolks. Put the bowl on top of the pot of water and whisk until the zabaglione is fluffy, stiff, and pale yellow, about 5 minutes. Divide among four shallow bowls and ladle the strawberries and wine on top. Serve with a few sprigs of mint in each bowl.

Bowl of Iced Summer Fruit

Some things are perfect: Hawaiian sunsets. A walk through the woods on a spring day. Lunch in the dappled sunlight at your favorite tree-shaded restaurant with someone you love. Vine-ripe tomatoes. Great summer fruits. With the ideal ingredients, nothing could be more perfect than tree-ripened fruit, herbs, and edible flowers floating in a clear glass bowl of cool water. Giving a recipe for something so simple seems absurd. Fresh fruit served in this manner is an Italian tradition, brought to North Beach.

The inspiration for this presentation came from my friend Lucinda Hutson, who grows a gardenful of rare culinary herbs at her Austin home. She makes amazing sangrias for parties, using herbs and sliced fruits served in glass jars.

¼ pound cherries
4 peaches or nectarines
4 plums or apricots
2 cups hulled strawberries or other berries
1 lemon, sliced
A few sprigs of herbs, such as thyme, lavender, basil, or rosemary, preferably with flowers
Petals of 1 garden rose or other edible, nonsprayed flower

Serves 4

Fill a large glass bowl half-full with cool water and ice (if you are feeling adventurous, you can freeze nasturtiums in ice cubes). Float the fruits, lemon slices, and herbs in the water, arranging them as much or as little as you wish. Begin with the fruit at room temperature and let it cool in the water for maximum flavor.

Sprinkle the flower petals over the top. Give everyone a plate, a sharp knife, and a fork, and let them choose their fruit.

Mixed Citrus Compote with Vanilla Ice Cream

- A selection of citrus fruits, such as 4 lemons, 6 tangerines, and 5 kumquats
- 1 pomegranate
- 1 tablespoon honey
- 4 sprigs thyme
- 1 pint to 1 quart premium vanilla ice cream

Serves 4 to 6

Citrus fruits are at their best in the winter, freshly picked, still fragrant from the sun. Much of their perfume is lost when they are cooked, as the difference between fresh-squeezed and pasteurized orange juice shows. Think of this fruit compote as a sort of citrus stew that has not been cooked. We combine different citrus fruits, add a bit of honey and pomegranate, and use the compote as a counterpoint for ice cream.

The subtle flavor of the thyme brings out the honey's floral quality. Look for honey made from bees that feed on herb flowers, such as lavender, thyme, or rosemary, and experiment with matching or contrasting that flavor with a fresh herb.

Peel and slice or section the citrus fruit (slice kumquats with their peel on—it is edible): You can cut wedge-shaped sections by cutting between the membranes that separate each segment, or simply cut round slices from the fruits. You may want to cut each fruit differently so that you have a variety of shapes as well as colors on your plate.

Put the fruit in a glass bowl. Cut the pomegranate in half. Squeeze one half over the fruit just as you would squeeze an orange half by hand. Remove the pomegranate seeds from the other half and sprinkle them over the fruit. Toss the fruit with the honey and throw in the thyme sprigs. Divide among four plates or bowls, arranging the fruit if you like. Serve with scoops of vanilla ice cream.

Strawberry Ice Cream

As early as the 1850s, plump and succulent strawberries were grown in San Francisco's Bayview Hunter's Point area. Italian truck gardeners augmented the sandy soil there with fertilizer swept up by fellow Italians who maintained the horse-drawn streetcar lines.

Today about seventy-five percent of the country's strawberry crop is grown in California, much of it south of the Bay Area, in Watsonville. The peak season is from March to May, but the crop is actually available from the first of the year through late fall. We always try to buy berries that have been organically raised, since strawberries are one of the most heavily sprayed food crop.

We make this ice cream at our booth at the Ferry Plaza Farmers' Market every Saturday when strawberries are in season. This recipe is quite easy, but it depends on good ingredients. Try to find whole milk that has not been homogenized. If you can't find it, add a can of evaporated milk to enrich whole milk. The cane syrup or light corn syrup gives the ice cream a silky texture. Other berries such as blueberries, raspberries, or blackberries can be used in place of the strawberries.

- 2 cups strawberries, hulled
- ¼ cup packed light brown sugar
- 2 tablespoons vodka (see Note)
- Finely grated zest of 2 lemons and 1 orange (about 1 tablespoon) or of 3 Meyer lemons
- 3 cups whole milk
- 1 cup heavy cream
- ½ cup cane or light corn syrup
- ¼ teaspoon kosher or sea salt

Makes about 1½ quarts

Mash the strawberries with the brown sugar and vodka in a large bowl. Let stand to dissolve the sugar, about 30 minutes.

Add the other ingredients and stir together. Pour into an ice cream maker and freeze according to the manufacturer's directions. Serve at once, while the ice cream is still soft.

Note

The vodka helps keep the strawberries from becoming icy in the ice cream.

Al Courchesne named his fruit farm in Brentwood Frog Hollow because he loves children's stories, particularly The Wind in the Willows, *and because there are so many frogs in the irrigation ditches they create a symphony at night—and because his last name is unpronounceable.*

Frog Hollow Farm has some of the best peaches and nectarines in the world. One fine summer morning, we went to find out why. "The best possible peach," explained Al, "is the peach that is just about to drop off the tree and then is allowed to age for three days." Al leaves his peaches on the trees longer than anyone else dares to.

"Everybody is always squeezing my peaches at the markets, and I just let them," says the engagingly cheery, handsome farmer, "but softness does not mean that the peach is necessarily ripe. It should be firm, with a bit of a give.

"Peaches," Courchesne says, "are bred for a dominant red color—the color most people look for in a juicy peach. But," he explains, "the dominance of the background color—a golden yellow—is the true indicator, and dullness is too. You don't want a shiny peach, and you don't want one that has a hint of green to it either."

It doesn't hurt that the soil and the climate in Brentwood, one hour east of San Francisco, is ideal for peach growing. Courchesne farms fifty-three acres with twenty varieties of peaches (Cal Reds are his favorite) and ten to fifteen varieties of nectarines. Harvest starts on May 20 and continues until the second week of October. Nectarines have a one-month season, in July.

On the way to the packinghouse, a discussion arises. There are a lot of peaches on the ground, and the possibility of grazing pigs on them is considered. The idea of cooking with prosciutto or pancetta made from a pig allowed to eat only the ripe fruit is all I can think of.

In the packinghouse office, Al gives us a little chemistry lesson. He explains that an instrument called a refractometer is used to determine the sweetness, or Brix, of a peach or nectarine. "Most peaches Brix out at 8. Mine," he proudly asserts, "Brix at between 12 and 18, 18 being the maximum on the scale. They call me Mr. Brix," jokes the former anthropologist.

Surprisingly, his peach yields didn't change as a result of going organic a few years back. Every single branch of fifteen thousand trees has to be pruned by hand anyway, so having two guys weed-whacking instead of spraying chemicals doesn't seem like much extra labor, even if it takes a month each season. "But really, at the end of the day," Courchesne says, "my desire as a farmer is to become a gardener again."

Frog Hollow peaches ripening on a wicker chair.

Farmers' Market Peach Ice Cream

3 cups peeled and diced peaches (or nectarines)
½ to ¾ cup sugar
1 cup heavy cream
1 cup whole milk
1 teaspoon vanilla extract
¼ teaspoon kosher or sea salt

Makes about 1½ quarts

At just about any farmers' market, when stone fruits such as peaches, nectarines, and plums arrive on the scene, the crowds grow and the level of the buying frenzy is heightened. San Francisco is no exception, particularly since it is warm and sunny at this time of the year. Perfect ice cream weather.

It's wonderful to make as much of a meal as possible from the food you buy at the market that day. If you use juicy, ripe, sweet fresh fruit, you don't have to fuss around with custard-based ice creams. Simply use quality whole milk and heavy, tree-ripe fruit. Try to buy your fruit picked when it is dead ripe; that's when the fruits' sugar levels are highest. We make this at the Rose Pistola booth at the Ferry Plaza Farmers' Market, where our friends at Frog Hollow Farm bring us peaches and nectarines that they have specially picked for us.

Peach ice cream is perfect when served soft, straight from the drum.

Frog Hollow peaches just picked and on their way to the farmers' market.

Mash the fruit together with ½ cup sugar in a bowl. You should have a slightly chunky puree; we use a potato masher. Add the cream, milk, vanilla extract, and salt and stir well. Taste and add more sugar if needed.

Pour into an ice cream maker and freeze according to the manufacturer's directions. Serve soft, straight from the machine.

Lemon and Pomegranate Snow Cones

Street fairs and festivals are historically as common in North Beach as they are in Italy. At the Rose Pistola booth at the Ferry Plaza Farmers' Market every Saturday, we are always trying to think of a dessert that reflects the carnival spirit. Executive chef Scott Warner came up with the idea of doing some outrageous snow cones. Instead of ice, the base of this recipe is granita, which is an Italian ice made of frozen juice. You can make all sorts of combinations—espresso with vanilla cream, peach with blackberry syrup, cherry with chocolate syrup, and more. The possibilities are endless. You can serve them in paper snow cone cones, in ice cream cones, or even in wineglasses—they are a gorgeous and light finish to a meal.

½ cup plus 2 tablespoons sugar
1 cup fresh lemon juice
1 cup fresh tangerine or orange juice
2 pomegranates

Serves 4

In a bowl, dissolve ½ cup of the sugar in the citrus juices. Pour the mixture into a 9- or 10-inch glass dish and put in the freezer. It will take about 2 hours to freeze; stir the mixture every 20 minutes or so with a fork to break up the ice crystals. You don't want it to freeze into a solid mass, but rather to look like shaved ice.

While the granita is freezing, make the pomegranate sauce: Cut the pomegranates in half. Reserve seeds from one half and set aside to sprinkle on top of the granita. Squeeze the other halves as you would oranges, right into a bowl. Mix the juice with the remaining 2 tablespoons sugar and refrigerate or set aside.

When the granita is ready, spoon it into paper cones or wineglasses. Pour the sauce over the top and sprinkle each one with a few pomegranate seeds.

Zuppa Inglese with Fresh Cherries

- 2 pounds cherries, pitted (about 6 cups)
- 2 cups sugar
- ¾ cup amaretto
- ¾ cup grappa or brandy
- 9 large egg yolks
- ¼ cup plus 2 tablespoons all-purpose flour
- 2 to 2½ cups whole milk
- 1 vanilla bean
- 1 teaspoon grated lemon zest
- 1 to 2 packages crisp Italian ladyfingers (at least 6 ounces)

Serves 8 to 10

Cherries are one of the most fragile fruits of late spring's and early summer's bounty. The blossoms are easily knocked off the trees by spring storms. Early summer rains can cause the fruit to rot, mold, or fall. But when they arrive in your kitchen, picked ripe, sweet, and barely soft, there is no better fruit. The uses of cherries are infinite—cherry pie, clafouti, tarts, ice cream, and so on. A handful of cherries goes superbly with a glass of wine, and they are wonderful preserved in grappa.

This zuppa is one of those gooey, boozy, old-fashioned Italian desserts that reflects the exuberance and joy of life the immigrants brought to North Beach. You can make versions of it throughout the year with berries or stone fruits.

Combine the cherries, 1 cup of the sugar, the amaretto, and grappa in a bowl. Set aside for at least 1 hour and up to 24 hours. Refrigerate if setting aside overnight.

Whisk together the egg yolks and the remaining 1 cup sugar in a bowl. Add the flour and whisk until smooth.

Pour 2 cups milk into a bowl. Split the vanilla bean lengthwise in half and scrape the tiny seeds into the milk, then toss in the bean pod as well. Add the egg mixture and the lemon zest and place in a heavy saucepan. Bring the ingredients to a simmer over medium heat, whisking furiously. Reduce the heat to low and stir or whisk constantly until thick and fluffy. If the sauce begins to seize or thicken too quickly, remove from the heat and add up to ½ cup more milk. When nicely thickened and frothy, scrape into a clean bowl so that it does not keep cooking.

Dip about half the ladyfingers, a few at a time, into the bowl of cherries and juice and use them to line the bottom and sides of a 3- to 4-quart deep clear glass bowl. Spoon about one-third of the cherries into the bowl. Remove and discard the vanilla bean pod and spoon about half of the sauce over the cherry layer. Dip the remaining ladyfingers, a few at a time, into the cherry juices and lay them on top. Top with half of the remaining cherries and then all of the remaining sauce. Spoon the remaining cherries on top.

Cover the bowl with plastic wrap and place a plate that fits snugly inside the bowl on top. Press it down firmly on the plastic wrap against the cherries. Refrigerate for at least 1 hour and up to 1 day.

Serve chilled from the refrigerator. Scoop out about ¾ cup per person, giving each a bit of each layer.

Note

Depending upon your bowl, the number of layers may be greater than what is described here; in other words, you might want to make more but thinner layers.

Fig Soufflé with Honey and Raspberries

½ pound fresh green figs, diced
⅓ cup honey
Juice of 1 lemon
1 teaspoon thyme flowers or thyme leaves
5 tablespoons unsalted butter, at room temperature
¼ cup plus 3 tablespoons granulated sugar
1 cup raspberries or other seasonal berries
¾ cup whole milk
2 tablespoons all-purpose flour
¼ teaspoon finely grated lemon zest
5 egg yolks
9 egg whites
Pinch of kosher or sea salt
Powdered sugar

Serves 4

Exotic and sensuous, figs are used in many ways in North Beach cooking. A few hidden fig trees still remain, and at the end of summer, old neighborhood denizens can be seen sneaking into backyards after the ripe fruit. However you get your figs, try this soufflé.

You will need a 1-quart soufflé dish or four 8-ounce ramekins for this recipe. At Rose Pistola, we serve individual soufflés, but at home it is probably easier to serve one large one.

Place the figs in a heavy nonreactive pot and stir together with the honey. Add the lemon juice and thyme and cook over medium-low heat, stirring frequently, for about 45 minutes, or until a thick jam is formed. To test if the jam is done, chill a plate and drop a teaspoon of the jam upon it. If it sets, it's done.

Preheat the oven to 400°F.

Butter a 1-quart soufflé dish or four 8-ounce ramekins with 1 tablespoon of the butter and coat with 2 tablespoons of the sugar. Shake excess sugar out of the dish(es) and discard.

Mix the berries with 1 tablespoon of the sugar in a bowl. Set aside.

Bring the milk to a boil in a heavy saucepan. Remove from the heat. Meanwhile, mix together the flour and the remaining 4 tablespoons butter in a small bowl. Slowly add the mixture to the milk, whisking continuously. Stir in the fig jam and lemon zest, then add the egg yolks and whisk to incorporate.

In a large bowl, whip the egg whites until frothy, then slowly add the remaining ¼ cup sugar and the salt and whip the whites to soft peaks. Whisk one-third of the whites into the soufflé base, then fold the base into the remaining whites.

Place the berries in the bottom of the soufflé dish(es). Top with the soufflé base. Place on a baking sheet in the center of the oven and cook until golden brown on top and set, 35 to 40 minutes for the large soufflé, about 12 minutes for the small ones. The soufflé should not jiggle when it is done. Remove from the oven, dust the top with powdered sugar, and serve at once.

Warm, Soft Chestnut Pudding

When the fog rolls in, North Beach moves inside. The neighborhood sidewalk caffès thin out, the streets grow quiet, and everyone searches out a warm, cozy place. I like to think of this tendency as North Beach's Italian heart, brash when the sun is shining, turning inward to home and hearth for reassurance when it is cold. And nothing's as satisfying during those cold spells as puddings.

In the winter, chestnut flour appears in Italian groceries in North Beach. It is classically used to make pasta, but, despite chestnut pasta's good flavor, it is often heavy and gummy. This pudding is a great alternative use of chestnut flour, combining techniques for making polenta. This pudding is something like an Indian pudding. Its flavor and texture actually come from the flour. The result is rich, smooth, light, and fragrant with chestnut. If you can find chestnut honey, by all means use it. Fairly common in Italy, it is becoming increasingly available here.

1 quart whole milk

3/4 cup chestnut flour, sifted (see Sources, page 264)

4 tablespoons unsalted butter, at room temperature

1/2 cup honey, preferably chestnut flower honey

1/4 teaspoon kosher or sea salt

2 large eggs, beaten

Whipped cream or vanilla ice cream, optional

Serves 4 to 6

Preheat the oven to 350°F.

Scald the milk (bring the milk nearly to a boil and then reduce to a simmer) in a heavy pot. Whisk in the chestnut flour, adding it in a steady stream. Bring to a simmer, whisking constantly, until thickened. Remove from the heat and let cool slightly. Add 3 tablespoons of the butter, the honey, salt, and eggs and whisk until smooth.

With the remaining 1 tablespoon butter, butter a 12 × 8½-inch gratin dish or similar-sized baking dish. Pour in the batter and bake for 1 hour, or until the top has caramelized nicely and the pudding is set. Remove from the oven and serve at once, with whipped cream or vanilla ice cream.

Persimmon Pudding

1½ pounds ripe Hachiya persimmons
1¼ cups all-purpose flour
½ teaspoon baking soda
½ teaspoon baking powder
⅛ teaspoon ground cinnamon
Scant ⅛ teaspoon kosher or sea salt
¾ cup sugar
3 large eggs
1½ cups whole milk
½ cup heavy cream
1 tablespoon honey
2 teaspoons vanilla extract
6 tablespoons unsalted butter

Serves 6 to 8

Many persimmon puddings taste like a spice cake. Not this one. It is exceptional because it really tastes of persimmons. There are two varieties of persimmons on the market. The most readily available ones are the acorn-shaped Hachiyas; they are almost pointed at one end. They ripen to a very soft gelatinous pulp, making them excellent for baking. The Fuyu is squat and round; it does not ripen to the same softness as the Hachiya does. Fuyus are most often eaten peeled and raw. Use Hachiyas here. If they are not completely ripe, freeze them for twenty-four hours to rid them of any bitterness.

Serve with whipped cream or good-quality softened vanilla or vanilla bean ice cream.

Preheat the oven to 325°F. Butter the bottom and sides of a round 10-inch Pyrex baking dish and line with waxed paper.

Scrape out the pulp from the halved persimmons, place in a food processor, and puree. Sift the flour, baking soda, baking powder, cinnamon, and salt into a large bowl.

In a bowl, combine the persimmon pulp with the sugar, eggs, milk, cream, honey, and vanilla. Gradually stir this mixture into the flour mixture. Allow the batter to stand for about 5 minutes, until it thickens slightly. Heat a small saucepan over medium-low heat for 1 minute and add the butter. Watching it carefully, cook the butter until it browns. Remove from the heat and add it to the mixture.

Pour the batter into the prepared pan. Bake for 3 to 3½ hours, until set. A wooden skewer inserted into the center should come out clean. Serve warm or at room temperature.

Flaky Pastry

This dough can be used for sweet or savory tarts, since there's no sugar in it. We use this recipe for the Rustic Nectarine and Berry Tart (page 248), the Caramelized Pear and Almond Tart (page 246), and any fresh fruit tart.

It is possible to make this dough by hand, as Rose Pistola might have done, but it is very quick and easy in the food processor. Be careful not to overprocess the dough.

1½ cups all-purpose flour
¼ teaspoon kosher or sea salt
8 tablespoons (1 stick) unsalted butter, cut into ½-inch pieces and very cold
4 to 5 tablespoons ice water

Makes enough for an 11-inch tart

Sift the flour and salt together and combine in a food processor. Add the butter to the flour mixture. Pulse until the butter is the size of hazelnuts. Add the water, 1 tablespoon at a time, and continue to pulse just until the water is incorporated. Remove the dough, including any little bits left in the bowl, before it forms a ball. (If you process the dough to the point where it forms a ball, it will be overmixed and tough.) Pat into a disc, wrap in plastic wrap, and chill for at least 1 hour and up to 2 days before baking.

Remove the dough from the refrigerator and bring it almost to room temperature before rolling. This will take about 1 hour, less, of course, if it is only chilled for 1 hour (then it will take about 15 minutes).

Proceed as directed in the recipes.

Caramelized Pear and Almond Tart

1 Flaky Pastry (page 245)
One 7-ounce tube almond paste
1 tablespoon amaretto
1 large egg
2 large egg yolks
1 cup heavy cream
¼ cup whole milk
3 ripe pears, preferably Bosc or comice, peeled and cut into quarters
½ cup sugar
1 tablespoon unsalted butter
2 tablespoons Calvados or Cognac

Serves 8

One of the joys of late fall is when winter's hard fruits, such as apples, pears, and quinces, come on the market. The aesthetic of Rose Pistola's North Beach Italian cooking—using seasonal, simple, clean, bright flavor combinations—is readily apparent in this dessert. The slightly smoky flavor of the caramelized pears goes nicely with the nutty flavor of browned pastry.

Tarts such as this can create timing problems—the crust browns before the sugar caramelizes, or the fruit gets mushy before the crust browns. We have circumvented all of that by separating the processes—first the crust is baked with an almond filling, then the fruit is caramelized and added to the crust. The result is wonderful. Serve with whipped cream or vanilla ice cream if desired.

Preheat the oven to 400°F.

Make the crust by tearing off small bits of the dough and pressing them into the bottom and up the sides of an 11-inch fluted tart pan with a removable bottom, covering it completely; the crust should be about ⅛ inch thick. Freeze the crust briefly before baking.

Line the crust with a piece of aluminum foil and fill it with dried beans to keep the crust from rising. Bake for 20 minutes, then remove the foil and weights. Return to the oven and bake until the crust is brown, about 10 minutes longer. Remove from the oven and set aside and cool. (Leave the oven on.)

Combine the almond paste, amaretto, egg, egg yolks, ¼ cup of the cream, and the milk in a food processor and process until smooth. Pour it into the tart shell and spread it evenly over the bottom. Bake for 15 minutes, or until set. Cool on a wire rack.

Toss the pears in a bowl with the sugar. Melt the butter in a heavy skillet over high heat. Add the pears—as they cook, they will throw off liquid that will blend with the butter and sugar. Cook over high heat until the sugar caramelizes to an amber color. When the pears are nicely browned, after about 7 minutes, carefully add the remaining ¾ cup cream. It will bubble and turn brown. Continue to cook until the syrup is thick, then add the Calvados or Cognac. Reduce again to a simmer and cook until thick, shaking the pan and spooning the sauce over the tops of the pears occasionally. Remove from the heat and let cool slightly.

Arrange the pears on top of the almond filling in the tart shell, with the narrow ends of the pears toward the center. Spoon the caramelized cooking liquid over the top. Allow the tart to sit until the caramelized liquid hardens slightly.

Rustic Nectarine and Berry Tart

- 1 Flaky Pastry (page 245)
- 3 to 4 ripe nectarines or peaches, unpeeled and cut into thin wedges
- 1 cup raspberries
- ⅓ cup plus 1 tablespoon sugar
- 1 tablespoon unsalted butter, cut into small pieces

Serves 8

This thin, crisp tart is easy to make, imprecisely beautiful, and absolutely delicious. It is important not to use too much fruit. The tart is really a sort of gratin, and the fruit must be in a thin layer so that the liquid from the fruit will evaporate rather than boil out and make the crust soggy.

Once you have mastered the basic technique of making this tart, you can vary it endlessly. Single fruits are wonderful—strawberries, pears, even jams work. Combinations of two are even more interesting—such as figs and raspberries with a honey glaze or, here, raspberries and ripe white nectarines, so redolent of early summer.

Serve the tart with whipped cream, mascarpone, or vanilla ice cream.

Preheat the oven to 425°F.

Dust a work surface lightly with flour. Roll out the dough into a round roughly 15 inches in diameter and ⅛ inch thick. Don't worry if the shape is not perfect. (Don't use too much flour to roll out the dough; flour you add will make the crust drier and tougher.) Line a baking sheet with parchment or use a nonstick baking sheet. Carefully transfer the round to the baking sheet.

Combine the nectarines and raspberries with ⅓ cup of the sugar in a bowl and toss. Spread the fruit over the dough, without arranging it, leaving a 2-inch border. Dot the filling with the butter. Fold the edges of the dough over part of the filling, roughly pleating the crust as you make your way around the tart. You should have a very rough approximation of a circle. Sprinkle the edges of the crust with the remaining 1 tablespoon sugar.

Bake for about 30 minutes, or until the crust is golden brown and you can cleanly lift an edge of the tart up off the baking sheet with a spatula. Serve warm or at room temperature. (This tart does not keep for more than a few hours in peak form; if you don't mind a slightly soggy crust, though, it is still delicious the next day and reheats well.)

Hazelnut-Chocolate Crust

This recipe makes two crusts. It freezes nicely for up to one month if wrapped well in plastic. Use one-half of the recipe for the Tangerine Tart (page 250).

2 cups all-purpose flour
¼ cup dark unsweetened cocoa powder
⅓ cup sugar
10 ounces butter (1 stick plus 2 tablespoons), chilled and cut into small pieces
1 cup hazelnuts, toasted, peeled (see page 191), and coarsely chopped
3 ounces bittersweet chocolate, grated
1 tablespoon grated tangerine zest (about 3 small tangerines; save the juice of the tangerines for Tangerine Tart filling or another use)
1 large egg
1 large egg yolk
Pinch of kosher or sea salt

Each crust makes one 10-inch tart

Sift together the flour, cocoa, and sugar into a bowl. Cut in the butter and blend until the dough is the size of peas. Stir in the hazelnuts, chocolate, and zest. Stir in the egg, egg yolk, and salt until a firm dough is formed. Knead together lightly. Wrap in plastic and refrigerate until firm, about 30 minutes. Divide the dough in half, freeze one-half for another use, and proceed with one-half.

Preheat the oven to 325°F.

Press the dough into a 10½-inch tart pan with a removable bottom and fluted edges. Bake for about 20 minutes until set. Cool completely on a rack.

Tangerine Tart

¼ cup fresh lemon juice
¾ cup fresh tangerine juice
5 large egg yolks
1⅓ cups sugar
1 tablespoon grated tangerine zest (about 3 small tangerines)
1 tablespoon cornstarch, sifted
5⅓ tablespoons unsalted butter, melted
½ recipe Hazelnut-Chocolate Crust (page 249)
1 seedless tangerine, sliced into paper-thin rings, skin on

Serves 8 to 10

In the late fall when tangerines reappear on the produce shelves and at citrus stalls at farmers' markets, buy them and make this rich holiday treat.

Any member of the citrus reticulata *family (tangerines, clementines, mandarins, or tangelos) may be used for this tart. California is a major producer of Satsumas, Mandarins, and other tangerines. The East Coast gets the bulk of their share, especially the popular Clementine from Spain and North Africa.*

The custard filling for this tart is a bit like a tangerine curd; the almost transparently thin slices of the fruit float fetchingly on the surface of the tart.

This tart is a delicious twist on more conventional chocolate and fruit combinations. Many such combinations rely on berries, but this one uses sweet-tart citrus fruit that loads down the trees in Liguria and that immigrants to North Beach continued to find in abundance in their new home.

You will need 6 to 7 tangerines for this recipe. The number of tangerines that you will need will depend upon their juiciness.

Preheat the oven to 325°F.

Whisk all of the ingredients, except the crust and tangerine slices, together in a bowl. Pour the batter into the cooled crust. Float the tangerine rings on top of the tart, placing them at even intervals around the edge.

Bake for about 40 minutes, or until the center is set. Cool on a wire rack and serve at room temperature.

Panna Cotta with Berries

Surrounded by mounds of fresh berries, this barely set, vanilla-scented cream means summer to me. The goodness of this dessert depends on the quality of the raw ingredients that go into it. If you can only get ultrapasteurized whipping cream, whisk ¼ cup mascarpone into 1¾ cups cream and substitute that for the 2 cups cream.

2 cups cream
¼ cup sugar
1 vanilla bean, split
1 teaspoon powdered gelatin
2 cups mixed berries
¼ cup crème de cassis

Serves 4

In a medium saucepan, scald the cream with the sugar and vanilla bean. Remove from the heat and dissolve the gelatin in the cream mixture to soften it, then strain. Cool. Pour the mixture into a 2½-cup mold, cover, and refrigerate until set, 2 to 3 hours.

Meanwhile, mix the berries with the cassis in a bowl and let macerate or sit for a few minutes.

Unmold the panna cotta onto a plate by tapping the inverted mold with the handle of a knife and serve the berries and their liquid around it.

Chocolate Budino

For the Budino

1 pound plus 1 tablespoon unsalted butter
1 pound excellent-quality semisweet chocolate
¼ cup espresso
¼ cup brandy
1¾ cups sugar
10 large eggs

For the Praline

6 tablespoons unsalted butter
¼ cup plus 2 tablespoons sugar
1 tablespoon light corn syrup
2 tablespoons heavy cream
¾ cup toasted and skinned hazelnuts (see page 191), chopped

For the Chocolate Crust

5 tablespoons unsalted butter, at room temperature
3 tablespoons sugar
1 large egg yolk
¼ teaspoon vanilla extract
Scant ½ cup all-purpose flour
½ cup sifted unsweetened cocoa powder

When we opened Rose Pistola, our first pastry chef, John Yengich, made a budino, the rich baked chocolate pudding—now the base of the cake—so typical of extravagant Italian neighborhood desserts. Although our dessert menu changes frequently, this favorite has remained on it to this day. We continued to tinker with it, though, and finally arrived at an absolutely sublime chocolate cake. To add texture and layers of flavor, we place the pudding on a chocolate crust and a praline layer and then top it with a layer of chocolate ganache and a thin layer of cake.

A cake decorating stand will make assembly easier, but is not essential. You will need a 3-quart stainless steel bowl, an 11-inch tart or cake pan, and a 9½-inch tart pan with a removable bottom. Prepare the dessert in stages; it is not hard to make, there are just a lot of steps. All the components of the cake can be made ahead, but it is best served within a few hours of assembly. If you are not feeling ambitious, just bake the budino alone, allow it to cool, and serve cut into wedges, with unsweetened whipped cream.

For the Budino

Preheat the oven to 350°F. Line a 3-quart metal bowl (with a diameter of about 11 inches at the rim) with aluminum foil, making the foil as smooth as possible. Grease the foil with 1 tablespoon of the butter.

Melt the chocolate and the remaining 1 pound butter in the top of a large double boiler. Combine the espresso, brandy, and sugar and stir into the chocolate. Continue to stir over medium-low heat until the sugar has dissolved, about 10 minutes. Remove from the heat.

Break the eggs into a bowl and lightly whisk them. Slowly pour the chocolate mixture into the eggs, whisking constantly to prevent the eggs from curdling. Whisk until the eggs and chocolate are very well combined.

Pour the batter into the prepared bowl and bake in the center of the oven for 1½ hours, or until the top is firm and slightly crisp but the center is still moist. When tested with a skewer, the skewer will not come out clean, but it should not be covered with liquid. Let cool; then refrigerate and chill completely, preferably overnight.

For the Praline

Preheat the oven to 350°F. Line a 9½-inch tart pan with a removable bottom with a round of parchment paper.

Place the butter, sugar, corn syrup, and cream in a heavy saucepan. Bring to a boil over medium-high heat. Add the nuts, lower the heat to medium, and stir until the mixture begins to pull away from the sides of the pan, about 2 minutes.

Pour the mixture into the center of the lined tart pan—it will spread out evenly to the edges. Place on a baking sheet and bake until golden brown all over, about 18 minutes. Begin checking for doneness after 15 minutes, and if the praline is browning unevenly, rotate the pan. Remove the pan from the oven.

When the praline is cool enough to handle, remove it from the tart pan. Set aside to cool completely, leaving it on the parchment.

For the Chocolate Crust

Cream the butter and sugar together in a small bowl. Beat in the egg yolk and vanilla. Sift the flour and cocoa together, then stir into the butter mixture. Cover with plastic wrap and chill for 1 hour.

Preheat the oven to 350°F. Line a 9½-inch tart pan with a removable bottom with a round of parchment paper.

Form the dough into a ball, then flatten it into a disc. Press it evenly over the bottom of the parchment-lined tart pan with your fingers. Bake for 8 to 10 minutes, or until the pastry has lost its glossy sheen, is dry to the touch, and is just cooked through, 8 to 10 minutes. Place on a rack to cool. When the crust is cool enough to handle, gently remove from the tart pan and set it aside to cool completely on a wire rack.

For the Roulade

3½ ounces semisweet chocolate, cut into small pieces
1 tablespoon espresso
1 teaspoon vanilla extract
4 large eggs, separated
½ cup sugar

For the Ganache

8 ounces semisweet chocolate
½ cup heavy cream
2 tablespoons unsalted butter, at room temperature

For Assembly

½ cup unsweetened cocoa powder

Serves 12

For the Roulade

Preheat the oven to 350°F. Line an 11-inch tart pan with a removable bottom or a cake pan with a round of parchment paper.

Melt the chocolate in a small heavy saucepan over low heat. Stir in the espresso, vanilla, and egg yolks. Remove from the heat.

In a large bowl, whisk the egg whites until frothy, then slowly add the sugar and continue to whisk until soft peaks form. Stir one-third of the egg whites into the chocolate mixture, then fold the chocolate mixture gently into the remaining whites. Do not overmix. Pour the batter into the lined pan and spread it out evenly.

Bake for 20 minutes, or until a skewer inserted in the center comes out clean. Remove the pan from the oven and cool completely on a rack.

For the Ganache

Grate the chocolate into a bowl. Bring the cream to a boil in a small saucepan. Pour it over the chocolate. Stir together until the chocolate is melted and well combined. Add the butter, stirring until well mixed. The ganache will be very fluid and spreadable, but it will thicken slightly as it cools. The ganache will be used to stick different components of the cake together.

To Assemble

Remove the chilled budino from the bowl but leave it in the foil. Spread a thin layer of ganache over the bottom of the budino. Place the praline on the ganache and press gently so it adheres to the budino. Carefully remove the parchment paper from the praline. Spread a thin layer of ganache over the praline. Place the chocolate crust on top and press down lightly to smooth.

Invert the budino onto a cake stand or plate. Remove the foil and spread a thin layer of ganache over the domed top of the budino. Invert the chocolate cake layer onto the budino, leaving the parchment paper on it as you press down gently. Remove the parchment paper. Trim off the excess edges, using a paring knife. Sift the cocoa powder over the top and serve.

Gorgonzola with Honey and Hazelnuts

Cheese as a final course has been a tradition of the North Beach table for more than a century and a half. For this quick and sophisticated dessert course, buy a nice, sweet, young Gorgonzola, known as Gorgonzola Dolcelatte. Gorgonzola Dolcelatte is a brand name for Gorgonzola produced by a company called Galbani. This "sweet milk" cheese comes to the market when it is underripe and quite young. It appeals to those who find the naturale, *the more traditional aged Gorgonzola, too strong.*

At Rose Pistola, this cheese offering bridges the gap between salad and dessert, because it includes honey, nuts, and cheese. We serve figs with this when they are in season. Drink an Amarone wine with this combination.

- 1/3 pound Gorgonzola Dolcelatte
- Wild thistle or wildflower honey, for drizzling
- 1/4 cup toasted hazelnuts (see page 191), peeled
- 4 thin slices grilled bread or 8 crackers

Serves 4

Divide the cheese among four plates. Drizzle the honey on top, so it dribbles down the sides. Scatter the hazelnuts over and around the cheese. Serve with the grilled bread or crackers.

Sacripantina

For the Meringues

6 large egg whites, at room temperature
1/8 teaspoon cream of tartar
2 cups sugar
1 teaspoon amaretto
2 teaspoons white vinegar

For the Genovese Butter Cake

7 large eggs
3 large egg yolks
1 cup sugar
1½ cups all-purpose flour
½ teaspoon baking powder
13 tablespoons unsalted butter, melted

For the Zabaglione Filling

8 large egg yolks
⅓ cup cream sherry
½ cup sugar
Finely grated zest of 1 orange
1 sheet gelatin (9 by 2½ inches) or 1 teaspoon powdered gelatin
1 cup heavy cream, whipped to medium-soft peaks

A North Beach christening, wedding, birthday, or other celebration would not be complete without a sacripantina. This rich old-fashioned cream cake is perfect with a caffè restretto at a neighborhood caffè.

We begin with a buttery genovese cake, the richer progenitor of the French génoise. We fill the cake with zabaglione lightened with whipped cream, frost it with whipped cream, and top it with amaretti crumbs.

This decadent dessert is made over two days, but it will be the best birthday present you ever give someone. Make the meringues and the genovese cake the first day and finish and assemble the cake the second day. Use an eight-inch metal or plastic cake ring to keep the cake straight while assembling it.

For the Meringues

Preheat the oven to 200° to 250°F. Line a baking sheet with parchment.

In a large bowl, beat the egg whites with an electric mixer until frothy. Add the cream of tartar and continue beating until soft peaks form. Lower the speed and gradually beat in the sugar. Add the amaretto and vinegar and beat at medium speed until stiff, glossy peaks form, about 8 minutes longer. Using a large kitchen spoon and your barely damp fingers, shape the meringue into twelve 4 × 3-inch ovals on the parchment-lined baking sheet.

Place on the lowest rack in the oven and bake for about 45 minutes, until golden brown. Cool on wire racks. Store in a tightly closed plastic container at room temperature.

For the Genovese Butter Cake

Preheat the oven to 350°F. Butter and flour an 8-inch springform pan.

In a large metal bowl, beat the eggs, yolks, and sugar with an electric mixer on high speed until tripled in volume, about 7 minutes.

Place the bowl over a saucepan of water, bring the water to a simmer, and whisk for 1 to 2 minutes to warm the eggs slightly. Remove from the heat.

Sift the flour and baking powder together and fold into the egg mixture. Transfer one-eighth of the batter to a small bowl and whisk the melted butter into it. Gently fold this mixture back into the batter. Pour the cake batter into the prepared cake pan.

Bake for 1 to 1¼ hours, or until a wooden skewer inserted into the center comes out clean. Remove from the oven and cool completely on a wire rack. (The cake can be made a day ahead if tightly wrapped in plastic.)

For the Zabaglione Filling

Make a water bath by filling a large deep pot half-full with water. Combine the yolks, cream sherry, sugar, and orange zest in a large bowl (preferably copper, to get more volume). Place the bowl over the water and, while whisking the eggs vigorously, bring the water to a simmer over medium-low heat. Continue whisking for about 5 minutes, or until the mixture thickens and is light and fluffy. Remove the bowl from the heat and let cool. (Leave the water bath over low heat.)

Place the gelatin sheet, if using, in cold water to soften. When soft, squeeze out the excess water, then whisk into the egg mixture. Or, for powdered gelatin, put 2 tablespoons cold water in a small dish and sprinkle the gelatin over the water. Let stand for 1 minute to soften, then whisk into the egg mixture. Return the bowl of egg mixture to the simmering water bath and whisk constantly over medium-low heat until the gelatin is fully dissolved, about 2 minutes. Be careful not to overcook the eggs, as they may curdle, and make sure when whisking to bring all of the mixture up from the bottom of the bowl. Refrigerate until cold, whisking occasionally, then fold in the whipped cream.

For the Cream Frosting

In a medium bowl whip the cream with the sugar, vanilla, and brandy to stiff peaks. Set aside in the refrigerator.

For the Cream Frosting

1 cup heavy cream

2 tablespoons sugar

1 teaspoon vanilla extract

1 tablespoon brandy

For the Simple Syrup

½ cup sugar

¼ cup cream sherry

For Assembly

1 cup amaretti cookie crumbs

Cocoa powder for dusting

Serves 12

For the Simple Syrup
Over medium heat, dissolve the sugar in ¼ cup water and the sherry.

To Assemble
Place the cake on a cake stand. With a long sharp knife, trim off the very top (about ⅛ inch) of the cake. To slice the cake into 3 equal rounds, score 2 evenly spaced lines all around the sides of the cake. Cut into the score lines about 1 inch deep all the way around the cake, then make a clean cut all the way through the cake to separate it into 3 layers. With a very sharp knife, trim off the outer brown edges of each layer.

Place the top layer of cake on a flat serving plate. Place the cake ring around the cake. Dip a pastry brush into the simple syrup and brush it generously onto the cake layer to moisten it. Spread about half of the zabaglione on top. Add the next layer of cake, brush with the syrup, and top with the remaining zabaglione and the final layer of cake. Brush with the remaining syrup and refrigerate for at least 30 minutes, or overnight, to set.

Remove the ring from the cake. Frost the whole cake with the cream frosting, spreading it very evenly and smoothly. (Use a cake comb if you have one.) Sprinkle the amaretti crumbs on top. Dust the tops of the meringues with cocoa, then press them lengthwise into the sides of the cake, spacing them evenly. Serve immediately, or refrigerate until ready to serve, or overnight.

The Bay Area Cheese-Making Tradition

Certain cheeses, such as teleme, or dried Monterey Jack, are quintessential North Beach. There once was a creamery across from Florence Ravioli on Stockton Street that made cheeses in the old days, and a tiny store on Union Street had its own aging room deep in the basement. Those places are long gone, but a devoted group of a new generation of great cheese makers in the Bay Area has taken up the cause.

Laura Chenel was the first person in the Bay Area, if not the entire country, to make goat cheeses. Laura's goat cheeses, and other artisanal, or farmhouse, cheeses have made their mark on the local and national culinary scene. Bellwether's crescenza and Toscano are becoming known nationwide, as are cheeses produced by very small makers such as the St. George Portuguese cheese and Humboldt Fog. The latter is a goat cheese made in the style of French Morbier, with a coating of vegetable ash and a line running through the center, also of the ash, intended to resemble fog. Cowgirl Creamery at Tomales Bay Foods in Point Reyes Station is producing fine crème fraîche, cottage cheese, quark, and mozzarella.

Cindy Callahan at Bellwether Farms, near Petaluma, with her famous Pecorino Pepato.

Acknowledgments

This book would not exist without the hard work and creative fire of my fellow chefs Scott Warner and Erik Cosselmon. Thank you. I am eternally grateful to Fred Hill for being not only a superb agent and teller of tales but for playing dealmaker above and beyond. Thanks to Barry for showing me the strength of the good and for being a pen pal through my many mistakes. To Laurie and Craig for being extraordinary friends and supporters. To Cass for his vision, support, and strength of will. To Marilyn, Steve, Peggy, Mickey, and Scott for their unwavering trust, support, and honesty. To Marjorie, Gene, Steven, and Barbara for their warmth, wisdom, and patience. To John for creating so much positive spirit and for embracing the real North Beach. To Angela, Serge, Tony, Irene, and Lisa for making every morning a good one. To Joe, Dan, Peter, Marta, Rose, Phil, and all the others who make this my "hood." To Ann for her spark, love, and wit. To Eleanor for always getting it and telling the truth—you are what I love about San Francisco. To Marion for her generosity of spirit and great wisdom. To Michael for suffering through the bear. To Christy for her unwavering passion, commitment, and spirit. To Lawrence for "Recipe for Happiness in Khabarovsk or Anyplace" and for some big pieces of who I am. To Coleman for continually opening my eyes a little wider. To Jonathan for being such a great friend through it all. To Nina, who wrote much of this book, inspired much of the food, and whose face is always a memory in my hands. To Peggy for introducing me to Rose, and always embodying the passion of North Beach. To Rose, the sexiest eighty-eight-year-old I ever met, we all miss you.

—Reed Hearon

I would like to thank:

Harriet Bell, our wonderful and patient editor.

Our supportive agents, Victoria Shoemaker and Fred Hill.

Scott Warner and Erik Cosselmon, for providing much of the creative force behind this book.

The Oldways Preservation and Exchange Trust-K. Dun Gifford and Sara Baer-Sinnott for making it possible to learn about the food of Liguria.

Kate Nowell Smith and Sharon Silva, for helping with recipes, format, and editing.

Alexis Levenson, for helping with all the communications for this book.

The many helpful and generous people at Rose Pistola who helped me, including Wendy Armstrong, pastry chef Galen Warner, pizza maker Vinny Montemayer, and chefs Laurence Searle and Jeff Powell.

Peter Birmingham and Ward Robilliard for the wine suggestions and John O'Neill for helping with tastings.

Librarian Ann Roberti from the Alice Statler Library at City College of San Francisco. To Adam, for computer graphics.

Laura Toomey, for her fantastic assisting skills.

The wonderful team of recipe testers Emmy Smith and Liz Levy.

Peggy's friends who helped test and taste recipes, including Cal Ferris, Ruthie Hunter, Jillian Clark, Hally Thatcher, Paula Wolfert, Bill Bayer, Terry Gamble, Keary Knickerbocker, and Francesca Quagliata.

Marion Cunningham, for her calm advice.

Laurie Smith, for her beautiful color photographs and Henrik Kam, for his amazing black-and-whites.

Nina Eberts, for helping us pull the book off, and Eleanor Bertino, for her integrity and friendship.

And to Flicka McGurrin with whom I began my culinary career and life in North Beach.

And to Reed who opened my mind and palate to another layer of the onion called North Beach.

And to Chris Pray for introducing us to Rose Pistola.

—Peggy Knickerbocker

Bibliography

Andrews, Colman. *Flavors of the Riviera: Discovering Real Mediterranean Cooking*. New York: Bantam Books, 1996.

Bittman, Mark. *How to Cook Everything*. New York: Macmillan, 1998.

Bugialli, Giuliano. *Bugialli on Pasta*. New York: Simon & Schuster, 1988.

Cinel, Dino. *From Italy to San Francisco: The Immigrant Experience*. Stanford: Stanford University Press, 1982.

Dillon, Richard, and Monaco, J. B. *The Italian Heart of San Francisco*. Novato, CA: Presidio Press, 1985.

Downie, David, and Harris, Alison. *Enchanted Liguria*. New York: Rizolli International Publications, 1997.

Field, Carol. *The Italian Baker*. New York: Harper & Row, 1985.

Fletcher, Janet. *Fresh From the Farmers' Market*. San Francisco: Chronicle Books, 1997.

Madison, Deborah. *Vegetarian Cooking for Everyone*. New York: Broadway Books, 1997.

Moose, Mary Etta, and St. Pierre, Brian. *The Flavors of North Beach*. San Francisco: Chronicle Books, 1981.

Plotkin, Fred. *Recipes from Paradise: Life and Food on the Italian Riviera*. Boston: Little, Brown, 1997.

Silva, Sharon, and Viviano, Frank. *Exploring the Best Ethnic Restaurants of the Bay Area*. San Francisco: San Francisco Focus, 1990.

Waters, Alice. *Chez Panisse Vegetables*. New York: HarperCollins, 1996.

Wolfert, Paula. *The Cooking of the Eastern Mediterranean*. New York: HarperCollins, 1994.

Sources

Corti Brothers
5810 Folsom Boulevard
Sacramento, CA 95819
Telephone: 916-736-3800
Polenta, extra virgin olive oils (a good selection of Ligurian oils), good vinegars, assorted other Italian products

Cowgirl Creamery
P.O. Box 717
Point Reyes Station, CA 94956
Telephone: 415-663-9335 (Wednesday through Friday)
Hand-crafted cheeses, including crescenza

Formaggio Kitchen
244 Huron Avenue
Cambridge, MA 02138
Telephone: 617-354-4750
Fax: 617-547-5680
Bottarga, Ligurian olive oils, vinegars, and other specialty items

Gray's Gristmill
P.O. Box 422
Adamsville, RI 02801
Telephone: 508-636-6075 (weekends only)
Organic, stone-ground coarse polenta

Hoffman Game Birds
Manteca, CA 95337
Telephone: 209-823-4028
Squabs, quail, and other game birds

Kalustyan's
123 Lexington Avenue
New York, NY 10016
Telephone: 212-685-3888
Fax: 212-683-8458
www.kalustyans.com
Chickpea flour, harissa

King Arthur Flour Company
The Baker's Catalog
P.O. Box 876
Norwich, VT 05055-0876
Telephone: 800-827-6836
Specialty flours such as chestnut flour for the Warm, Soft Chestnut Pudding, and what they call "Italian-style flour," which is the American version of the "00 Pastiticio flour" that we use in our pasta dough for ravioli and other handmade pastas. You might be able to track down 00 flour in an Italian deli, or mail-order this version.

Phipps Ranch
P.O. Box 349
Pescadero, CA 94060
Telephone: 800-279-0889
Fax: 415-879-1622
Dried beans

The Spanish Table
1427 Western Avenue
Seattle, WA 98101
Telephone: 206-682-2827
Fax: 206-682-2914
E-mail: tablespan@aol.com
Calamari ink

Sur La Table
1765 Sixth Avenue South
Seattle, WA 98134-1608
Telephone: 800-243-0852
www.surlatable.com
Utensils and cookware

Williams-Sonoma
10000 Covington Cross
Las Vegas, NV 89134
Telephone: 800-541-2233
www.williamssonoma.com
Utensils, cookware, oils, vinegars, etc.

Zingerman's
422 Detroit Street
Ann Arbor, MI 48104
Telephone: 888-636-8162; 313-769-1625 (in Michigan)
Olive oils from Liguria, cheeses, salt-packed anchovies

Early morning tai chi in Washington Square Park, North Beach.

Index

Wine bottles lined up on the bar at Rose Pistola;
spicy breadsticks in the background.